This is the first book-length study in any language dedicated specifically to lute, guitar, and vihuela performance. Written by specialists in this music, it is intended for players, teachers, and scholars who are interested both in the history of performance and in the specific interpretation of lute, guitar, and vihuela music from the end of the fifteenth century to approximately 1850. It brings to light various new ideas about performance and technique for a wide range of instruments – fifteenth-, sixteenth- and seventeenth-century Italian lute, archlute, theorbo, French Baroque lute, vihuela, and Baroque and classical guitar – as well as for lute-accompanied English and Italian song. The articles in this book decode the unwritten traditions of these instruments, and examine various performance issues through a combination of performance experience and a fresh, innovative look at traditional problems.

Performance on Lute, Guitar, and Vihuela

This series provides a forum through which the most important current research may reach a wide range of musicologists, performers, teachers, and all those who have come to regard questions of performance practice as fundamental to their understanding of music. Each volume contains contributory essays on various aspects of a particular theme in performance history.

Published titles

Perspectives on Mozart Performance
ed. R. Larry Todd and Peter Williams

Plainsong in the Age of Polyphony
ed. Thomas Forrest Kelly

Performing Beethoven
ed. Robin Stowell

Music and Performance in the Weimar Republic
ed. Bryan Gilliam

English Choral Practice
ed. John Morehen

Performance on Lute, Guitar, and Vihuela
ed. Victor Anand Coelho

PERFORMANCE ON LUTE, GUITAR, AND VIHUELA

Historical Practice and Modern Interpretation

Edited by

VICTOR ANAND COELHO

Professor of Music
The University of Calgary, Alberta

CAMBRIDGE
UNIVERSITY PRESS

PUBLISHED BY THE PRESS SYNDICATE OF THE UNIVERSITY OF CAMBRIDGE
The Pitt Building, Trumpington Street, Cambridge CB2 1RP, United Kingdom

CAMBRIDGE UNIVERSITY PRESS
The Edinburgh Building, Cambridge CB2 2RU, United Kingdom
40 West 20th Street, New York, NY 10011–4211, USA
10 Stamford Road, Oakleigh, Melbourne 3166, Australia

© Cambridge University Press

First published 1997

Printed in the United Kingdom at the University Press, Cambridge

Typeset in Bembo 10.25/14

A catalogue record for this book is available from the British Library

Library of Congress cataloguing in publication data
Performance on lute, guitar, and vihuela: historical practice and
modern interpretation / edited by Victor Anand Coelho.
p.   cm. – (Cambridge studies in performance practice; 6)
ISBN 0 521 45528 6 (hardback)
1. Lute – Performance – History. 2. Guitar – Performance – History.
3. Vihuela – Performance – History. 4. Performance practice (Music)
I. Coelho, Victor. II. Series.
ML 1003.P47   1997
787.8'143 – dc21   96–47888   CIP

ISBN 0 521 45528 6 (hardback)

SN

For Gerald Armand Milette

CONTENTS

List of plates   *page*   xi
List of tables   xii
General preface   xiii
Preface   xv
List of abbreviations   xviii
Note on pitch   xix

1   An invitation to the fifteenth-century plectrum lute: the
    Pesaro Manuscript   1
        Vladimir Ivanoff (Munich, Germany)

2   Lute tablature instructions in Italy: a survey of the *regole* from
    1507 to 1759   16
        Dinko Fabris (Conservatorio di Bari)

3   The performance context of the English lute song, 1596–1622   47
        Daniel Fischlin (University of Guelph)

4   *Per cantare e sonare:* accompanying Italian lute song of
    the late sixteenth century   72
        Kevin Mason (Chicago, Illinois)

5   Authority, autonomy, and interpretation in seventeenth-century
    Italian lute music   108
        Victor Anand Coelho (University of Calgary)

6   Performance instructions for the seventeenth-century French lute
    repertory   142
        Wallace Rave (Arizona State University)

7   The vihuela: performance practice, style, and context   158
        John Griffiths (University of Melbourne)

8   Performing seventeenth-century Italian guitar music: the question
    of an appropriate stringing   180
        Gary Boye (Duke University)

9   Essential issues in performance practices of the classical guitar,
    1770–1850   195
        Richard Savino (California State University, Sacramento)

    General index   220
    Index of first lines and titles   230

PLATES

1   Jan Brueghel ('Velvet Brueghel', 1568–1625), 'Hearing' (Madrid, Museo del Prado, no. 1395). By permission of Art Resource   *page*   56

2   'Sanguigno per l'aria', Cesare Ripa, *Iconologia* (rpt Padua, 1611)   57

3   *Se scior si ved'il laccio*, from Antonelli, *Il primo libro delle napolitane ariose* (Venice, 1570)   80

4   *Ancor che col partir*, Gasparo Fiorino, *La nobiltà di Roma* (Venice, 1571)   80

5   Texted intabulation, *Mentre io campai*, from *Cavalcanti*   84

6   18-course theorbo by Matteo Sellas (*ca.* 1630), Paris, Musée de la Musique, Cité de la Musique. Inv. E 547   121

7   *Perugia*, p. 114, *Ceccona per A* (courtesy of the Archivio di Stato, Perugia)   131

8   Orpheus playing the vihuela, from Milán, *El Maestro* (1536)   174

9   Arion playing the vihuela, from Narváez, *Los seys libros del Delphín* (1538)   174

10   Charles Doisy, *Principes Généraux de la Guitare* (Paris, 1801)   198

11   Frederico Moretti, *Principi per la Chitarra* (Naples, *ca.* 1792)   201

12   Dionisio Aguado, 'Tripodium' from the 1843 *Nuevo Método*   204

13   Fernando Sor, [on the right hand] from *Method for the Spanish Guitar* (*ca.* 1850)   210

TABLES

1.1   Instances of plectrum technique in the Pesaro Manuscript   *page*   10

2.1   Italian prints and manuscripts containing instructions for the
lute (1480–*ca.* 1759)   18

2.2   Non-Italian prints containing instructions for the lute before 1600   21

4.1   Songs with mensural voice parts and Italian lute tablature
accompaniments   77

4.2   Texted intabulations of polyphonic Italian vocal music   81

4.3   French tablature accompaniments of Italian polyphony   86

GENERAL PREFACE

No doubt the claim, heard frequently today, that 'authentic performance' is a chimera, and that even the idea of an 'authentic edition' cannot be sustained for (most) music before the last century or two, is itself the consequence of too sanguine an expectation raised by performers and scholars alike in the recent past. Both have been understandably concerned to establish that a certain composer 'intended so-and-so' or had 'such-and-such conditions of performance in mind' or 'meant it to sound in this way or that'. Scholars are inclined to rule on problems ('research confirms the following . . .'), performers to make the music a living experience ('artistry or musicianship suggests the following . . .'). Both are there in order to answer certain questions and establish an authority for what they do; both demonstrate and persuade by the rhetoric of their utterance, whether well-documented research on the one hand or convincing artistic performance on the other; and the academic/commercial success of both depends on the effectiveness of that rhetoric. Some musicians even set out to convey authority in both scholarship and performance, recognizing that music is conceptual *and* perceptual and thus not gainfully divisible into separate, competitive disciplines. In general, if not always, the scholar appears to aim at the firm, affirmative statement, often seeing questions as something to be answered confidently rather than searchingly redefined or refined. In general, with some exceptions, performers have to aim at the confident statement, for their very livelihood hangs on an unhesitating decisiveness in front of audience or microphone. In the process, both sometimes have the effect, perhaps even the intention, of killing the dialectic – of thwarting the progress that comes with further questions and a constant 'yes, but' response to what is seen, in the light of changing definitions, as 'scholarly evidence' or 'convincing performance'.

In the belief that the immense activity in prose and sound over the last few decades is now being accompanied by an increasing awareness of the issues arising – a greater knowledge at last enabling the question to be more closely defined –

the Cambridge Studies in Performance Practice will attempt to make regular contributions to this area of study, on the basis of several assumptions. Firstly, at its best, Performance Practice is so difficult a branch of study as to be an almost impossibly elusive ideal. It cannot be merely a practical way of 'combining performance and scholarship', for these two are fundamentally different activities, each able to inform the other only up to a certain point. Secondly, if Performance Practice has moved beyond the questions (now seen to be very dated) that exercised performance groups of the 1950s and 60s, it can widen itself to include any or all music written before the last few years. In this respect, such studies are a musician's equivalent to the cry of literary studies, 'Only contextualize!', and this can serve as a useful starting-point for the historically minded performer or the practically minded scholar. (The Derridaesque paradox that there is no context may have already affected some literary studies, but context is still clearly crucial across the broader field of music, the original Comparative Literature.) Cambridge Studies in Performance Practice will devote volumes to any period in which useful questions can be asked, ranging from at least Gregorian chant to at least Stravinsky.

Thirdly, Performance Practice is not merely about performing, neither 'this is how music was played' nor 'this is how you should play it in a concert or recording today'. (These two statements are as often as not irreconcilable.) In studying all that we can about the practical realization of a piece of music we are studying not so much how it was played but how it was heard, both literally and on a deeper level. How it was conceived by the composer and how it was perceived by the period's listener are endless questions deserving constant study, for they bring one into intimate contact with the historical art of music as nothing else can. It is the *music* we fail to understand, not its performance as such, if we do not explore these endless questions. As we know, every basic musical element has had to be found, plucked out of thin air – the notes, their tuning, compass, volume, timbre, pace, timing, tone, combining – and they have constantly changed. In attempting to grasp or describe these elements as they belong to a certain piece of music, it could become clear that any modern re-realization in (public) performance is a quite separate issue. Nevertheless, it is an issue of importance to the wider musical community, as can be seen from the popular success of performers and publications (records, journals, books) concerned with 'authenticity'. In recognizing this practical importance, Cambridge Studies in Performance Practice will frequently call upon authoritative performers to join scholars in the common cause, each offering insights to the process of learning to ask and explore the right questions.

PETER WILLIAMS

PREFACE

Performance, like language, evolves over time and across geographical space, varies between individuals, contemporaries, generations, and genres, and changes according to rhetorical demands, purpose, and context. It is a professional public activity, but also a private amateur pastime, a business, an education, a diversion, a necessity, and now a history with its own historians. Performance traditions vary; they are read, written, memorized, and extemporized. Conventions of practice, even those that are considered sacrosanct, are corruptible, malleable, and mutable in the hands of players as they rethink, revive, relive, and – perhaps most importantly – interpret history; for musical performance is not only a historical mirror reflecting the practice of the past, it is an open window to modern conventions that secure the relevance of this music for the future. For lutenists, vihuelists, and guitarists, the scope of these perspectives challenges them to seek information about performance not only in conventional source materials, such as treatises, tutors, prefaces, scholarly editions, and occasionally paintings, but also in areas that have not been traditionally validated by either musicology or pedagogy: amateur and street music, household books, orality, living traditions (traditional and folk music), popular music, modern recordings, and the subjective experience. The integration of these areas defines the relationship between historical performance and modern interpretation, which is the central theme of this collection of essays.

Combining modern, critical approaches to source material with fresh insights about execution and context, this book attempts to show how earlier players – from professionals to amateurs, and from court to countryside – conceived of themselves not just as musicians but as *interpreters*, solving technical problems and making autonomous musical decisions. Needless to say, these essays move significantly beyond the collecting of historical fact and the collating of data from treatises, archival sources, and eyewitness accounts. The nine authors of *Performance on Lute, Guitar, and Vihuela,* aim to integrate their knowledge of what was written about performance with their *experience* in how music was actually performed, occasionally penetrating into the unwritten and oral traditions that are part of the ancestry of lute, vihuela, and guitar performance. These essays will also illuminate the umbral area of pedagogy – that is, the craft experience between master and student as codified in hundreds of manuscripts, paintings, and literary accounts, which has been ignored in modern studies despite the crucial importance pedagogy played in the skills of improvisation, accompanying, and composing.

Appropriately, Vladimir Ivanoff begins the volume by examining the performance issues that reside in the heart-shaped Pesaro Manuscript, the central fifteenth-century tablature containing works for the plectrum lute. Copied during the transition from plectrum to finger technique, the manuscript contains many fascinating clues about performance on the pre-Petrucci lute, which are decoded for modern players by Ivanoff, a specialist on the instrument and the author of a complete study of the manuscript. Turning from plectrum to finger technique, Dinko Fabris offers a detailed survey of the commercially available 'rules' for playing the lute that publishers appended to Italian printed books from Petrucci's earliest volumes to 1750. Such rules can inform about the musical competence of the largely amateur public for which these rules were intended, as well as show the relationship between rules, the public, and the commercial market over several generations of Italian lute music.

The following two articles by Daniel Fischlin and Kevin Mason employ completely new methodologies towards studying the performance of English and Italian lute song, respectively. Using literary, iconographic, and mythographic sources, Fischlin argues that 'interiority' and 'privacy' constitute the main aesthetics of the English lute ayre – a genre whose performance conventions are practically undocumented – rather than models of 'oratory' and 'Orphism' as proposed by other writers and performers. Mason, a specialist on continuo playing, confronts the much-disputed question about the proper accompanimental style for early monody by investigating sources that precede monody, specifically lute song arrangements of vocal polyphony, rather than rely on the stylistically inconsistent sources contemporary with monody and after, as most other writers have done.

Since seventeenth-century lute music in France and Italy is preserved primarily in manuscript, rather than print, knowledge of these sources and the information about performance practice they contain remains limited to only a few specialists in the field. Victor Coelho and Wallace Rave make similar distinctions between sources in their respective surveys of seventeenth-century Italian and French music. Their essays show the wide variety of approaches and flexibility that characterized performance practice in lute music of this period – a flexibility that would occasionally startle a modern player – and both agree that manuscript variants are the key sources for understanding this style. Coelho sees the issue as toggling between respect to tradition (authority) and interpretation (autonomy); similarly, Rave sees a French lute piece as 'less an unalterable, finished composition than a core idea to be enhanced anew in performance'.

The final triad of essays investigates performance issues of three consecutively related instruments of the guitar family: the vihuela, the five-course Baroque guitar, and the 'classical' guitar. John Griffiths, drawing on an impressive variety of Spanish sources, combines musical and cultural insights about vihuela performance towards an integrated summary of style, taste, and instrumental technique. Gary Boye focuses on the thorny problem of unison or octave stringing of the five-course guitar in seventeenth-century Italy, and in the process illuminates an important repertory of mostly Bolognese and Roman guitar music. Lastly, Richard Savino discusses the performance conventions and techniques of the classical guitar based on the little-known guitar sources and manuals from the early nineteenth century, as well as his personal experience as one of the foremost players of the nineteenth-century guitar today.

The problem of editing a book of essays about performance practice, it must be said, is that the contributors invariably live complicated lives that are divided unequally between performing, teaching, and writing. I wish to thank the other eight contributors for managing to carve out the necessary time to complete this project, and for their belief in its importance. Other thanks must go to my wife, Brita, for her consistently sensible advice and warm encouragement, as well as to George V. Coelho for his continued support of my endeavours that can only be described as *incalculable*. Much of the preparation of this volume was accomplished during my appointment as visiting professor of music at Cornell University in 1995, whose splendid library and staff greatly facilitated the chores of editing. Closer to home and for similar reasons, I am grateful to the library and staff at The University of Calgary for their assistance and cooperation, to Thomas Peattie for some last-minute help with the final typescript, to Miles Dempster for producing the tablature examples, and to Lucy Carolan for the improvements she made to the text. Penny Souster of Cambridge University Press has been extremely supportive, patient, and a pleasure to work with at all times, and I have also benefited from the advice and recommendations of the series editor, Peter Williams.

VICTOR ANAND COELHO

ABBREVIATIONS

AcM	*Acta Musicologica*
BJhM	*Bäsler Jahrbuch für historische Musikpraxis*
CM	*Current Musicology*
EM	*Early Music*
FAM	*Fontes artis Musicae*
GL	*Gitarre und Laute*
GSJ	*Galpin Society Journal*
JAMS	*Journal of the American Musicological Society*
JLSA	*Journal of the Lute Society of America*
JMR	*Journal of Musicological Research*
LSAQ	*Lute Society of America Quarterly*
LSJ	*The Lute Society Journal*
Ma	*Musique ancienne*
MD	*Musica Disciplina*
MQ	*The Musical Quarterly*
PRMA	*Proceedings of the Royal Musical Association*
RM	*Revista de Musicología*
RdM	*Revue de Musicologie*
RIM	*Rivista Italiana di Musicologia*
RISM	*Répertoire internationale des sources musicales*
Sm	*Studi musicali*

NOTE ON PITCH

Pitch registers are indicated by the following scheme:

AN INVITATION TO THE FIFTEENTH-CENTURY PLECTRUM LUTE: THE PESARO MANUSCRIPT

VLADIMIR IVANOFF

Modern performance of the so-called 'early Renaissance' lute repertory continues to be restricted to a small circle of sources and composers, generally revolving around Joanambrosio Dalza, Francesco Spinacino, and Vincenzo Capirola. Consequently, many of the works by these composers have assumed the status of 'masterworks', but whether they offer an historically accurate portrait of lute practice in the late fifteenth and early sixteenth centuries is open to debate. The purpose of this article is to examine the issues of performance practice that are offered by a central lute source of this period, the heart-shaped 'Pesaro Manuscript' (Pesaro, Biblioteca Oliveriana, Ms. 1144, hereinafter *Pesaro*).[1] The subject of several studies by musicologists but still largely neglected by performers, *Pesaro* allows for a close look into conventional or 'every-day' lute practices from about the 1460s to the beginning of the sixteenth century. The following discussion, which, by necessity, can illuminate only a few aspects of solo performance on the plectrum lute, is thus intended as an invitation to lutenists to investigate more deeply the music and issues of performance practice that are transmitted by this unique source.

THE LUTE IN THE FIFTEENTH CENTURY: A RESEARCH SUMMARY

According to Peter Danner,[2] who provided the first introduction to the history of the fifteenth-century lute, the instrument was mainly a plectrum lute used for playing single-voiced lines. Lutenists performed in duos or larger ensembles, almost always as improvisors.[3] Danner suggested that extant polyphonic *basse danses* might

---

[1] For a complete bibliographical, historical, and palaeographical study of this manuscript, see Vladimir Ivanoff, *Das Pesaro-Manuskript. Ein Beitrag zur Frühgeschichte der Lautentabulatur*, Münchner Veröffentlichungen zur Musikgeschichte 45 (Tutzing, 1988) and Vladimir Ivanoff, *Eine zentrale Quelle der frühen italienischen Lautenpraxis. Edition der Handschrift Pesaro, Biblioteca Oliveriana, Ms. 1144*, Münchner Editionen zur Musikgeschichte 7 (Tutzing, 1988).

[2] Peter Danner, 'Before Petrucci: The Lute in the Fifteenth Century', *JLSA* 5 (1972), pp. 4–17.

[3] See also Oswald Körte, *Laute und Lautenmusik bis zur Mitte des 16. Jahrhunderts*, Publikationen der Internationalen Musikgesellschaft: Beihefte 3 (Leipzig, 1901; rpt Wiesbaden, 1974), p. 77.

preserve the stylistic nature of lute music from the fifteenth century, with the arrangements of chansons by Spinacino[4] and Capirola[5] providing further hints. Danner also pointed out the close relationship between lute and organ that existed during this period.

In a later study on the fifteenth-century lute duet, I was able to show that Francesco Spinacino's prints preserve the only extant examples of a long and important tradition of lute duets.[6] Using evidence obtained from archival and iconographical sources, I traced the development of the harp–lute duet from the first half of the fifteenth century to the lute–lute duet in the second half of the century. This latter combination (with two lutes) featured specific roles for each of the two participating lutenists: while one of them extemporized single-note lines using traditional plectrum technique, the other lutenist accompanied him using the newly developed 'polyphonic' finger technique, a combination that literally 'outran' the traditional accompanying instrument, the harp. The fifteenth-century lute was also deeply influenced by the organ, and it can be said that organists set the models of performance for all other instrumentalists during this period. I have shown that certain pieces in the central fifteenth-century tablature manuscript for organ, the 'Buxheimer Orgelbuch', reveal particular stylistic, structural, and ornamental characteristics that also suggest a lute–lute or lute–harp duo.[7]

The main studies on extant fifteenth-century tablatures (probably) for lute are those by David Fallows[8] and Christopher Page.[9] Page discussed several interesting sources that also give an insight into fifteenth-century lute pedagogy, while Fallows's contribution provides an excellent survey and detailed analysis of some early tablatures for plucked instruments. Finally, Morrow's article on fifteenth-century lute sources gives only a very general summary,[10] and Päffgen's study[11] is a short but detailed survey of recent musicological research on the fifteenth-century lute.[12]

4   Francesco Spinacino, *Intabulatura de lauto, libro primo / libro secondo* (Venice, 1507). See Henry L. Schmidt, 'The First Printed Lute Books', Ph.D. diss., University of North Carolina, 1963; Vladimir Ivanoff, 'Die Lautenduos in Spinacinos "Intabulatura de lauto" (Ven. 1507)', M.A., University of Munich, 1984.

5   Chicago, Newberry Library, Acq. No. 107501. For a modern edition, see Otto Gombosi, ed., *Compositione di Meser Vincenzo Capirola. Lute-Book (circa 1517)* (Neuilly-sur-Seine, 1955).

6   Vladimir Ivanoff, 'Das Lautenduo im 15. Jahrhundert', *BJhM* 8 (1984), pp. 147–62.

7   For more recent documentation of the fifteenth-century lute duet, see Keith Polk, 'Voices and Instruments: Soloists and Ensembles in the 15th Century', *EM* 18 (1990), pp. 179–98, Table I.2. On German lute practice in the fifteenth century, see Rudolf Henning, 'German Lute Tablature and Conrad Paumann', *LSJ* 15 (1973), pp. 7–10, and Hiroyuki Minamino, 'Conrad Paumann and the Evolution of Solo Lute Practice in the Fifteenth Century', *JMR* 6 (1986), pp. 291–310.

8   David Fallows, '15th-Century Tablatures for Plucked Instruments: A Summary, a Revision and a Suggestion', *LSJ* 19 (1977), pp. 7–33.

9   Christopher Page, 'The 15th-Century Lute: New and Neglected Sources', *EM* 9 (1981), pp. 11–21.

10 Michael Morrow, 'Fifteenth-Century Lute Music: Some Possible Sources', in *Le luth et sa musique* II, ed. J.-M. Vaccaro (Paris, 1984), pp. 31–3.

11 Peter Päffgen, 'Lautenmusik vor 1500', *GL* 6 (1987), pp. 58–61.

12 For an introduction into plucked instruments and into ensemble playing in this period, see the short but valuable contributions by Hopkinson Smith and Crawford Young in Tess Knighton and David Fallows, ed., *Companion to*

THE PESARO MANUSCRIPT

Pesaro assumes a central position among early sources for the lute. It contains the earliest extant tablatures of genuine lute pieces,[13] and among these works are the only known pieces for the plectrum lute. My palaeographical study[14] of *Pesaro* showed that the heart-shaped manuscript was bound and prepared for the entering of six- and seven-line lute tablature between *ca.* 1480 and 1490, probably at Fabriano or Venice. The first pieces, then, were only entered after the completion and binding of the manuscript. In its present state *Pesaro* contains thirty-eight complete pieces: nine arrangements of polyphonic compositions, twenty-five instrumental pieces of the *recercare* genre, and three dances, two of them for the *lira da braccio*. This repertory was notated by four scribes in five different tablature notations, four of them for the lute or similar instruments (labelled Tablature A to D in my study), and the remaining one for the *lira da braccio*.

The first owner of *Pesaro* (Scribe 1) entered the earliest layers of tablature (types A and D) after *ca.* 1480. Tablature layer A contains instrumental arrangements of chansons that were popular in the period between *ca.* 1470 and 1490, and Italian songs from before *ca.* 1495. Frottole by composers of the younger generation, such as Marco Cara or Bartolomeo Tromboncino (which are prominent in collections after 1500), are entirely absent in *Pesaro*. From this evidence we can assume that the lute pieces in tablature layers A and D were notated somewhere between *ca.* 1490 and 1495. Many features in the notational script of the tablatures – among them numerous scribal errors – prove that the lute pieces in *Pesaro* were copied from a number of other (today unknown) sources, mostly of single leaves.[15] This is a common and well-documented method in teacher–pupil relationships, in which the student copied lute tablatures into his personal collection from single leaves provided by his teacher, as Gombosi has noted in his history of the Capirola Lute Book of 1516–17:

Medieval and Renaissance Music (New York, 1992). Concerning the lute, solo lute performance, and its participation in different ensembles in Germany, see Keith Polk, *German Instrumental Music of the Late Middle Ages: Players, Patrons and Performance Practice* (Cambridge, 1992), pp. 22–30.

[13] Although the 'Königsteiner Liederbuch' proves the existence of 'German lute tablature' in the last third of the fifteenth century, it does not contain any actual lute music: tablature notation is used only as a space-saving means to give the melodies of monophonic German songs; see Paul Sappler, ed., *Das Königsteiner Liederbuch*, Münchener Texte und Untersuchungen zur deutschen Literatur des Mittelalters 29 (Munich, 1970), pp. 7, 325–7, 375–80; see also Hans Tischler, 'The Earliest Lute Tablature?', *JAMS* 27 (1974), pp. 100–3, and Ivanoff, *Das Pesaro-Manuskript*, pp. 12–13.

 The fragment Bologna, Biblioteca Universitaria, MS 596. HH.2⁴ *(Bologna)*, which has been considered by some scholars to contain the earliest extant lute tablatures, has some stylistic features in common with the chronologically latest repertory in *Pesaro*. The date of its origin can therefore be roughly placed between *Thibault* and *Capirola*; see Ivanoff, *Das Pesaro-Manuskript*, pp. 14–20. *Bologna* has been published in facsimile and thoroughly studied by Fallows in '15th-Century Tablatures'.

[14] For details on methods and results, see Ivanoff, *Das Pesaro-Manuskript*, pp. 30–49.

[15] *ibid.*, pp. 85–90.

The composer of the pieces lived in Venice in the years 1516/17. The writer of the manuscript took lute instruction from him and incorporated some of the pieces he got from his master at the outset. As witnessed by the technical difficulty of some of the pieces he learned to play the lute well. This must have taken several years. The manuscript was obviously written within a short time: the writer copied earlier notations in a neatly planned and systematically ornamented manuscript.[16]

Pesaro shares two significant tablature concordances with another important early lute source, the so-called 'Thibault Manuscript', Paris, Bibliothèque Nationale, Rés. Vmd. ms. 27 *(Thibault)*, dating from *ca.* 1495–1505.[17] The scribal errors in these concordances reveal that Scribe 1 in *Pesaro* and the scribe of *Thibault* copied their material from the same sources; it is probable that both scribes were taught by the same lute teacher.[18] Most of the pieces in *Thibault*, including the two significant concordances with *Pesaro*, are signed with the letter *H*, which could be the initial of the teacher's name.

Through some common features, such as didactic function, notational similarities, and concordances, *Pesaro* can be grouped with other important early lute manuscripts: *Pesaro* (tablature layer A), *ca.* 1490–5; *Thibault, ca.* 1495–1505; Fribourg, Bibliothèque cantonale et universitaire [CH Fcu], Ms. Cap. Rés. 527 (fragment), *ca.* 1513–14; *Capirola, ca.* 1515; and London, British Library, Add. 31389, *ca.* 1520.[19] These sources were most likely copied by bourgeois amateur lutenists in Venice as documentation of their lute lessons. Moreover, they share many common features in their outer appearance, notation, and repertory, as well as in the musical structure of the pieces and in issues of performance practice.

READING (AND PLAYING) TABLATURE A IN PESARO[20]

In Tablature A, systems of six lines represent the six courses of the lute, with the lowest line representing the lowest sounding course *(basso)* and the highest line for the highest sounding string *(canto)*. The letters *a–i* – which would become known

---

[16]   Gombosi, *Compositione*, p. xxii.

[17]   This source has been studied in the following. (1) Geneviève Thibault, 'Un manuscrit italien pour luth des premières années du XVIᵉ siècle', in *Le luth et sa musique*, ed. Jean Jacquot (Paris, 1958), pp. 43–76. Thibault dated the manuscript to *ca.* 1505, studied its provenance, and published the first transcriptions from it. (2) François Lesure, ed., *Tablature de luth italienne . . . Facsimile du ms. de la Bibliothèque Nationale, Paris. Rés. Vmd. ms. 27 . . .* (Geneva, 1981). (This facsimile edition is of poor technical quality. Many details from the original are not visible or blurred, and some blots in the reproduction do not appear in the original and can be misread as being part of the tablatures. Furthermore, some pages have been trimmed at the edges and the last page of the manuscript is missing entirely.) (3) Lewis Jones, 'The Thibault Lute Manuscript: An Introduction, Part 1', *The Lute* 22 (1982), pp. 69–87; 'Part 2': *The Lute* 23 (1983), pp. 21–6. Jones gives a detailed description of the manuscript as well as some transcriptions. (4) Ivanoff, *Das Pesaro-Manuskript*, pp. 152–76, 303–15. (5) Ivanoff, *Handschrift Pesaro*, pp. 25–48.

[18]   For details see Ivanoff, *Das Pesaro-Manuskript*, pp. 165–74.

[19]   *ibid.*, pp. 150–76, 215–17, 223–5.

[20]   Edited and transcribed in Ivanoff, *Handschrift Pesaro*, pp. 1–150.

as 'French' tablature after Attaingnant's *Tres brève et familière introduction* (Paris, 1529) – on the tablature lines represent the open sounding string *(a)* and the eight fret positions *(b–i)*. The letter *m* in the tablature indicates a string that has to be dampened by the player (see Ex. 1.7c; *Pesaro*, p. 30, edition, p. 13).[21] To play this chord, one of the left-hand fingers that is used to stop an adjacent string is straightened far enough so that one of its joints touches the open string and dampens it. This technique would be unnecessary, of course, if the two lowest notes of the chord were plucked by the thumb of the right hand, and the upper two by the index and middle finger, as was practised later in sixteenth-century lute playing. In other words, the technique of dampening the middle course becomes necessary when the strings of the instrument are plucked with only *one* of the fingers or with a plectrum. If the middle course is not dampened a dissonant note would sound in the chord, in this case a non-chord tone G clashing with a chord built on F. (A similar technique is used by folk, jazz, and rock guitar players using plectrum-based chordal playing styles.) The 'm' symbol is only one of several elements in Tablature A that reveal the affinity of some of the pieces with the plectrum lute, and this specific technique provides the only extant hints preserved in tablature of plectrum lute performance.

String dampening is necessary in many other places as well in Tablature A, though without being indicated by special signs (see Ex. 1.1). The tablature indications that I have placed in brackets produce dissonant notes in their respective chords if sounded, so dampening them becomes necessary. Most of the chords with these 'dissonances' on open strings occur immediately after fast ornamental formulas. Lute players know that placing all the necessary fingers to produce a full chord after fast passages is not always easy. The dampening of the open string in Ex. 1.1 allows the player to use only two or three fingers of the left hand.

Ex. 1.1   *a recercar* (*Pesaro*, p. 46; edition, p. 63)

---

[21] Following the word 'edition' I am indicating the appropriate place where the tablature and transcription of a specific example can be located in Ivanoff, *Handschrift Pesaro*, which also contains an explanation of the editorial guidelines and specific conventions used in this edition (pp. xxvi–xxxi).

What was the tuning of the 'Pesaro lute'? If we compare the lute arrangements of polyphonic models to their original settings in mensural notation, we are confronted with several possible solutions:

1. Relative G-tuning ($G/g–c/c^1–f/f^1–a/a–d^1/d^1–g^1$) for *De tous biens playne* (*Pesaro*, pp. 65–8; edition, pp. 101–9)
2. Relative A-tuning for *J'ay pri(n)s amours* (*Pesaro*, pp. 61–4; edition, pp. 93–100), *Contento in foco* (*Pesaro*, pp. 70–1; edition, pp. 115–18), *Fortuna desperata* (*Pesaro*, pp. 31–5; edition, pp. 15–26) and *Ocultamente* (*Pesaro*, pp. 68–70; edition, pp. 111–14)
3. Relative B-tuning for *A Ladri* (*Pesaro*, pp. 43–5; edition, pp. 57–64)

De tous biens playne and *A Ladri* were obviously transposed a whole tone up and a whole tone down, respectively, to facilitate performance on a lute in A-tuning. Since the other three intabulations of models in mensural notation are clearly designated for a lute in relative A-tuning, we can safely conclude that all of the pieces in Tablature A were intended for a lute in this tuning.[22]

The scribe of Tablature A positioned the following symbols[23] above the tablature letters, most probably to convey rhythmical and metrical information:

Ex. 1.2

By comparing the six lute arrangements listed above with their models, it is possible to arrive at some answers regarding the meaning of the three signs in Ex. 1.2. The T-sign may be an abbreviation of the term *Tactus*. In a German organ manuscript from the first half of the fifteenth century, the term *Tactus* stands for a stereotypical melodic formula consisting of four semibreves.[24] They are divided into three groups according to their movement in upward or downward direction, or by their function as an ornamentation of the same note. In his edition of the organ manuscript, Theodor Göllner presented these formulas in a table, using abbreviations to define their melodic movement (see Ex. 1.3).[25] Two of these *Tactus puri* may be combined

---

[22] Other reasons for transpositions of mensurally notated models in lute arrangements are given in John Ward, 'Le problème des hauteurs dans la musique pour luth et vihuela au XVIᵉ siècle', *Le luth et sa musique*, pp. 171–8, and John Ward, 'Changing the Instrument for the Music', *JLSA* 15 (1982), pp. 27–39.

[23] In the text of this article these symbols are represented by the signs 'T', '&' and '^'.

[24] Munich, Bayerische Staatsbibliothek, Cod. lat. 7755, fols. 276–80; ed., Theodor Göllner, *Formen früher Mehrstimmigkeit in deutschen Handschriften des späten Mittelalters*, Münchner Veröffentlichungen zur Musikgeschichte 6 (Tutzing, 1961), pp. 155–94.

[25] *ibid.*, p. 62.

to form a larger, composite *Tactus*. When this *Tactus* is set above a tenor-note in the lower voice, the initial notes of its first and second half will have to form a consonance with the tenor-note. It is preferable if a consonance in the first half of a composite *Tactus* is followed by a wider consonant interval in the second half. In *Pesaro* similar formulas are combined according to similar rules. The first note starts the formula type A1 with the interval of an octave with the lower voice, followed by an identical formula beginning with the interval of a tenth (see Ex. 1.4).

Ex. 1.3   *tactus puri*: A: *Ascendentes*; D: *Descendentes*; I: *Indifferentes*

Ex. 1.4   *arecercare* (*Pesaro*, p. 27; edition, p. 7)

The T-signs in *Pesaro* obviously define similar formulas, constructed from semi-minims, which follow the same rules of consonance. Tablature A in *Pesaro* contains many passages with this structure. The T-sign does not define the length of a single note; it should be understood as a position mark, indicating the beginning of a new melodic formula and hence, a new metrical unit. It appears more frequently in arrangements of mensurally notated models than in *recercari*. While the intabulations are based on models in fixed metres, the *recercari* are non-derivative works of an improvisational nature: very few of them suggest a fixed metre. It is possible that the scribe of Tablature A intended a freer performance of these pieces and for this reason did not add many *Tactus* signs. When the sign does appear in the *recercari*, it is used exclusively in places where metrical precision is of crucial structural importance, for example, in *penultima-clausulae* (see Ex. 1.5).

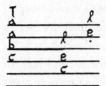

Ex. 1.5   *arecercare* (*Pesaro*, p. 29; edition, p. 11)

Symbols that are similar to the & sign were employed in the fifteenth and sixteenth century by many humanistic scribes as decorative alternatives for the letters s and t;[26] In humanistic calligraphy the sign was used exclusively as an ornamental internal ligature inside a word. In *Pesaro* it probably designates an abbreviation for semibreve or *tactus*. It is used as an alternative for the T-sign, having the same function in most cases. The ∧ sign is positioned almost exclusively above note values of short duration, such as *minimae, semiminimae,* or *chromae,* without any distinction between these values. A closer look at the script of Tablature A shows that the ∧ signs are most likely hastily written variants of the & sign. In fact, the scribe used only two different signs above the tablature letters, and only one of them offers accurate metric or rhythmic information.[27]

The scribe obviously checked his copying and erased (by razoring) incorrect tablature letters. None of these erased letters has a rhythmic sign placed above it. From this we can conclude that our scribe wrote down the tablature letters first, adding the signs above them only during a second phase, while checking his writing.[28] This procedure was also used in the Capirola Lute Book. Here, the scribe crossed out complete bars that were copied incorrectly; none of these bars bear any rhythmic signs. The scribe of *Thibault* (the source that has the closest relationship with *Pesaro*) ignored rhythmic signs entirely. It thus appears that in early lute tablature sources rhythmic indications did not have an important function.

Vertical lines, similar to bar lines, appear rarely and irregularly in Tablature A. In most cases they are found behind chords that initiate a new melodic formula and metrical unit.[29] Points that appear under the letters indicate an upward stroke either by the plectrum or by the index finger of the plucking hand; single notes without points are to be plucked downwards by the plectrum or by the thumb.[30] The dot (.) signs that are generally used in tablatures to indicate this upward–downward

[26] Different examples can be found in Vespasiano Amphiarco's calligraphy manual (Venice, 1554). See the facsimile in James Wardrop, *The Script of Humanism, 1460–1560* (Oxford, 1963), Table 56.

[27] The second sign is used as a variant of the T-sign, mostly above shorter note values.

[28] For further hints at this procedure in *Pesaro*, see Ivanoff, *Das Pesaro-Manuskript*, pp. 98–100.

[29] Only in a few cases did the scribe place the vertical lines in the position of later tablature lines or modern barlines.

[30] In his 'Regola per quelli che non ianno [*recte*: sanno] cantare', included in Spinacino's collection of 1507, the publisher Ottaviano Petrucci provides the first description of this now-well-known thumb–index technique. See Francesco Spinacino, *Intabulatura de lauto, libro primo / libro secondo* (Venice, 1507; facsimile rpt Geneva, 1978), fol. 2v.

technique also provide the lutenist with a certain orientation to where he is within a bar at a certain moment in his playing. They enable the player in most cases to reconstruct the metrical and rhythmic values of the tablature letters. Therefore, the scribes of early manuscript sources for the lute, like *Thibault,* could mostly dispense with additional indications of rhythm, like the headless rhythmic flags that appear above the staff (or, in Petrucci's books, *within* the staff) in most later tablatures. Earlier players who were familiar with the repertory of their time could obviously glean enough information about rhythm and meter by the (.) signs. Furthermore, many manuscript tablature sources, even from the seventeenth and eighteenth centuries, lack rhythmic indications. They may have served as an *aide-mémoire* for amateurs and beginners who were just learning the repertoire or, as Petrucci stated in his lute prints from 1507, 'for those who don't know to sing [from notation]' *(per quelli che non [s]anno cantare).*[31]

In my study and edition of *Pesaro,* the intabulations of given models in Tablature A, together with analyses of the tablature script, the indications given by the (.) signs, and the vertical tablature lines, were combined with a statistical analysis of grouping and frequency of occurrence of the additional signs used in Tablature A.[32] From all of this evidence there emerged detailed information concerning the rhythmic interpretation of the works in *Pesaro.* Nevertheless, the pieces still leave the final decisions to the lutenist who performs them; for in this repertory, one that exists within a long tradition of *ad hoc* performance and improvisation, personal choices of interpretation assume a large importance.

PLAYING AND UNDERSTANDING TABLATURE A

Numerous iconographical documents show that until at least around 1450, the lute was invariably plucked with a plectrum made from a bird's feather. Paintings and drawings show that lutenists generally held the plectrum between the index and middle fingers and plucked the strings with a shaking movement of the forearm and wrist. From around 1410, the little finger of the right hand was usually positioned on the soundboard of the instrument to give the plucking hand a more precise orientation. The up-and-down movement of the thumb–index technique is a residual of this plectrum technique and was preserved well into the seventeenth century. Again, numerous visual sources show that the transition from plectrum to thumb–index technique took place approximately between *ca.* 1460 and 1500. Until *ca.* 1500 both techniques existed simultaneously.[33]

---

[31]   Spinacino, *Intabulatura,* fol. 2v.

[32]   For details on the methods of statistical analysis that led to the rhythmical interpretation used in my edition of Tablature A in *Pesaro,* see Ivanoff, *Das Pesaro-Manuskript,* pp. 91–107.

[33]   Concerning details on this transition, see Ivanoff, 'Das Lautenduo im 15. Jahrhundert', pp. 151–6.

Folk, jazz, and rock guitar players use the plectrum (or 'flatpick') for playing single lines as well as for chordal playing. Similarly, present-day lutenists who perform fifteenth-century music use their instrument for playing both single lines and polyphony, often in a technically awkward combination of plectrum and finger technique. Some of the pieces contained in Tablature A provide ample evidence of a performance technique on the plectrum lute that combines single-line and chordal playing. This style provides a satisfactory solution for lutenists seeking to integrate the musical repertory from the second half of the fifteenth century into their solo lute playing.

Table 1.1 lists pieces in *Pesaro* that show specific features of plectrum technique. It should be noted that only the pieces indicated in Tablature A, which is the chronologically earliest layer of the manuscript, can be performed entirely with a plectrum; the repertory in the later tablature layers B and D shows some elements of plectrum technique incorporated in a musical context (for example notes on non-adjacent strings that have to be played simultaneously) that can only be realized through finger technique. Nevertheless, all of the plectrum pieces share the following features in common:

Table 1.1 *Instances of plectrum technique in the Pesaro Manuscript*

Tablature A		
arecercare,	*Pesaro*, p. 29	edition, p. 11
(a recercar)	p. 45	edition, p. 63
(interlude for *e Ladre*)		
A recercar,	p. 46	edition, p. 65
a recercar	p. 54	edition, p. 83
(postlude to *de tus biense*)		
ja pregamore	p. 61	edition, p. 93
de tus bie(n)se	p. 65	edition, p. 101
a recercar	p. 84	edition, p. 145
Tablature B		
Recercate d. Gasp.:		
Nr. 16.3.	*Pesaro*, p. 91	edition, p. 159
Nr. 16.4.	p. 93	edition, p. 161
Nr. 16.7.	p. 96	edition, p. 169
Nr. 16.8.	p. 171	edition, p. 171
Tablature D		
a recercar	*Pesaro*, p. 197	edition, p. 183

1. Chords of 5–6 notes on adjacent strings introduce single-line passages in equal note values (see Ex. 1.7a [*Pesaro*, p. 29; edition, p. 12]).
2. With the plectrum it is impossible to realize any independent voice leading of polyphonic compositions. Therefore, many pieces in *Pesaro* introduce a technique that is similar to the medieval *hoquetus*, in which the notes of two voices are performed in alternation, rather than simultaneously (see Ex. 1.6).

Ex. 1.6   *ja pregamore* (*Pesaro*, p. 63; edition, p. 98)[34]

In Ex. 1.6 the ornamented cadential formula in the top voice is interrupted by a note of the lower voice; the final a[1] appears after some delay.

THE RECERCARI

In the *recercari*, stereotyped melodic formulas *(Tactus)* are combined in sequential melodic patterns. This method of construction allowed the lutenist/composer to achieve longer structural units by a very simple method, as shown in Ex. 1.7b (*arecercare: Pesaro*, p. 30; edition, p. 14).

One of the main differences in how organists and lutenists employed these ornamental formulas was the ambitus/intervals these formulas covered. On the organ, awkward stretches or jumps of the hand were avoided by using formulas that generally did not exceed a third. Because of the completely different playing technique of the lute (strings in intervals of fourths plus a third), formulas covering much larger intervals were preferred.[35] These patterns differ fundamentally from the slightly later means of ornamentation used, for example, in the Capirola Lute Book.[36]

While most of the *recercari* in Tablature A appear to have a rather improvised, spontaneous nature, some details in these pieces show that they constitute carefully planned forms. *Arecercare* (*Pesaro*, p. 29; edition, p. 11), given as Ex. 1.7, unfolds in

---

[34] The blackened note heads show the notes that the arrangement shares with the polyphonic model *J'ay pri(n)s amours a ma devise*.

[35] In *Pesaro*, formulas D 2 and A 2 (Göllner's abbreviations) are the most preferred ones.

[36] This ornamentation technique has been described in detail in Howard Mayer Brown, 'Embellishment in Early Sixteenth-Century Italian Intabulations', *PRMA* 97 (1970/71) pp. 49–83.

four sections (marked I–IV) of roughly equal length. The first (I), introduced by a six-note chord on A, explores the hexachord a^1–f^2 in single-line technique. The final a^1 is reached by a downward melodic movement. The first chord of this piece already shows the contrast between melodic movement and tonality that is a common feature of early organ and lute music. The $c\sharp^1$ in the introductory 'A major' chord contrasts with the lower major second g^1 that follows, which is one of the typical elements of the Aeolian mode. As a further contrast, twenty notes later the note a is reached from the 'leading-note' $g\sharp$.

The second section (II) is a variation of the first, but in the lower octave; in the third section (III) an octave scale beginning A–a is stated five times in sequence at different pitch levels; and in the fourth and last section (IV) the melodic formula 'D 1' (Göllner's classification) is transposed and repeated on f^2–d^2–c^2–b^1–a^1–g^1–f^1. The final scale b–B deceptively targets the *finalis* A, and the piece ends unexpectedly with a chord on C.

The replacement of a chord with another chord on the parallel lower or higher third (or, in tonal terms, the relative major or minor chord) is a procedure that can be found in all of the works in *Pesaro*. This compositional technique is based on a succession of parallel tenths, for example:

$$b^1 \quad a^1 \quad g^1$$
$$g \quad\ \ f \quad\ \ e$$

Many pieces can, in fact, be reduced to a chordal pattern that is based solely on the fluctuation of relative minor or major chords. A *recercar* (*Pesaro*, p. 45; edition, p. 63), which obviously serves as an interlude between the two parts of the intabulation *e Ladre,* opens with a B♭ chord, which is followed by the 'relative minor' on g that begins a small series of chords. They are all built on the stepwise downward movement g–f–e, anticipating an arrival on d. The final chord in this downward movement, however, is instead the lower relative third B♭, which is followed again by the lower relative third g and a final cadence F–B♭.

To make the parallel intervals shown above playable on the plectrum lute, the intabulator must 'fill the space' with chords. Through this simple method, successive chains of tenths and sixths – a common element in vocal music of the late fifteenth and early sixteenth century – were adapted for the plectrum lute and transformed into a genuinely instrumental idiom. Most works in the *recercare* genre employ a cantus firmus supported by parallel tenths in the lowest voice; these intervals are enriched by chords, suitable for the plectrum lute. *Clausulae* provide formal structure to the pieces according to the tetrachords through which the upper voice is moving, while ornamental melodic formulas connect the single notes of the cantus firmus. Pieces structured in this manner could have been (and still can be) improvised by any lutenist familiar with the rudimentary instrumental techniques of the time.

Ex. 1.7   (1.7 a–c; 1.7 I–IV) *arecercare* (*Pesaro*, p. 29–30; edition, pp. 12–14)

Such pieces cannot be classified as true 'compositions'. Like many tablatures in the *Buxheimer Orgelbuch* and other organ sources of the fifteenth century, they are *exempla* – good or typical examples of an *ad hoc* or improvised performance.

THE INTABULATIONS

All of the structural elements that are present in the *Pesaro* ricercars can also be found in the arrangements of models in mensural notation or vocal models. The arrangements of the earliest two vocal models, the chansons *De tous biens playne* by

Hayne van Ghizeghem and *Jay pri(n)s amours* by Johannes Japart (both dating from *ca.* 1470–80), were notated one after the other in Tablature A. The scribal errors, along with the many musical similarities between the two works, show that the scribe most probably copied them from the same source. The arranger of *De tous biens playne* intabulated the superius and the chordal pattern of his model quite accurately, but he was obviously not interested in following the rondeau structure of the model. The cadences that define the original composition according to the rondeau form in the superius and tenor are evaded by the contratenor (according to Zarlino's well-known rule *fuggire le cadenze).* The intabulator obviously concentrated on the tenor–superius structure of the chanson, which he used as a kind of cantus firmus, connecting the single chords by ornamental melodic formulas, as in the *recercari.* While he left about three-fourths of the notes from these voices unchanged, the arranger metrically displaced about half of the notes from the contratenor and eliminated about one fourth. The vocal model thus served as a frame for the construction of a genuinely instrumental composition with the original tenor–superius pair acting as a structural aid, in the same way as a given cantus was used in fifteenth-century organ music.

PLAYING THE CORRECT INSTRUMENT

The pieces in Tablature A call for a six-course lute in relative A-tuning. The left-hand fingering of some of the larger chords can be comfortably executed on a lute with a rather short string length (approximately 50–5 cm between bridge and nut). Unfortunately, there is only one extant lute from the first third of the sixteenth century that has come down to us in a presumably original state. This lute was most probably built in Venice and was in the collection of Laurence C. Witten II that is now at the Shrine to Music collection in South Dakota. Friedemann Hellwig has dated this instrument to shortly after 1500.[37] Other than the fact that the instrument has only five courses, it is perfectly suited to play the pieces in Tablature A. It has a string length of 50 cm and the ribs are made from ivory. The distance between the lowest and highest strings is 2.6 cm at the nut and 6.8 cm at the bridge. The wide distance between the courses at the bridge is an advantage for plectrum technique, while the narrow span at the nut allows the use of the left-hand thumb for fingering; this technique furthermore makes the fingering of the widely stretched five- and six-note chords in Tablature A a bit easier.

In the absence of any relevant European descriptions, information concerning the appropriate lute plectrum is offered by the partly still-living tradition employed by *al-'ūd* players in the Islamic world. According to tradition, the *'ūd* player Ziryāb

---

[37] Friedemann Hellwig, 'Lutemaking in the late 15th and 16th Century', *LSJ* 16 (1974), pp. 24–38.

(d. 852), introduced a new type of plectrum *(midrāb al-'ūd)* made from an eagle's feather. This type of plectrum is still made in the following way: the upper (softer) end of the feather is spliced with a sharp knife to a length of about 8–10 cm; the surface of one half of the spliced piece is then smoothed and cleaned from the spongy substance in the interior part; finally, the tip of the plectrum is rounded and smoothed again.

CONCLUSION

From the above, it will be seen that a number of pieces in *Pesaro* were originally intended for the plectrum lute, although in their notation they do not differ much from the other pieces in the manuscript. Most of the works in *Pesaro* were copied from earlier, still unknown, sources. During the time when the copying of the manuscript took place, plectrum technique and finger technique were both used on the lute. The lutenist who copied the pieces into Tablature A had either already made the complete transition to finger technique, or used finger and plectrum technique alternately, according to the musical structure of the pieces. Pieces employing the originally plectrum-based technique of strumming full chords and connecting them with single-line passages echoed well into the sixteenth century, as the dances *zum durchstreichen* ('to strum') in German tablature sources show.[38] Present-day lutenists have both options at their hands – or plectrum!

[38]   A good example is the *Gassenhauer* by Hans Newsidler contained in his *Ein Newgeordent künstlich Lautenbuch* (Nuremberg, 1536), fol. x.

2

LUTE TABLATURE INSTRUCTIONS IN ITALY: A SURVEY OF THE *REGOLE* FROM 1507 TO 1759

DINKO FABRIS

The introduction of music printing in Venice at the beginning of the sixteenth century appears to have resolved a long-standing problem of achieving a wide commercial distribution for musical rules or *regole*. Such publications were intended for use by amateurs who may not have had access to a teacher or were ignorant of musical notation. But despite the breadth and quantity of the subjects they cover, no single sixteenth-century treatise quite satisfies our desire to understand fully the music of this period. When the *Prattica di musica* (Venice, 1592/1622) appeared, its author, Ludovico Zacconi, was accused by contemporary professionals of having dared to expose the innermost secrets of music, and thus undermining and devaluing the importance of the personal transmission of an art that, by tacit consensus, no one had ever fully revealed.

The case of the lute is particularly revealing. Despite its popularity, especially in Italy, the instrument inspired relatively few instruction books for the instrument, and the information contained in any one print is insufficient. Lute instructors in modern times who have tried to teach the instrument based on sixteenth- and seventeenth-century practices are well aware of this problem. As Diana Poulton points out, 'one of the great difficulties of reconstructing a "method" for the Renaissance lute is the fact that, during the period of its greatest flowering, no really complete book of instruction was ever produced'.[1]

Musicologists, too, have sought to integrate the role of instructions and rules into the history of the lute.[2] Nevertheless, almost all research has concentrated on non-

---

[1] Diana Poulton, *A Tutor for the Renaissance Lute* (London, 1991), p. 1. For other modern manuals based on early instruction books, see, for example, Howard Mayer Brown, *Embellishing 16th-Century Music* (London, 1976), Oscar Ohlsen, *Aspectos tecnicos esenciales en la ejecucion del Laud* (Santiago, 1984), and Roland Stearns, 'A Manual of Lute, Vihuela, and Guitar Tablatures with Surveys of Transcription Practice, Instrumental Technique, and Beginning Pedagogy', Ph.D. diss., University of Idaho, 1978; for information on specific aspects of lute technique, see Paul Beier, 'Right Hand Position in Renaissance Lute Technique', *JLSA* 12 (1979), pp. 5–24.

[2] See Daniel Heartz, 'Les premières "instructions" pour le luth (jusqu'à vers 1550)' in *Le luth et sa musique,* ed. Jean Jacquot (Paris, 1957), pp. 77–92, and Karl Scheit, 'Ce que nous enseignent les traités de luth des environs de 1600',

---

Italian lute instructions and methods, and until now the only article to confront Italian sources up to 1550 remains that of almost forty years ago by Daniel Heartz, which is cursory and incomplete. The present study seeks to fill this gap with an analysis of all known Italian manuscript and printed sources containing rules from the end of the fifteenth century to around 1750. The sources are listed in Table 2.1 (pp. 18–20) and are compared to non-Italian printed lute instructions, which are listed in Table 2.2 (pp. 21–2).

RULES FOR READING TABLATURE

From the very first Venetian edition of tablature printed by Petrucci in 1507, the lute enjoyed a commercial prosperity that was unrivalled by any other instrument for over a century. All of Petrucci's lute publications for a period of fifteen years began with the *Regole per quelli che non sanno cantare,* which were occasionally reprinted in Latin, in addition to the usual Italian, in order to attract a wider international public. These rules were intended to provide untutored dilettantes with a basic knowledge of the rudiments of music so that they might learn the pieces contained in each collection by themselves and for their own amusement. One might compare such anthologies with some modern guitar methods intended for the complete beginner. But the few sentences contained in these rules could never have served as a comprehensive self-instruction, nor could they have aided the lutenist to play the more difficult compositions, which were probably intended for professionals. Rather than a 'method' for learning to play the lute, these rules may be considered as a synthetic and simplistic reduction of the musical theory of the time – the minimum information necessary to make sense of the works to be performed – that were intended, literally, for 'those who don't know how to sing'.

The main topic that these rules seek to address, however, is the interpretation of lute tablature, suggesting that this system of essentially graphic musical notation was not yet very well known. German lutenists and theorists of the same period – such

---

in *Le luth et sa musique,* pp. 93–105. See also the following articles in the same volume that deal with rules and instructions for the lute: Diana Poulton, 'La technique du jeu du luth en France et en Angleterre', pp. 107–19, and Thurston Dart, 'La méthode de luth de Miss Mary Burwell', pp. 121–6.

A study that examines both Italian and non-Italian rules is Hiroyuki Minamino, 'Sixteenth-Century Lute Treatises with Emphasis on Process and Techniques of Intabulation', Ph.D. diss., 2 vols., University of Chicago, 1988. Other useful studies of non-Italian lute instructions are H. Sommer, 'Lautentraktate des 16. und 17. Jahrhunderts in Rahmen der deutschen und französischen Lautentabulaturen', diss., University of Berlin, 1922; W. S. Casey, 'Printed English Lute Instruction Books, 1568–1610', Ph.D. diss., University of Michigan, 1960; and Jean-Michel Vaccaro, *La musique de luth en France au XVIe siècle* (Paris, 1981), pp. 91–117. Such studies are almost completely lacking in Italian; a first approach was attempted by the Gruppo di Studio del Conservatorio di Milano, which produced a series of summary investigations on 'La tecnica esecutiva degli strumenti a tastiera e del liuto nelle fonti storiche', in *Praxis: Studi e testi sull'interpretazione della musica* (Rovereto, 1983), part II: 'La tecnica del liuto', pp. 154–62.

Table 2.1: *Printed books and manuscripts produced in Italy (1480–ca. 1759) containing rules or instructions for lute*

Date	Author of rules	Title/abbrev.	City of origin	Type of rules	Observations
1480–90?		*Bologna*	Naples	10	
1490–1500		1490–1500		3, 6	
1507	Petrucci	1507_1 and 1507_2	Venice	1, 2, 4	No extant copy; Rules = 1507_1
1508	Petrucci	[1508_1]	Venice	1, 2, 4	Rules = 1507_1
1508	Petrucci	1508_2	Venice	1, 2, 4	Rules = 1507_1
1509	Petrucci	15091	Venice	1, 2, 4	Rules = 1507_1
1511	Petrucci	15111	Venice	1, 2, 4	Rules = 1507_1
ca. 1517	Capirola	*Capirola*	Brescia/Venice	3, 4, 5, 8, 9	
1520	Petrucci	$152?_1$	Venice	1, 2, 4	Rules = 1507_1
1533	Lanfranco	*Scintille*	Brescia	3, 4, 6, 9, 10	
1536	Francesco da Milano?	*Libro I e II d.Fortuna*	Naples	2, 4	
before 1540?	Strambi	Rules	Rome	7	Only copy in Bologna
1540–50	T. Biondi?	*Pesaro*		3	Later section in an older ms., Neapolitan tab.
1543	Ganassi	1543_2	[Venice]		
1546	Barberiis	$1546_{2–4}$	Venice	2, 4, 9	
after 1546 but after 1603?	[Cavaliere del Liuto?]	Ms. addition in 1546_5	Rome	4, 8	In the Sorau copy, not extant. Ms. in Latin and Polish
1546	?	1546_8	Venice	2, 4	Also instructions on the choice of dances
1546	?	1546_{11}	Venice	2, 4	'Regola alli lettori'; rpt 1548
1546	?	Ms. addition in 1546_{13}		2, 10	In the copy in London, British Library. 1 fol. added with ms. Notes on theory and hexachords
before 1550?	M. Pagano	Rules	Venice	7	Only copy in Stockholm
1559	B. Lieto	1559_5	Naples	2–6, 8, 9, 10	The first lute treatise, Neapolitan tab.
1566	V. Dorico	1566_1	Rome	2, 4	
1568	V. Galilei	1568_2	Venice	2, 4, 8, 9, 10	First intabulation method
1569	V. Galilei	1569_8	Venice	2, 4, 8, 9, 10	Rpt = 1568_2 second part only
1582	Brambilla, M.	[1582_2]	[Rome?]	7	Broadside sheet for cittern or lute? No extant copy
1584	V. Galilei	1584_5	Venice	2, 4, 8, 9, 10	
1585	M. Carrara	1585_5	Rome	7	Copy in Florence; engraving Brambilla, ed. Ruberti = 1594_4 modified

ca. 1580		Ms. Florence	Lyon or Italy?	3, 10	
ca. 1580–90		Ms. Genoa	Genoa	3, 10	
1590–*ca.* 1605		Ms. Turin, BN Mus. IV. 43/2		3, 10	Ms addition to the edition of Orso da Celano, Venice, 1567
1594	M. Carrara	1594$_4$	Rome	7	Copy in Florence; ed. Ruberti = 1585$_5$ modified
end 16th century		Ms. Florence	Florence	10	Small treatise on basso continuo for lute
beg. 17th century		Ms. Paris BN, Rés. 50	Florence	3, 9	See Coelho, *Manuscript Sources*, pp. 128–9
1601	S. Cerreto	*Della musica . . .*	Naples	3, 4, 6, 8, 9, 10	Section dedicated to the lute in a musical treatise; Neapolitan tab.
before 1603	Lorenzini	Rules	[Rome]	3, 4, 5, 8, 9	Edited by Besard, Dowland et al.
1608–9		Ms. Florence BN Magl. 106	Florence	3, 10	See Coelho, *Manuscript Sources*, pp. 80–2
1608–12		Ms. Nuremberg 33.748/271 [4]	Florence	10	Example of b.c . figured and realized in lute tab. See Coelho, *Manuscript Sources*, p. 116
1613	P. Cerone	*El Melopeo*	Naples	3, 4, 5, 9, 10	Section dedicated to the lute in a theoretical treatise in Spanish.
1614	Melii	*Libro II*	Venice	4, 5, 9	Instructions
1615	M. Carrara	Rules	Rome	7	Only copy in Paris, BN = 1585$_4$ modified
1616	Melii	*Libro III*	Venice	3, 4, 5, 9	Instructions
1616	Melii	*Libro IV*	Venice	3, 4, 5, 9	
1620	Melii	*Libro V*	Venice	4, 5, 9	
1623	Piccinini	*Libro I*	Bologna	3, 4, 5, 8, 9	
1627–49		Ms. Rome, Barb. Lat. 4145	Rome	10	Basso continuo exercises and elementary music theory; See Coelho, *Manuscript Sources*, pp. 145–7
1630–40		Ms. Nuremberg 33.748/271 [8]		3, 10	French lute and harpsichord; 1 work for archlute
1636	Valentini	Rome, Ms. Barb. Lat. 4395	Rome	2, 3, 4, 8, 9, 10	Treatise with examples
1640	Kapsberger	*Libro IV di chitarrone*	Rome	3, 4, 5, 9	Instructions for theorbo

ca. 1650	Valentini	Rome, Barb Lat. 4433	Rome	2, 3, 4, 5, 8, 9	Theoetical treatise with examples
1657–ca. 1666		Ms.Venice, Marciana 1793		3, 10	Lessons for b.c. and diminutions; See Coelho, *Manuscript Sources*, pp. 162–3
1670–5	Bertacchini? Estense Mus. 239	Ms. Modena, Biblioteca	Modena	4, 10	Contains over 90 intabulated *cadenze finale* for theorbo
1759–17??	F. Dalla Casa	Ms. Bologna	Bologna	2, 3, 4, 6, 9, 10	Large theoretical section, with rules for basso continuo and scales for lute and theorbo

Column 3

The dates refer to Howard Brown, *Instrumental Music Printed before 1600* (Cambridge, MA, 1980); for manuscripts, see the list below;

Column 5

 1 rules for reading tablature in Latin
 2 rules for reading tablature in Italian
 3 tuning systems
 4 general indications on performance practice
 5 ornaments and other signs
 6 drawings of instruments or players
 7 broadside sheets (containing almost all of the other categories)
 8 intabulation methods
 9 organological indications
10 correspondence between mensural notation and tablature or between different tablatures; rules for general music theory

as Virdung, who published the first printed example of German organ tablature in 1511, or Martin Agricola and Hans Judenkünig, who published books in 1528 and 1523, respectively – speak of tablature as if it were as recent an invention as the rise of finger technique over plectrum technique. Since the earliest manuscript sources of lute tablature are roughly contemporary with the first tablature prints, it would seem that Italian tablature could not have been in use earlier than the last years of the fifteenth century. According to tradition, German lute tablature derived from organ tablature around the time of the blind lutenist and organist Conrad Pauman (the earliest source, the *Königsteiner Liederbuch,* is dated 1470–3). On the assumption that this is accurate, then French tablature possibly derived from the German system, transliterating the letters from the Gothic alphabet. At present we know of only one source written in French tablature prior to 1500, the heart-shaped 'Pesaro Manuscript', while the first published source in French tablature, printed by Attaingnant, appeared only in 1529.[3]

---

[3] On fifteenth-century tablatures, see Vladimir Ivanoff's chapter in this volume.

    It is not the intent of the present study to deal with evidence pertaining to fifteenth-century lute sources (for which the reader is referred to Vladimir Ivanoff's chapter in this volume) or with the wealth of indirect evidence on the practice and organology of the instrument, which, even if limited to Italy, would occupy an entire book in itself, considering the theoretical treatises, chronicles, archival documents, and, above all, iconography.

Christopher Page has put this traditional hypothesis into doubt with his sugges-tion that the earliest French tablature might be recognized in a late fourteenth-century treatise.[4] The clear derivation of the 'presumed French tablature' of Page's source from the most common medieval system of didactic notation, the alphabet, is striking. Moreover, in the tablature fragments at the University Library in Bologna, dated 1480 and considered as the earliest written source of Italian tablature, letters from medieval alphabet notation are written under the tablature numbers, presu-mably to clarify the musical significance of a notation that was still hardly known.[5]

The connection between the earliest tablatures and theoretical and pedagogical questions is revealed yet again in an enigmatic Venetian treatise dated between 1490 and 1500. In a diagram of the instrument's strings (significantly, there are already six courses with the sixth tuned to D), the frets, including the nut, are indicated by the numbers 1 to 8, and the open and fretted positions for each string are labelled with the corresponding letter of alphabet notation.[6] Here, then, the two notational sys-tems co-exist. What this important document does not help to clarify is which type of tablature is derived from which; it seems probable that the universal diffusion of alphabet notation favoured the birth of French tablature, while Italian tablature seems to have originated from a mechanical indication of the frets. But it is equally significant that the numbering of the frets in this diagram starts with 1 (indicating the nut, rather than the first fret), as in the so-called 'Neapolitan tablature', and not 0, as in normal Italian tablature. It is no coincidence that the Bologna fragments as well as the small amount of Italian tablature contained in the Pesaro manuscript use the Neapolitan system. This type of notation must have been much more common than extant sources reveal, because otherwise it would not have made sense to include rules for reading it in popular broadside tablature sheets, which I will discuss further on; on the other hand its use may have been limited to Naples.

Rules for playing from Italian tablature appear in the first edition of lute music published by Petrucci in 1507, and the same rules are to be found, with slight modifications, in practically every lute book published up to 1520. We know that

---

4   See Christopher Page, 'A French Lute Tablature in the 14th Century?' *EM* 9 (1981), pp. 488–92. Page admits, in fact, that the diagram shown in the treatise examined (Berkeley, University of California Library, MS 774, p. 51, dated after 1375) is not necessarily French tablature but might in some way be related to alphabet notation.

5   Bologna, Biblioteca Universitaria, MS 596.HH.2/4. See David Fallows, '15th-Century Tablatures for Plucked Instruments: A Summary, a Revision and a Suggestion', *LSJ* 19 (1977), pp. 18–28 and Dinko Fabris, 'Prime aggiunte italiane al volume RISM B/7', *FAM* 28 (1982), p. 105. As late as the second half of the sixteenth century, lutenists required charts to convert letter tablature to number tablature, as seen in 'Instruction de la Tablature de Luth' that opens the *Premier Livre de Tablature de Luth of M. Jean Paul Paladin* (Lyon, 1560); see Dinko Fabris, 'Influenze stilistiche e circolazione manoscritta della musica per liuto in Italia e Francia nella prima metà del Seicento', *RdM* 77 (1991), p. 312.

6   The diagram is found on a page added to Venice, Biblioteca Nazionale Marciana, Ms Lat. 336, coll. 1581 (fol. 1r). It is reproduced, but with no indication as to the presence of lute tablature, in Don Harrán, 'Intorno a un codice veneziano quattrocentesco', *Sm* 8 (1979), p. 49, fig.1. I wish to thank Franco Pavan for attracting my attention to this document.

Table 2.2: *Non-Italian printed books containing rules or instructions for lute, published before 1600*

Date	Author of rules	Title / abbrev.	Country	Type of Rules	Observations
1511	Virdung	*Musica Getuscht*	Germany	1, 3, 4, 6, 9, 10	
151?	Judenkünig	$151?_1$	Germany	1, 3, 4, 5, 9	
1523	Judenkünig	1523_2	Germany	2, 3, 4, 5, 6, 9	No extant copy; Rules = 1507
1530	O. Finé	1530_2	France	1, 3, 9, 10	Instruction manual printed by P. Attaingnant
1503	?	Ms. Addenda to 1530_2	France	10	Annotations in Italian in the names of the notes
1532	H. Gerle	1532_2	Germany	2, 3, 4, 6, 9	
1536	L. Milán	1536_5	Spain	2, 3, 4, 9	
1536	Newsidler	1536_6	Germany	2, 3, 4, 9	
1538	Narváez	1538_1	Spain	2, 3, 4, 9	
1544	Newsidler	1544_{1-3}	Germany	2, 4, 9	Rules = 1536_6
1545	Phalèse	1545_3	France	2, 4, 9	
1546	H. Gerle	1546_9	Germany	2, 3, 4, 9	
1546	Mudarra	1546_{14}	Spain	2, 3, 4, 6, 9	
1547	Newsidler	1547_4	Germany	2, 4, 9	Rules = 1536_6
1547	Valderrábano	1547_5	Spain	2, 4, 9	
1547	Phalèse	1547_{7-8}	France	2, 4, 9	Rules = 1543_3
1549	Bermudo	1549_3	Spain	2, 3, 4, 6, 9, 10	See also 1550_1, 1555
1549	Newsidler	1549_6	Germany	2, 4, 9	Rules = 1536_6
1549	Phalèse	1549_8	Germany	1, 4, 9	1545_6 but in Latin
1550	Wyssenbach	1550_4	Germany	2, 4	
1551?	Le Roy	$[1551_9]$	France	2, 3, 4, 9	Cf. successive editions
1552	Pisador	1552_7	Spain	2, 4	
1553	de Rippe	1553_7	France	3	
1554	Fuenllana	1554_3	Spain	2, 4	
1557	Henestrosa	1557_2	Spain	2, 4, 9	
1560	Paladin	1560_3	France	2, 3	
1562	Heckel	1562_{3-4}	Germany	2, 4	
1563	Wyssenbach	1563_{10}	Germany	2, 4	
1565	Santa Maria	1563_{10}	Spain	2, 3, 4, 5, 9, 10	
1568	Le Roy	1568_3	England	2, 3, 4, 9	= 1555_9 but in English
1570	Le Roy	1570_2	France	1, 3, 4, 9	= 1555_9 but in Latin
1572	Jobin	1572_1	Germany	2, 4	
1574	Le Roy	1574_2	England	2, 3, 4, 9	= 1555_9 but in English
1576	Daza	1576_1	Spain	2, 4	
1592	Cabezón	$[1578_3]$	Spain	2, 3, 4, 9	
1592	Adriaensen	1592_6	Holland	2, 10	
1592	Waissel	1592_{12}	Germany	2, 4	

Column 3
The dates refer to the bibliography of printed books in Brown, *Instrumental Music*

Column 5:
1 rules for reading tablature in Latin
2 rules for reading tablature in the national language
3 tuning systems
4 general indications on performance practice
5 ornaments and other signs
6 drawings of instruments or players
7 broadside sheets (containing almost all of the other categories)
8 intabulation methods
9 organological indications
10 correspondence between mensural notation and tablature or between different tablatures and rules for general music theory

in 1498 the Signoria of Venice granted Petrucci a twenty-year privilege to publish and sell books in both mensural notation and lute tablature, and that the lutenist Marco dall'Aquila was also granted a similar ten-year privilege limited to lute tablature in 1505, but apparently no tablature book was published until 1507.[7] Who was the author of the *Regole?* It would be difficult to imagine Petrucci using rules by his competitor Marco dall'Aquila, so perhaps the rules were written by Francesco Spinacino, the first 'intabulator' in the service of Petrucci, or by the publisher himself, who in 1513 obtained another privilege from Pope Leo X to print the first organ tablature, of which he declared himself 'inventor'. Whatever the identity of their author, the *Regole* were extraordinarily successful, especially when one considers that they were reprinted essentially unaltered in all of Petrucci's lute publications and were even borrowed by other publishers up to at least 1548. Between 1507 and 1520 the *Regole per quelli che non sanno cantare* are identical not only in their content (there were occasionally a few corrections or additions to the various editions) but in the typographical setting as well. Even more surprising is the existence of a practically identical version in the *Primo libro della Fortuna* of Francesco da Milano (Naples, 1536).[8] The volume by Francesco da Milano and Pietro Paolo Borrono of 1546 (rpt 1548) reproduces once again rules based on the Petrucci prototype, but the variants start to become increasingly significant, as already seen in the title: *Regola per quelli che non sanno la Intavolatura*.[9]

The first completely new rules for playing from tablature that can be attributed without question to a single author appear in the tablatures printed in Venice by Girolamo Scotto in 1546. These consist of rules 'For those who have no [knowledge of] music, and who also have little practice in playing the lute . . .' signed by Melchiorre de Barberiis and inserted into his *Quarto, Quinto,* and *Sesto* lute books.[10] In addition, Joan Maria da Crema, in his *Regola alli lettori* of the *Libro Terzo* of 1546 (but curiously not in the *Libro Primo* of the same year) declares his intention to 'aid beginners as I desire' ('giovar come desidero à prencipianti'), beginning with an explanation of the 'style of tablature described by others at other times, who composed similar characters, strings and signs, in the easiest possible way. Conceding

7   The privilege granted to Marco dall'Aquila is printed in Howard Mayer Brown, *Instrumental Music Printed before 1600* (Cambridge, MA, 1980), pp. 11–12. The dedication (reprinted by Brown) might be interpreted as a claim to the invention of Italian tablature on the part of Marco dall'Aquila, but it more probably refers to the first application of movable type (carved by the lutenist himself?) to the printing of lute tablature.

8   The differences between the edition of 1536$_1$ and Petrucci, other than a change in typeface from italics to Roman type, are purely orthographical, and the concluding sentence is new.

9   In 1546$_8$, line 1, the beginning is changed a little, from 'Prima deve intendere' to 'Prima doveti sapere'; the new elements concern the names of the courses (defined as consisting of double strings) and the performance of chords with a dot printed next to them, the updating of rhythmic signs with rhomboid note heads from contemporary mensural notation, and the introduction of a legato sign for held notes.

10   'Per dichiarare a quelli che non hanno musicha, & etiam hanno pocca pratica nel sonar de Liuto io li mostrerò qui disotto per ragione, e per pratica . . .'

in everything, however, to those who know better.'[11] Barberiis's instructions occupy two densely written pages and aspire for the first time to take the reader beyond the mere reading of tablature.

Essentially, the rules contained in Italian lute books from the first half of the sixteenth century discuss the following issues:

- The correlation between the six lines of tablature and the six courses on the lute (the names of the courses and their disposition as double strings are cited for the first time in 1546_{11} – the subset refers to Brown, *Instrumental Music Printed Before 1600*. The disposition of Italian tablature, with the top line representing the 'contrabasso' is never discussed, except in the 1536 *Libro secondo della Fortuna*, where, due to the use of Neapolitan tablature, a different ordering of the lines is used.[12]

- The correlation between the tablature numbers and the frets of the lute up to the twelfth fret. Carrara, writing in 1585, claims to have been the first to have added frets on the body of the lute up to the rose (seventeenth fret!) in order to play cleanly ('aggionti tutti i tasti sino à la Rosa per comodità di sonar le corde nette').

- The explanation of rhythmic signs, from breve to fusa, placed above the tablature. Signs for ternary rhythm and rhythmic proportions are included up to 1520; after that date, the rules describe a new method of placing the rhythmic signs, whereby the sign is only set in the tablature when there is a change in rhythm and not over every note. The *Libro Primo della Fortuna* of 1536 adds dotted rhythmic signs (with a printing error at the third sign). From 1546 the graphic form of printed rhythm signs change.

- Basic indications of right-hand technique. Tablature characters with a dot underneath must be played upwards with any finger except the thumb, usually the index; those without the dot must be played downwards with the thumb. The placement of a dot to the side of a character in 1546_{11} indicates the simultaneous execution of the notes of a chord.

- Indications for left-hand performance technique. These are mostly limited to the sign for legato ♯, introduced in 1546_{11} in both the rules and the music. That this was considered an important aspect of performance is confirmed in the Capirola manuscript. Marks indicating a left-hand grace (trill or appoggiatura), consisting of an open and closed parenthesis enclosing the two tablature characters to be

---

[11] 'modo della Tabolatura altre volte dimostrato d'altri che hanno composto simil Caratteri, corde & Segni con quel più facil modo che sia possibile. Remettendoci però in ogni cosa à chi più ne saperà.'

[12] The rules of the *Libro secondo della Fortuna* of 1536 say, in fact, 'al contrario degli antichi, li quali tenevano la prima corda de sopra per contrabasso, e noi la tenemo per lo canto' (line 2). Line 5 of the same rules declare that tablature without the zero is an entirely new invention: 'Gli antichi mettevano un zero, ò vero .o. che significava vacante, & pero quando serà signato .1. significa che se toccha quella corda, dove é tal segno vacante . . .' In order to facilitate reading the early Italian texts quoted in the present study, I have transcribed them to conform to modern Italian, normalizing the spelling and expanding abbreviations.

ornamented, are used and described for the first time in the 1548 reprint of Borrono's *Secondo libro:* 'and where you find a circle with this form ( ), two fingers must be placed on the given string and [you must] firmly hold down the finger which is on the lower number . . .' ('e dove trovereti uno circolo in tal forma ( ) se ha da amettere duo deta sopra detta corda et tenere fermo il detto qual e sopra il menor numero . . .').

In 1546 Barberiis and Joan Maria da Crema added more detailed instructions, dealing with:

- the possibility of intabulating from one to four voices (but possibly five or six voices as well).
- a more detailed explanation of the legato sign ♯. Barberiis: 'Wherever you find these signs ♯♯, in that place you must hold your hand, that is, the finger [must be] held down firmly while you accompany that note for many shorter notes, because in the music those notes are long, so therefore you must firmly hold down [the notes] marked by the ♯ . . .';[13] Joan Maria: 'The finger must not be moved from the fret until it has played the value of four successive [notes] or of two held more or less as is needed. Indeed, the finger must be held a short or a long time as well as possible, because it is important for the harmony . . .'[14] Later, Joan Maria enters into greater detail about the importance of rhythm in music, 'because one must not hide or be silent about things that might help the student'.
- the first meticulous description in an Italian source about alternation in right-hand fingering as applied to diminutions. Barberiis: 'when you find some dots . . . those strokes that have a dot must be made upwards, and those quick notes that do not have a dot need to be made downwards with the big finger [the thumb]. And when you find quick notes on or above the tenor [fourth course], you must play them downwards with the big finger, and when they are on or beneath the tenor, they must be played upwards with the first finger next to the thumb, for great agility and speed of the hand . . .'[15] Barberiis then explains how to handle cases of erroneously printed dots in lute books: 'If the quick notes are of an odd number, the first must be played upwards, and if they are of an even number, play the first downwards . . . to be more precise, I tell you that this rule must always be obeyed: in diminution, the last stroke before the chord must always be played

---

[13] 'Dove ritroverai questi segni ♯♯ in quello loco li debbi tenir la mano, cioè il dito firmo fina tanto che pagi quella nota con tante minute, perche quella nota son longa nel canto, et per tanto fa bisogna tenir fermo dove sono le ♯'

[14] 'ne si dee movere il dito dal Tasto sin che non habbia sonato il valore di .4. seguenti o di due tenute o piu o meno come sia di bisogno. Et in somma si dee tener il dito o poco o assai meglio che si puo, percioche importa all'Armonia'

[15] 'quando ritroverai alcuni ponti . . . quella botta dove son el ponto dar si debbe in suso. Et quella minuta che non hanno ponto dare se bisogna in giu con lo dito grosso. Et quando troverai dal tenore in suso una minuta dare si debbe con el dito grosso in giu, et quando sara dal tenor in giu, dare si debbe in suso con el primo dito appresso el polize, per una tanto commodità et prestezza di mano . . .'

upwards, because [in this way] the hand is comfortable, and is quick to reach its positions.'[16]

The advice that publishers of lute books evidently considered sufficient for amateurs may be evaluated by a comparison with the only extant early sixteenth-century manuscript instructions by a professional lutenist. The rules transcribed by the student Vidal in the Vincenzo Capirola manuscript (*ca.* 1517) have been amply studied, so I will limit myself to an overview of their main concepts.[17]

- Capirola excuses himself for having included 'at the beginning and somewhat further along . . . some trifles, easy or of little importance ('nel principio, et più oltra scorendo . . . qualche choseta facile, o di pocho momento . . .'). The same excuse is made by Dalza (1508) who promises in the future to publish more difficult works for those who are more advanced in the art, and by Joan Maria (1546); and yet much of the music found in these collections seems far from appropriate for just mere beginners.
- *Indications for the left hand:* the placement of the fingers on the neck of the instrument and insistence on the necessity of holding legato notes.[18] The most innovative indication, unique in the literature, refers to the production of a double sound on one of the inner courses. The technique consists of separating the two strings of a 'mezzano' course with the little finger of the left hand so that one of them can be stopped on the fret and the other played in open position. There is a practical example in the manuscript, in the *Paduana discordata*, where an extra line is added to the tablature indicating the split course. According to Capirola, one cannot easily describe this technique: it must be observed in practice. Another startling practice hinted at is the use of the thumb to stop the sixth course, although his advice is not to use it often: 'et manco che adoperi el deo groso, e piu bel al veder sul manego' (to paraphrase: the neck of the lute is prettier the less you use the thumb). The use of this technique in the first half of the sixteenth century, which may seem strange to us now but has a parallel in folk and rock guitar technique, is corroborated by at least one authoritative

---

[16] 'se le minute son disparo la prima si debbe daro in suso. Et se le minute son paro la prima darai in giu . . . per piu chiaro ti dico e questa regula e ferma che sempre in diminutione la ultima botta avanti el picego, dare si debbe in su, perche la man se accomoda, e é presta alli suoi luoghi.'

[17] See Otto Gombosi, ed., *Compositione di Meser Vincenzo Capirola. Lute-Book (circa 1517)* (Neuilly-sur-Seine, 1955). A facsimile edition of the manuscript has been published with an introduction by Orlando Cristoforetti (Florence, 1981). See also the English translation of Capirola's rules in Federico Marincola, 'The Instructions from Vincenzo Capirola's Lute Book: A New Translation', *The Lute* 23 (1983), pp. 23–8. Capirola–Vidal, too, calls the instructions at the beginning of the manuscript 'regola', provided so as to help the lutenist understand 'il notare de dito libr.º e li bono modi del portar de la mano e quelo oservar tu de'.

[18] In discussing legato, Capirola divulges 'il più bel segreto et arte' as if citing an Aristotelian maxim: 'avertisi nel sonar sempre tenir ferme le bote col deo, over dei sul manego fina che trovi altre bote che te sia forza lasarlle [*sic*], cusi sempre farai de man, in man, per che l'importa asai, e tuti non l'intende'.

theoretical treatise which will be discussed shortly, that of Silvestro Ganassi. It is also to be seen in numerous iconographical sources, such as the Raphael drawing on the cover of the present volume, as well as the recently discovered painting at the Pinacoteca of Como, which has been identified as possibly a portrait of Francesco da Milano.

- *Indications for the right hand:* upward and downward strokes with alternate fingers, as in the printed rules. The first written evidence of the practice of moving the thumb to the inside of the fingers in diminutions is found here.
- *Chords:* care must be taken in making each note of the chord sound well, particularly inner notes that risk being underplayed. The use of the *barré* is recommended in chords to facilitate playing legato.
- *Gracefulness in the placing and carriage of the hands:* Capirola uses the word 'galanteria' in accordance with the contemporary aesthetic theories of Castiglione's *Il Cortegiano*. It, too, cannot be described but has to be demonstrated 'live'.
- *Rhythm:* this is limited to advice on playing groups of quavers and semiquavers, which are often confused by beginners.
- *Ornamentation:* this is the most important and innovative section of the rules.[19] There are a number of types, otherwise unknown in contemporary lute prints except for the one described above in 1546_{11}:
  - (a) Tremolo, indicated by a number written in red dots. It is described generically as a 'thing that trembles, where you don't hold the finger still' ('cosa tremolizzante che non si tien fermo il deo'), to be used mainly on long notes, 'and those who know how to play, do them of their own initiative where they please' ('et chi sano sonar i fano da sua posta dove li piace').
  - (b) Held notes (tenuto), indicated by three different signs: X on single held notes; X to denote the beginning of sections where there are several notes or chords to be held; O to denote the end of a tenuto section initiated by the previous sign.

Capirola ends his rules with an important section dedicated to 'secrets of the strings'. The courses are given their usual names and there are technical details about stringing, tuning, and other 'secrets' for making the lute perfect, such as the positioning of the nut and the gut frets. He advises to keep the nut as low as possible. The strings should be set as close as possible to the frets, for in doing so the strings become 'harp-like'.

---

[19] It should be noted that the Italian lute manuscript tablature Paris, Bibliothèque Nationale, Rés. Vmd. 27 (Ms. 'Thibault'), *ca.* 1505, uses signs for ornaments or other performance practices that are completely different from those indicated by Capirola and in the lute prints of the early sixteenth century. The exact meaning of these signs is not yet entirely clear. Professional lutenists probably created their own individual set of signs to represent what might have occurred in performance.

After about 1550, rules 'for those who don't know how to sing' disappear almost completely from lute publications; even in manuscripts they become rare and less extensive, limited, for the most part, to tuning directions. Knowledge of tablature and of elementary musical notation was by now taken for granted, as seen in a note found in Ms. 223 (fasc. I, Cantus, fol. 1v) of the Accademia Filarmonica of Verona (*ca*. 1550): 'Those who do not know how to play or sing should not drive themselves crazy with this book' ('Chi non sa sonare e cantare non s'impazza in questo libro'). On the other hand, tablatures for the lute and other instruments had reached widespread popularity and diffusion. In 1600, the music theorist Giovanni Artusi, the famous adversary of Monteverdi, commented on the reasons that led to the invention of tablature and its 'regole' a century earlier:

> Those first inventors, after having heard several chords and diverse harmonies pleasing to the ear, wished to make clear the exact positions whereby one could have such chords. They realized that they needed to give a name to each of the strings and then, with some sign, mark out the points that would with certainty be equivalent [to the notes] on the said strings. Thus, a way of making heard all of the compositions on this instrument that one may wish could be reduced to universal rules. As one can see, they did this, and by giving to the public a great variety of tablatures they served everyone, whether intelligent or ignorant of music, nor was it possible to do otherwise . . .[20]

By the early seventeenth century the inclusion of rather extensive sets of rules at the beginning of publications was once again made necessary by innovations in technique, instrument building, and the changing roles of lutenists. The rules provided by Pietro Paolo Melii (1614–20) and Giovanni Girolamo Kapsberger (1640) are limited to explanations of the new tunings for archlute and theorbo and the signs used for ornamentation, arpeggios, and other performing practices. Kapsberger refers the reader wishing more information to his book *Il Kapsperger della Musica. Dialogo* which, unfortunately, has not survived, if it was ever written.

With the emergence of the Spanish guitar at the beginning of the seventeenth century, along with the new system of musical notation created for it, *alfabeto*

---

[20] *L'Artusi overo delle imperfettioni della moderna musica* (Venice, 1600), p. 10: 'quei primi inventori, dopò lo haver sentito diversi accordi, e diverse Harmonie all'udito grate; volendo dare ad intender i luochi particolari, dove si potessero havere simili accordi, s'accorgessero, che le facea di bisogno poner il nome à tutte le corde, & dipoi con qualche segno, significare à quante parti, di dette corde, si potessero di certo haver questi confronti per ridure sotto regole universali, il modo di far sentire le Compositioni tutte, siano quali si vogliano in questo Instromento, come si vede, che hanno fatto con il dare nel publico tante, e tante variate Intabolature, che servono à ogni intelligente, & ignorante della Musica, nè era possibile poter fare altrimenti . . .'

Artusi speaks next of lute fretting. The frets were placed by chance and without rules in ancient times, according to what he was told by Mr Venere 'che a' giorni nostri è stato valente huomo, e singolare nell'Arte di fare li Lauti nella Città di Padoa', even if 'buoni Maestri' succeeded in recapturing the perfection of the tuning by practice, and some even tried to re-propose the theoretical division of the string into the eighteen parts of Aristoxenus. On early treatises and instructions for tuning and temperaments for the lute see Mark Lindley, *Lutes, Viols and Temperaments* (Cambridge, 1984).

tablature, the situation is the same as that of the lute a century earlier. For several decades, all of the Italian publications for guitar were accompanied by simple rules on tuning and how to read *alfabeto*, along with basic practical advice, again destined 'to those who don't know how to sing'. But for instruments of the lute family such elementary advice was no longer considered necessary, as shown in a remark by Bellerofonte Castaldi at the beginning of his *Capricci a due stromenti cioe Tiorba e Tiorbino* (Modena, 1622; rpt Geneva, 1982), who contrasts the music intended for beginners with his more difficult compositions: 'The instructions, of how to accent the [notes], of dots for striking upwards with the finger, of slides and trills, of forte and piano, of equality and velocity in playing arpeggiated figurations, of tuning in conformity to given [diagrams], and other such things, will not be given [here], because those who have the good sense to play this tablature with confidence, will have it as well for such odds and ends . . .'[21]

THEORETICAL TREATISES AND INTABULATION MANUALS

The first Renaissance theorist in Italy to discuss the lute within the context of a general treatise on music was Giovanni Lanfranco in 1533.[22] Lanfranco concentrated exclusively on problems of tuning and temperament, which, as he explains, constitute the potential perfection of the lute. His most interesting contribution is the diagram he includes of the neck of a lute with five double courses and a single top string. The usual 'Renaissance' tuning is given (courses tuned at intervals of fourths with a third between the third and fourth courses), and for the first time there is an indication as to which courses are tuned at the unison and which ones at the octave. As noted above, a diagram of a lute neck is also found in the heart-shaped Pesaro Manuscript, a Venetian treatise from the end of the fifteenth century – albeit in a section of the manuscript written by Tempesta Biondi after 1545. It consists of two similar neck designs accompanied by two sonnets that contain rhyming instructions for tuning the lute.[23]

---

[21] 'Gl'avvertimenti, come d'accentar la corda, di punti per metter le dita approposito e per l'insù, di strisci, di trilli; di forte, e piano; d'uguaglianza, e velocità nel battere i gruppi Arpeschi, d'accordar lo stromento conforme a la mostra, et altri non si danno, perche chi havra giuditio per sonar sicuro questa intavolatura, l'havrà ancora per cosi fatti rimansugli . . .'

[22] Giovanni Lanfranco, *Scintille di musica* (Brescia, 1533), 'Parte Quarta: Del Liuto', pp. 140–1. Brescia was also the birthplace of Vincenzo Capirola and one of the most renowned centres for the construction of lutes and other plucked-stringed instruments during the first half of the sixteenth century.

[23] See Vladimir Ivanoff, *Das Pesaro-Manuskript. Ein Beitrag zur Frühgeschichte der Lautentabulatur*, Münchner Veröffentlichungen zur Musikgeschichte 45 (Tutzing, 1988), pp. 128–31, which includes a reproduction of the sonnets and the diagram. As late as the mid-sixteenth century the tuning of the lute continued to be a problem for players, rendering it necessary for Melchiorre de Barberiis to add to his 1546 rules 'Il nuovo modo di accordare il Lautto posto in fine'.

As announced in its long title, the *Lettione seconda* of Ganassi (1543) contains a 'new lute tablature enriched with many and useful secrets pertaining to the requirements of the virtuoso of that instrument . . . a most useful work for those who take pleasure in learning how to play'.[24] The author's purpose was to treat subjects that had been neglected in previously published rules. Ganassi's main principles are as follows:

- *Held notes (tenuto):* He reiterates the importance of tenuto 'because the lute needs this [more than] any other instrument according to its nature' ('perche il liuto da di bisogno & ogni altro Stromento per il suo naturale'). The signs used to indicate tenuto are similar to those given by Capirola – semicircles above and beneath the note – and anticipate by a few years their appearance in Borrono's print of 1548, which uses them to indicate left-hand graces.

- *Left-hand fingering:* This is the first use in Italy of a system for indicating fingering. Ganassi's system does not seem to have been used elsewhere, as it lends itself easily to printing errors and misinterpretations. The different fingers are represented by the position of a small dot placed around the tablature cipher: above left = index; below left = middle finger; above right = ring finger; below right = little finger. Ganassi also advocates 'the thumb to be that which helps the hand, by keeping it steady, to serve the fingers' ('il dedo police per essere quello che aiuta essa mano in servigio delle deda che è il tenirla ferma'), and reiterates Capirola's unusual advice that 'sometimes one can use it to play the contrabass string on any fret' ('alla volte el si puo accomodarsi su la corda contrabassa su ogni tasto').

- *Right-hand fingering:* Ganassi recalls that the use of a dot below the tablature cipher to indicate the upward stroke of a finger has become standard. He adds indications for the middle finger (a dot over the cipher) and ring finger (a short line underneath the cipher), while the little finger is not used because 'it is that which holds the hand steady in [order to] assist the [other] fingers' ('e quello che ferma la mano in servitio de le deda'). These concepts are further elaborated in a chapter wholly dedicated to the subject, 'The way of using the fingers in their strokes' ('Modo che regola le dede nel suo picigo'), which also contains instructions on how to execute chords of two or more voices.

Brevity and succinctness are not among the strong points of Ganassi's writing, and his treatise repeats the same things over and over again, assisted by many examples in tablature. Nevertheless, occasionally one comes upon an extremely well-planned chapter, such as the 'Discorso del travagliare la corda in suso con el dedo police', in which the practice of plucking the string upwards with the thumb is represented by a small line placed above the tablature cipher. Furthermore, Ganassi describes here a

---

[24] 'nuova tabulatura di lauto adottata di molti et utilissimi secreti a proposti nell'effetto dil valente di tal strumento . . . opera utilissima a chi se diletta de imparare sonare'.

characteristic technique of playing chords 'with the thumb, by strumming down-wards with the thumb as if ripping up all of the strings, which [way of playing] will be made known by means of dots and signs . . .'[25]

The *Dialogo Quarto di Musica* (Naples, 1559), by the Palermitan priest Bartolomeo Lieto, is the first complete method dedicated to the art of intabulation and playing the lute, and it reflects the traditional ambivalence between the lute and the viola da mano encountered in that city.[26] At the beginning of the dialogue, 'maestro' Lieto suggests to Rosso, a lute virtuoso ignorant of music theory and who plays only by ear, to try out 'a new method, not yet invented by anyone else, for intabulating musical works easily and perfectly, without your having otherwise to work hard to learn music'.[27] The method is based on two fundamental principles: how to set music into score, and how to intabulate. Various levels of difficulty are established. First, Lieto discusses the main concepts of rhythm, comparing the 'figure della musica' (the notes) with those of the 'sonatori' (the rhythmic signs); the first level also discusses dotted rhythms, rests, and black notes, but not ligatures, as 'they aren't used' ('tanto più che non s'usano'). Other details about reading music, such as the variety of clefs and the ancient use of proportional signs, which he says were abandoned by the moderns because of the difficulty of using them in practice, are discussed throughout the book, even in the section devoted to intabulation.[28]

---

[25] 'con il dedo police nel trascorrere zoso con el dedo come squarzar su tutte le corde le quale se fara conoscere per il mezzo de ponti e segni'. The pages of the original edition are not numbered; our citations are from chapters VII–XIV, foliation letters C–D–E. For an explanation of tablature, Ganassi refers the reader to one of his earlier publications, the *Regola Rubertina* (Venice, 1542), dedicated exclusively to the viola da gamba. There are, in fact, many more important observations on lute technique than I have been able to refer to in the text of the present study. I would like at least to note a few additional arguments about which the author furnishes interesting details: (1) the number of frets on the fingerboard; (2) playing on the soundboard above the frets; (3) tuning by ear; (4) keeping the little finger on the soundboard; (5) the use of index/ring-finger alternation; and (6) adding diminutions while respecting the harmonic structure of a composition.

[26] In his dedication, Lieto discusses his 'fatica . . . ch'è d'intavolatura per Liuto o per Viola a mano . . .' and promises 'altre maniere di intavolature per altre sorti di stromenti'. It might be noted in this context that in Naples in this period a number of contracts were signed between teachers and pupils for learning how to read tablature and to play the viola da mano. For example on 27 February 1551, maestro Giovanni Geronimo de Andriolo consented to teach the 'viola ad mano sopra la intavolatura' to Giovanni Alfonso Imparato for the fee of 13 carlini per year, 'con misura, tutte le opere che gli saranno poste per le mani . . . con promessa di andare ogni giorno in sua casa': cited in Gaetano Filangieri, *Documenti per la storia, le arti, le industrie delle provincie napoletane* (Naples, 1883–91), vol. V, p. 91.

[27] 'un nuovo modo, non piu d'altri inventato de intavolare le opere Musicali, con facilita et perfettione, senza ch'altramente vi habbiate a travagliare d'imparare Musica'.

[28] Lieto's contention, that it is 'ben vero che alcuni ignoranti (è rari sono) che alle volte l'osservono, perche si persuadono essere segni pertinenti alla Prattica, e sustantia di Theoria' leads to the incongruous advice that the student read and learn only those works in [C] or [¢] and if other metres appear, 'lasciatela quell'opera, che se voi voleste vo sentire l'accidente che vi succedono, andariano troppo a longo, e tanto più che vi pervenirano rarissimamente'. The author then speaks of 'certi compositori poco prattici nella scientia di Musica' who criticize his works because they do not use proportional rhythm signs, and presents arguments in his defence. Other important theorists in the second half of the sixteenth century, such as Vicentino and Bottrigari, agree with Lieto on this point.

According to Lieto, one learns the art of intabulation through a number of simple procedures:

- Write out the six lines of tablature corresponding to the strings of the lute and divide them into sections (bars), each of which indicates one unit of time (a 'Compasso, over Tempo'). The bars must be wide enough to be able to insert four to sixteen tablature ciphers horizontally.
- Consult the seven tables provided in the book showing the correlation between the musical notes and the ciphers of the tablature. The seven tables, provided 'for those of you who don't know singing' ('per Voi che non sapete Cantare'), are accompanied by another seven tables for the flat keys.
- Follow an order, from the lowest to the highest, in intabulating the various voices of the composition. This rule is contradicted later by the suggestion that, to avoid confusion caused by unisons in the various voices, the top voice be intabulated first, then the bass, and finally the others, which can sometimes be left out, since 'Players who are not observant leave intervals that they shouldn't' ('Sonatori di poca avertenza, lasciano Consonanze che non devono'). A 'Tavola dell'unità dei suoni' follows for the purpose of inserting as many of the unisons as possible.

Advice regarding the choice of instrument, tuning, and temperament follows: the instrument should be chosen by calculating the ideal size of lute body that can be accommodated in one's arms. The size of the neck is then calculated in proportion to the body. There is a rare mention of tuning pegs, called 'biscari over piretti'. To place the frets one must follow Pythagorean proportions (octave = 1:2, fifth = 2:3, etc.), but since false intervals are often generated in this way, the lutenist must adjust the frets with the help of a special table for the division of the string (which is based on a lute tuned in E). Then the tuning is made 'più perfetto' by playing the unisons, as one might tune the modern guitar. A brief mention of 'tasti geminati' (twin frets), as distinct from ordinary frets, indicates the existence of special temperaments that use smaller fret subdivisions, but Lieto does not explain how to produce them. Finally, the Sicilian author expresses his ultimate concept of music in a 'universal' rule at the conclusion of his treatise: 'Facility is not subject to reason, for as the whole world knows, singing naturally (spontaneously) is easiest' ('Della Facilità non accade a ragionare, perch' è noto a tutto il Mondo che il Cantare naturale è più facile').

If the Bolognese musical theorist Ercole Bottrigari was not familiar with the work of Bartolomeo Lieto, he is at any rate close to Lieto in his thinking. In the 'terza giornata' of his manuscript treatise *Il Trimerone* (1593–9), he repeats his admonition about the cosmetic uselessness of mensural signs ('vanissime vanità') and discusses extensively the musical 'ziffre' that one can 'reasonably enumerate and the characters and signs used by players of the lute and "arpicordo" or "clavacembalo" in their, as they call it, tablature'.[29] Bottrigari begins with the usual description of the tablature stave of six lines representing the six lute strings. In speaking of the 'Letters of the alphabet, used by ancient lutenists, instead of which the moderns use our arithmetical characters' ('Lettere dello Abcdario, usate dagli antichi lautisti, invece delle quali i moderni adoperano i nostri caratteri aritmetici'), he appears to believe that Italian tablature is derived from German or French tablature, apparently unaware of the continuing diffusion in Europe of these systems.[30]

Pietro Cerone bases much of the organological information found in his *El Melopeo y Maestro* (Naples, 1613) on another, better-known treatise of Bottrigari. But inasmuch as they are derived from a distinctive Neapolitan-Spanish tradition, his rules 'para poner en la Vihuela obras de Canto de Organo' (Ch. XX, p. 1059) are quite original. The difference with respect to Lieto is that by now the ability to 'cantar un poco de Canto de Organo' (i.e. a knowledge of counterpoint) is considered to be necessary. Indeed, Cerone insists that there is no need even to discuss it, 'because one cannot desire enough that others have discussed it [already]' ('porque no podre dezir tanto, que otros no lo ayan tractado'). After the usual explanation of the six lines of the tablature stave, the division into bars, and the figures to be used as rhythmic signs, he comments about the small dots written in the spaces between the six lines, that 'serve as a guide to the [tablature] numbers that are to be played together' ('sirven de guiar los numeros que se han de dar juntos'), that is, indicate chords to be played without arpeggiating. As for the tuning and temperament of the lute (Ch. XVII, pp. 1055–7), the instructions of Lanfranco are copied word for word, reproducing the same diagram of the lute's neck, but adding a 'practical advice on how to tune the lute' ('aviso para templar el Laud por pratica'), along with a new table of correspondences that recommend the user to 'take much notice of this table, since it seems to me very clear and easy' ('tengase mucha cuenta con esta tabla, pues me parece harto clara y facil').[31]

A much more detailed chapter devoted to the lute appears in another Neapolitan treatise, Scipione Cerreto's *Della prattica musica vocale et strumentale,* published in 1601. The information contained in Chapter VIII of 'Libro Quarto', entitled 'Regola dove s'impara l'Intavolatura, e d'intavolare sopra lo Strumento del Liuto' ('Rules that teach tablature and how to intabulate for the lute'), may be summarized as follows:

[29] 'ragionevolmente connumerare e i caratteri e i segni usati da' sonatori di lauto e di arpicordo o clavacembalo nelle loro, com'essi le chiamano, intavolature'.

[30] On the autograph manuscript of Ercole Bottrigari, preserved in Bologna, Civico Museo Bibliografico Musicale, Ms. B 44, see Giuseppe Vecchi, 'Primi accenni ad una storia della semeiografia musicale nel "Trimerone" (Giornata III) di Ercole Bottrigari', *Quadrivium* 12 (1971), pp. 321–46 (the section on tablature is on pp. 139–41 of the original).

[31] See Franco A. Gallo, introduction to the facsimile edition of Pietro Cerone, *El Melopeo y Maestro* (Bologna, 1969), pp. 1ff.

- The tablature used is a form of Italian tablature, but reference is made to the Neapolitan system 'del 1'. It uses a staff of eight lines corresponding to the strings of an eight-course lute. The rhythmic indications are called 'tempi' or 'bandiere' and are placed above the tablature in order to allow even 'those who have no knowledge of song . . . to play all things perfectly' ('a quelli, che non hanno cognition del Canto . . . sonaranno tutte le cose perfettissimamente'). The author remarks that some players used to mark the rhythm directly on the lines of the tablature, but 'this way of intabulating only serves those who have knowledge of written music' ('questo modo d'intavolare serve solamente à quelli, che hanno cognitione del Canto Figurato'). Cerreto explains that the dots encountered in dotted rhythmic indications are different from the ones found underneath the tablature characters, which indicate the upward stroke of the index finger, while the lack of a dot indicates the downward stroke of the thumb. When dots are missing under the appropriate notes in diminutions or single notes, Cerreto continues, the player must apply the rule of beginning the passage with the index finger if the notes are of an odd number, and with the thumb if the notes are even.
- The usual recommendation is given to hold the notes of a chord with the fingers of the left hand until the next chord must be played, even if there are melodic passages in between the two chords. Rather unusual, however, is his advice to use, when possible, the finger of the left hand corresponding to the tablature number, i.e. the index finger on fret 1, the middle on fret 2, and so on.
- Prior to learning intabulation on the lute, 'one must not only know song, but one must have a good knowledge of how to use the [Guidonian] hand as well' ('non sol bisogna saper cantare, ma ancora havere buona cognitione dell'introduttione della Mano'). The correlation between the musical notes and their positions on the fingerboard is presented in two special tables, one in mensural notation and one for the player 'who has no notion of written music'.
- The principles of intabulation are similar to those of Lieto, including the recommendation to leave out inner voices that are too difficult to play. Like Galilei, Cerreto includes an example of a four-voiced composition written out in both score and in tablature. Appearing at the end of the treatise are eight chromatic scales corresponding to the first eight frets of each of the eight courses of the lute, and a large diagram of correspondences between the notes and the lute's fingerboard (probably modified from the one in Lieto).

There are no other important sixteenth-century instructions for the lute that have come to light, but it would be no surprise if others were to be found still buried in the compendious mass of neglected sources.[32]

---

[32] It is a pity that in the *Dolcimelo* of Aurelio Virgiliano (MS treatise in Bologna, Civico Museo Bibliografico Musicale, written at the end of the sixteenth and beginning of the seventeenth centuries), the page that was to have contained rules on 'Come si accordi il lauto', with a corresponding diagram, was left unfinished, as was most of the third part of the treatise; see the facsimile edition by Marcello Castellani (Florence, 1979).

Until now we have examined rules and instructions intended for amateurs or for players without prior knowledge of music. Vincenzo Galilei, however, addresses an entirely different audience in his famous treatise entitled *Fronimo. Dialogo . . . sopra l'arte del bene intavolare, et rettamente sonare la musica negli strumenti artificiali . . . & in particulare nel Liuto.* Published for the first time in two separate volumes in 1568, it met with considerable success, so much so that the author claims to have been begged to reissue it 'as it is no longer found in bookstores' ('per non trovarsene piu alle Librerie'). In 1584 the volume was reprinted 'enriched, and embellished with new ideas and examples' ('arricchito, et ornato di novità di concetti, et d'essempi'). The differences between the two editions, and the changes they reflect within the evolving taste and maturity of the author over two decades, has been treated comprehensively in a recent study.[33] It will suffice here to provide a synthesis of the most relevant innovations in Galilei method. The author begins with the reasons that motivated him to publish his treatise:

I myself am sometimes amazed at how there has never been anybody (of all those who, in the profession of the lute, have succeeded in becoming almost divine) who has taught us the art and the rules of intabulating vocal music for the lute, since, as for the music of sounds [i.e. non-vocal music], the lute is the least imperfect instrument we have. Nor do I see any reason for this, except that maybe these [great players] thought it too lowly to teach certain small technicalities, necessary to be observed in this art, as for them it was sufficient to know perfectly how to do them . . .[34]

Galilei hopes that his rules will be of use not only to those untutored in the art of music, but also to professionals ('rari contrappuntisti'), and this is the most significant innovation of the book. A glance at the table of contents shows that over half of the book is dedicated to the rules of counterpoint, from the easiest to those of medium difficulty, forming a true composition manual for the lutenist. Subjects treated include authentic and plagal modes, voice leading and intervals, and diminutions and modulations, and there is no shortage of references to ancient and modern theorists. Included in the section dedicated to the lute, or rather, to the rules for intabulating, is a diverse array of musical examples, in mensural notation and in tablature, amounting to 120 complete compositions (counting the works in both editions), a quantity of music previously unheard of in an Italian publication for the lute.

[33]   See Philippe Canguilhem, 'Les deux éditions de *Fronimo* (1568 et 1584) et la place du luth dans la pensée musicale de Vincenzo Galilei', doctoral thesis, 2 vols., Université François Rabelais, Tours, 1994. See also the introduction by Orlando Cristoforetti to the facsimile edition of Vincenzo Galilei, *Libro d'intavolatura di liuto* (Florence, 1992)

[34]   'mi son tal'hora da me medesimo maravigliato, come non vi sia stato alcuno (di tanti che nella professione del liuto sono riusciti quasi divini) che ci habbi insegnato l'arte & le regole d'intavolare in esso le cantilene, il quale pur di musica di suoni è il meno imperfetto strumento, che habbiamo. Ne ci sò vedere altra ragione, se non che forse gli paresse cosa troppo bassa ad insegnare certe minutie cosi fatte, che intorno a questa arte sono necessarie da osservarsi, & bastasse loro sapere perfettamente farlo . . .' (p. 1).

After reviewing the usual premises about notes and their corresponding positions in tablature, Galilei first takes exception to the rules of counterpoint caused by specific properties of the lute (p. 13), discusses repeated notes and chords, particularly in cadences, with advice on where and where not to add diminutions (p. 109), and gives observations on how to write syncopations, rests, and proportional signs in tablature (pp. 114–15). Next, Galilei considers the importance of the legato sign + (p. 14), stresses the necessity of respecting the contrapuntal texture of the work being intabulated and the problems encountered if it is not respected (p. 38), and gives advice on handling unisons (p. 108). There is also a discussion of the benefits of unequal fret placement, but a new proposal for fret placement is also formulated (pp. 102, 108). It is argued that the classic six-course lute is sufficient for intabulating with ease and is perfect for all types of musical composition, and the fashion of adding extra bass strings to the lute (the first experiments in this would eventually lead to the invention of the archlute) is met with sarcasm and dislike (p. 104).

While the central didactic purpose of *Il Fronimo* concerns the acquisition of the counterpoint necessary for 'those who want to intabulate correctly' (p. 57), the treatise is, in reality, a method for the lutenist who intends to turn professional (and lute teachers nowadays should take more notice of it). But it is also a rare example of how to conduct an analysis of Renaissance music 'from within', and in this, *Il Fronimo* might still be considered relevant today.

At about the time of the second printing of Galilei's dialogue in Venice, an enigmatic lutenist known as the 'Cavaliere del Liuto' was establishing himself in Rome as one of the foremost players in Italy. The identity of this mysterious figure probably, but not necessarily, corresponds to the virtuoso lutenist Lorenzini; in any case, contemporary sources tend to confuse the two names. Despite scant biographical information, the international celebrity of the Roman master is established by a number of important and widely circulated anthologies of lute music that immortalized his name. Foremost among these is the *Thesaurus Harmonicus Divini Laurencini Romani . . .* by Jean-Baptiste Besard (Cologne, 1603; rpt Geneva, 1975), and the *Varietie of Lute-Lessons* by Robert Dowland of 1610 (rpt London, 1958). In an appendix to the *Thesaurus,* Besard printed a short treatise of seven pages, entitled 'De Modo in Testudine Studendi Libellus', that declares to have been taken 'ex Laurencini, & aliorum passim observatione, ac ipso tandem usu annotare potui, sequentibus aliquot regulis comprehensum etiam hic habes . . .'. Thus, the treatise reflects, at least in part, the teaching of the great Roman lutenist, with whom Besard probably studied in Rome.[35]

Such was the favour with which these rules were received in Europe that they were republished many times: in English translation in Robert Dowland's print of

---

[35] As Besard writes on fol. 3 of the preface: 'hic Divinus ille artifex Laurencinus Romanus instructor quondam meus . . .' On the enigmatic Lorenzini, see Paul Beier's forthcoming study to appear in the *JLSA*(1994).

1610 (the translation was probably by John Dowland himself, who, as with his son, expressed great admiration for Lorenzini); in Besard's *Novus Partus* of 1617; and in a German translation in another work by Besard, the *Isagoge in Artem Testudinariam*, also in 1617, as well as in a number of contemporary manuscripts.[36] It would have been interesting to compare the instructions of Lorenzini/Besard to those transcribed into Latin and Polish that appear in the appendix to a group of eight Venetian lute books of 1546–7, formerly at Sorau but missing since 1942. Entitled 'Instructio tradens eiusmodi Tabellatura intelligentiam, quoad tactum Testudinis', these rules were edited by a Polish student who was probably in contact with the 'Cavaliero maestro di Roma' whose name appears in the manuscript.[37]

Alessandro Piccinini was another of the great Italian masters of the lute at the end of the sixteenth and the beginning of the seventeenth centuries. In the years he spent at Rome he was in contact with the Cavaliere del Liuto (the Cavaliere died in 1608), as he relates in the preface to his *Libro primo . . . di Liuto, et di Chitarrone* (Bologna, 1623). In this work, begun in 1614 and encompassing Alessandro's entire experience as a lutenist and theorbist, we find the last and perhaps most lucid set of rules on lute playing to be found in any Italian source. It is nearly encyclopedic in scope and includes an organological section in which Piccinini claims to have invented the archlute.[38] The following is an overview of the thirty-four chapters in which Piccinini organizes his rules 'A'gli studiosi del Liuto' (pp. 1–10):[39]

[36] The 'De Modo in Testudine Studendi Libellus' was translated in Dowland's book as 'Necessarie observations belonging to the Lute, and Lute playing' (London, 1610); it was slightly expanded for insertion into the small treatise *Novus Partus* and entitled 'Ad artem testudinis, brevi citraque magnum fastidium capescendam, brevis et methodica Institutio' (Augsburg, 1617). The two Latin versions were merged and translated into German in *Isagoge in Artem Testudinariam* (Augsburg, 1617). In 1603, Philippe Hainhofer, a friend of Besard, copied the whole of the instructions into his vast anthology of lute music in Italian tablature (Wolfenbüttel, Herzog-August-Bibliothek, Codex Guelf.18.7–8 Aug. 2⁰, part III), and there is another German translation in Nuremberg, Bibliothek des Germanischen National Museums, Ms. 3148 /M.260 (*ca.* 1630).

In the Latin instructions inserted into the Hainhofer manuscript (Part III, fols. 45r–48v), the musical examples are transcribed into Italian tablature instead of being in French tablature, as they appeared in Besard. On fol. 48v Hainhofer includes instructions for reading French and German tablature, but leaves unexplained his choice for using Italian tablature in the rest of the anthology. On the instructions of Lorenzini–Besard, see Julia Sutton, 'The Lute Instructions of Jean-Baptiste Besard', *MQ* 51 (1965), pp. 345ff.

[37] See Brown, *Instrumental Music,* p. 79, 1546₆ note 1; *RISM* B VII (Munich, 1978), p. 324.

[38] The first facsimile edition of Piccinini's *Libro Primo* was edited by Mirko Caffagni, 2 vols. (Bologna, 1965). It was republished together with the *Secondo Libro* (Bologna, 1639) with an important introduction by Orlando Cristoforetti (Florence, 1983). The rules by Piccinini have been translated into French by Joël Dugot and Marco Horvat in *Ma* 19 (1985), pp. 21–39, and in English in both Stanley Buetens, 'The Instructions of Alessandro Piccinini', *JLSA* 2 (1969), pp. 6–17, and in *Alessandro Piccinini: Sämtliche Werke von Laute solo,* ed. D. Perret, R. Correa, and M. Chatton, 2 vols. (Wilhelmshaven, 1983). On Alessandro Piccinini, with numerous documents on his activities as instructor of the lute, see Dinko Fabris, 'Frescobaldi e la musica in casa Bentivoglio', in *Girolamo Frescobaldi nel IV Centenario della nascita,* ed. Sergio Durante and Dinko Fabris (Florence, 1986), pp. 63–85, and Fabris, *Mecenati e musici: Documenti sul patronato artistico dei Bentivoglio di Ferrara nell'epoca di Monteverdi* (Lucca, 1997).

[39] Since Piccinini's original text is widely available in facsimile and modern edition (see n. 38 above), only an English translation will be given here.

- Ch. I. General introduction: 'I know by experience how important a good foundation is for those who desire to become excellent players. My instructions therefore will be made in such a manner, dealing with the most important things . . .'
- Ch. II. *On playing cleanly:* 'such that every minimum stroke of the string be as limpid as pearls, and those who do not play in this way are little to be esteemed'.
- Ch. III. *On playing piano and forte:* a prerogative of the lute. Indicates where to play piano and forte and 'for variety at times it works well to play as they do in Naples: on the dissonances repeat several times that same dissonance, now piano, now forte, and the more it is dissonant, the more they repeat it . . .'
- Ch. IV. *Where the lute produces the best 'harmony':* with the right hand placed between the rose and the bridge.
- Chs. V–VIII. *Of the right hand.* The thumb must be stretched out and the little finger placed on the soundboard.
  How to use the thumb: with the fingernail 'not long', and after plucking the string it must rest on the string beneath it until needed again.
  How to use the index, middle and ring fingers: with fingernail 'not long', and care must be taken to pluck the two strings of the course simultaneously.
  With which fingers to play chords of two notes: always use the combination thumb/middle finger unless there is a dot underneath, in which case use index/middle finger.
- Chs. IX–XII. Ornamentation.
  The 'gruppo' and how difficult it is to play.
  How to play 'Tirate' and 'Gruppi' (with the index finger alone or with the thumb and index alternatively).
  Arpeggi: what it means and how it is executed.
- Chs. XIII–XIX. *Of the left hand:* Only the thumb is in constant contact with the fingerboard.
  When the fingers have to be held on the fingerboard: holding legato notes is a fundamental concept – 'Holding the fingers firm on the fingerboard where necessary . . . is a thing of such importance that without it the playing cannot be good, nor enjoyable . . . and those who know music know how important it is.' Piccinini indicates the notes to be held with a small dot above the tablature character.
  Which finger to use in going from one fret to another and from one string to another.
  Of the three kinds of 'tremoli': the long tremolo, made by restriking the plucked string with the left hand only; the quick tremolo, a short trill or mordent begun from the note above; and a third tremolo, used infrequently, in which the string is made to wave by pulling it down on the fret.
  The places in which one must use tremoli.

- Chs. XXI–XXVII. *Information on the signs used in the book:*

  Tirate (diminutions or running passages) *without dots underneath,* to be played with the thumb only.

  Tirate with dots underneath, alternating the index and thumb or middle finger.

  Rules for knowing with which finger to start the tirata: with the thumb on the first note and the index on the last note if the number of notes are even, or the index on the first note if the number is odd (the same rule was published twenty years earlier by Cerreto, whose treatise was possibly known by Piccinini).

  The Punto fermo, i.e. the sign for held notes, which was already explained in Ch. XIV.

  The Strascino for the lute and the chitarrone: the sign used to indicate them and how to play them when they are ascending and descending. The scale is always started with the thumb and continued with the left hand only, and 'I don't like it on the lute unless played rarely for caprice and novelty . . . while on the chitarrone it is a most appropriate style . . .'

- Chs. XXVIII–XXXI. After having spoken about the origin of the chitarrone and of the pandora and providing important organological information about these instruments, Piccinini discusses in greater detail typical ways of playing chords on the theorbo, providing written-out examples both of normal arpeggios and of several special ones indicated in the tablature by the numbers 2 and 4. The playing of ornaments, discussed earlier, is taken up again, but with some specific indications for the theorbo, such as the playing of piano and forte as on the lute, 'but normally [the theorbo] needs to be played quite energetically, and always precisely and cleanly . . . and I say this for those who want to rise above mediocre playing'.

- Ch. XXXII. The conclusion consists of advice to the beginner on how to use the rules contained in the book, and ends with a reflection worthy of Vincenzo Galilei: 'One acquires the science of music by working hard at counterpoint and by putting the works of others, such as ricercars, motets, and other compositions, into score and by playing from those scores, so that, by means of the counterpoint, one arrives at being able to manage on one's own.'

The remaining chapters deal with music 'per suonare il Liuto, & Organo, con il Basso continuo, & ancor il Chitarrone, & Organo, & a due, e tre Liuti concertati insieme', and with Piccinini's claim to have invented the archlute. Finally, a table of 'Riccordi' (Reminders) summarizes (as in the prints of Melii and Kapsberger) the tunings of the lute and theorbo, of two and three lutes played together 'in concerto', and the signs used in the book, such as the *arpeggi* indicated by the numbers 2 and 4, the *strascino,* and the dot indicating *tenuto.*

By the time of Piccinini's death (which is mentioned by his son in the *Secondo Libro di Liuto* (Bologna, 1639), the Roman theorist Pier Francesco Valentini had written, in manuscript, one of the last treatises dedicated to the lute (*ca.* 1636). Beginning with a description of the 'Order . . . to be followed in playing and intabulating for the eight-course lute' ('Ordine [. . .] il quale serve a sonare, et a intavolare nel Lauto di otto ordini') its contents are summarized by the author as follows:[40]

Just six years ago, I, Pier Francesco Valentini, composed a work not yet published, where I demonstrate and teach a way to intabulate for the lute and to play transposing on all of its frets, that is, in the twelve semitones contained in whatever octave. In this work I describe twelve orders, or tones (as they are commonly called) to play and to intabulate; and in each of these I have fashioned an aria on the Ruggiero, with the figures for playing thoroughbass added as well. . . .[41]

Some years later, around 1650, Valentini revised and condensed the Ordine in the first part of a new treatise to which he gave the title *Il Leuto Anatomizzato* ('The Dissected Lute' [Ms. Barb. Lat. 4433]), adding a second part (probably also a revision of some earlier work that has not survived) that consists of *Regole e maniera d'intavolare nel Leuto*. According to Cristoforetti, these rules reveal the essential principles of Valentini's didactic method, which connect directly to Galilei's *Fronimo:* the examples he cites come from the 1584 edition of Galilei's treatise.

The concluding section of the *Leuto Anatomizzato,* which gives the treatise its name, consists of original analytic research on several aspects of the 'modern' classification of harmony and musical technique, such as transposition, both according to the harmony and to the tablature, and the execution of cadential formulas. An innovative terminology is used here: 'botte o chiavi di harmonia', 'chiavi maggiori', and 'chiavi minori', 'chiavette', 'ponticelli minori' (that is, minor chords), and 'archetti'. Not lacking are organological indications, such as the difference between the eight-course lute, the 'Leuto Teorbato', the tuning of the 'Leuto alla Francese', and information on notation, such as the differences between Italian, French, and Neapolitan tablatures. A strange rule is given on re-intabulating works for the greater pleasure of the curious lutenist, in which eleven intabulations of the *Aria della Folia* are presented, each beginning on a different semitone. At the end of the treatise appears a summary of the basic rules of counterpoint that draws on every important treatise from Galilei to Piccinini.[42]

---

[40]   Rome, Biblioteca Apostolica Vaticana, Ms. Barb. Lat. 4395. See the informative introduction to the facsimile edition of the two lute treatises of Valentini by Orlando Cristoforetti, 2 vols. (Florence, 1989). The citations in the present study come from this introduction.

[41]   'Già sei anni sono, Io Pier Francesco Valentini, composi un'opera non data ancora in luce, dove dimostro et insegno il modo d'intavolare nel Leuto, et di sonare trasportato in tutti i tasti di esso, cioè nei dodici semitoni contenuti in qualsivoglia Ottava, nella quale opera descrivo dodici Ordini, o Toni (come volgarmente si dice) di sonare, et intavolare; et in ciascuno di essi da me è formata un'aria di Ruggiero, con esservi poste anco le chiavi per sonare sopra la parte . . .'

[42]   'Arte di raffinato contrapunto dove oltre le regole di esso, compendiosamente et praticamente si tratta delle consonanze et dissonanze et di altre cose necessarie in tal professione Opera di Pier Francesco Valentini Romano', in appendix to *Il Leuto Anatomizzato,* facsimile edn, pp. 56ff.

Thus, Valentini has created the first true synthesis of all of the rules and instructions produced in Italy over the preceding century and a half. Information relating to performance practice in the widest possible sense is given, pertaining not only to solo playing but also to the practice of playing continuo. Typical of Valentini is the fact that the two main types of lute referred to in the rules are the eight-course lute, which was by then an archaic instrument, and the new theorboed lute. To these practical considerations are added a series of technical arguments in which the author takes a strong stand, as for instance against the attempt, proposed by such illustrious theorists as Lanfranco, Zarlino, Artusi, and Cerreto, to use equal temperament on the lute: 'I realized that the way [the lute] has been used up to the present day, it is not [tuned] entirely with equal tones and semitones . . . in this, not only common folk but also the most serious authors have erred, writing that on the said instrument there is equality in the tones and semitones . . .'[43] Valentini's description of fret placement furthermore makes it clear that he is describing some form of meantone temperament: 'regarding the lute, as well as the cittern and other similar instruments, one can see clearly that the third fret is wider than the second, which shows that there is a larger semitone on the third fret than on the second. One also sees that the first fret greatly exceeds the second [in width].'[44]

The last Italian instructions for the lute are dated to 1759, but they remained in use possibly as late as 1811, the year that their author, Filippo Dalla Casa, aged seventy-four, decided to donate the manuscript of sonatas containing them, together with his archlute, to the Accademia Filarmonica of Bologna. Pompously entitled 'Rules of music and also rules for accompanying above the bass, for playing basso continuo, and for the French archlute and for the theorbo. To be used by me, Filippo Dalla Casa, the player of these [instruments]' ('Regole di Musica, ed'anco le Regole per accompagnare sopra la Parte per Suonare il Basso continuo & per l'Arcileuto Francese e per la Tiorba. Per uso di me Filippo Dalla Casa Suonatore di essi'), they turn out actually to be a thoroughly ordinary collection of mundane notions of music theory.[45] The last three pages contain scales for the theorbo and the archlute and a few 'Avertimenti' for the theorbo, limited to showing the difference between its tuning and that of the archlute. By now all trace of lute tablature is gone; even the sonatas are written in staff notation on two staves.

---

[43] 'accorgendomi che nel modo che sino al presente giorno si è usato [il liuto], non è in tutto con toni et semitoni eguali . . . in tal cosa non solo il Volgo; ma anco gravissimi Autori hanno errato con scrivere che detto istrumento ha in se l'eguaglianza de Toni et de semitoni . . .'

[44] 'nel riguardare il Leuto, come anco la Cethera, et altri simili istrumenti si vede manifestamente ch il terzo tasto è più largo del secondo, il che dimostra, in esso terzo tasto essere un semitono maggiore di quello che si ritrova nel secondo tasto. Si vede anco il primo tasto eccedere, et avanzare di gran lunga il secondo.'

[45] Bologna, Civico Museo Bibliografico Musicale, Mss. EE.155, (I) *Suonate di Celebri Autori per l'Arcileuto Francese, per servizio di me Filippo Dalla Casa, Suonatore d'Arcileuto, e Compagnatore sopra le Parti, e Professore di Pittura,* and (II) *Regole di Musica...* (rpt Florence, 1984, with an introduction by Orlando Cristoforetti).

BROADSIDE SHEETS AND THE DISSEMINATION OF THE RULES

In his *Monochordo,* Pier Francesco Valentini recalls having heard 'not only by word of mouth, but also on a sheet printed in Rome in 1641 . . .' about attempts to tune the harpsichord and the organ through adopting a system of equal temperament based on that for the lute ('non solo a bocca, ma anco con un foglio stampato a Roma nel 1641 . . .').[46] This 'folio' is no longer extant, but it was probably one of the last examples of a minor and little-studied print tradition that had its beginnings in Rome in the third decade of the sixteenth century. In fact, at least seven editions of these 'fogli volanti', or broadside sheets, are known, spanning nearly a century. Engraved only on one side, the sheet typically contains the figure of a lute, a short piece of vocal music transcribed into several different types of tablature, and brief rules for reading music and intabulation. The production of these broadside sheets must have been much more fervent, but the expendable nature of such a product has impeded their survival, so much so that of the seven editions we know of, which must have been printed in large enough numbers to have made them commercially viable, only one example of each has generally survived. Rules for the lute made for broadside sheets were presumably written for a more popular market than those intended for the usual prints of lute music, and were circulated by itinerant merchants or specialized shops, as with contemporary English ballad broadsides. Unfortunately, this aspect of sixteenth-century publishing, which is connected to sociological issues involving the popular consumption of music, has been virtually ignored in modern scholarship.[47] There were probably many other broadside sheets printed in Italy containing elementary rules about music that, while not necessarily concerning the lute, were used by lutenists. Some confirmation of this is found in a sheet (taken from a lost original) that was hand-copied and inserted at the beginning of Philip Hainhofer's lute manuscript of 1603. Entitled *Regola Universale facile Et sicura di trova tutte le Note overo Mutationi di canto in qual si voglia CHIAVE,* a cartouche indicates that it was printed at Rome in 1587 by Nicolo van Aolst. The original must have followed the typical format of lute broadsides, i.e. the insertion of brief rules and musical designs filling up the entire sheet. The only part of the sheet not written out by hand, but apparently cut out from a printed sheet or book, is the illustration of the

---

[46]   Cited by Orlando Cristoforetti in *Il Leuto Anatomizzato,* facsimile edn, p. 12.

[47]   There is not, for example, a single musical example listed in Alberto Di Mauro, *Bibliografia delle stampe popolari profane del fondo 'Capponi' della Biblioteca Vaticana* (Florence, 1981). An analogous situation to the broadside sheets for the lute can be found in the rare examples of editorial catalogues printed in the same format. Only nineteen of these are known from the sixteenth century and they contain very few indications of music editions. See the important study by Iain Fenlon, 'Il foglio volante editoriale dei Tini, circa il 1596', *RIM* 12 (1977), pp. 231–51, which gives more information on these broadside catalogues and relevant bibliography.

Guidonian hand. It is not clear whether this was cut out from a damaged original of the broadside in question, or from a different source altogether.

The earliest broadside sheet was printed in Rome, probably in the 1530s, by Antonio Strambi, a publisher not particularly known for his musical ouput.[48] Almost all of the elements found in successive editions can be seen in this first prototype, which places particular emphasis on rules for tuning ('Come se ha d'accordare il lauto' and 'La prova da veder quando il lauto e accordato'), on the principles of solfège and the Guidonian hand, on the correspondences between the notes and the positions on the fingerboard, and on the names of rhythmic indications. Occupying the central position on the broadside are rules for playing from tablature in which we find, once again, the usual instructions as handed down from the time of Petrucci: the correlations between tablature line and lute string, and note and fingerboard position; the meaning of the rhythmic signs; and, the upward stroke to be used on tablature characters with a dot underneath. The choice of musical examples is also rather archaic: a frottola arranged in score in the style of Bossinensis, with the superius in mensural notation and the tenor and bass parts in tablature underneath. A rhythmic sign is indicated for each note in the tablature, and the text is placed between the two staves.

About twenty years later, a Venetian printer working 'in Frezaria al segno della Fede', Mutio Pagano, unknown until now, reproduced the entire contents of the Roman broadside without alteration, including the figures of the lute and the hand, the rules, and even the composition with tablature. That the plate was newly engraved for the print-run is noticeable from several graphic modifications.[49]

In 1582, Ambrogio Brambilla, a well-known Milanese engraver active in Rome – the preferred centre, evidently, of this particular publishing initiative – produced a copper plate to print a broadside sheet that apparently contained instructions for playing the cittern along with an intabulation of a psalm. Unfortunately, no copy seems to have survived.[50] It is possible that the author of the cittern instructions was one Michele Carrara, who, three years later, put his signature to the *Regola ferma e vera per intavolare nel liuto* on an engraving signed 'Ambrosius Bramb[illa] F[ecit]/ 1585' and published in Rome by Ettore Ruberti.[51]

---

[48] The only copy is in Bologna, Museo Civico Bibliografico Musicale, B 145.

[49] The only specimen is conserved in Stockholm, Kungl. Biblioteket, Kart och bildsektionen Musikalier, Skap 6c, Hylla 23 and has been discussed in Kenneth Sparr, 'An Unknown and Unique Broadside Lute Instruction', *The Lute* 27 (1987), pp. 30–4 (includes a facsimile of the broadside).

[50] See Georg Nagler, *Die Monogrammisten (1879–1919)*, I, n. 946. He summarizes the title as follows: 'Anleitung die Zither zu spielen, nebst Noten eines Psalmes. Ambrosius Brambilla fecit 1582, gr.qu.fol' (cited in Brown, *Instrumental Music*, p. 309: 1582_2).

[51] See Benvenuto Disertori, ed., *Intavolatura di Liuto di Michele Carrara MDLXXXV* (Florence, 1957). The only known copy survives in the Landau–Finaly collection of the Biblioteca Nazionale in Florence. See Brown, *Instrumental Music,* p. 342: 1585_5. In fact there is a second copy, identical to the 1585 edition but lacking any indication as to the printer, Carrara's name, and the dedication. This could be a pirate edition, possibly prior to 1594. I wish to thank Oscar Mischiati for providing me with a reproduction of this broadside.

Two more reprints of the Carrara broadside, in 1594 and, finally, in 1618, are known. The former contains numerous graphic modifications from the 1584 edition, which proves that it was made from a new plate. The latter might be a plagiarized or pirate edition.[52] The most interesting of these is the one reprinted in 1594, which contains a cartouche that declares its author as 'M. Michele Carrara, able player of the lute and excellent musician' ('Autore M. Michele/Carrara perito sonato- / re di liuto, et musico / eccellente'). A *Regola ferma, et vera di novo corretta per l['']intavolatura del liuto* has been inserted in which Carrara displays his knowledge of the Pythagorean science of intervals, concluding that the division of the tones and semitones is realised on the lute in the least imperfect way, and 'one can set there into score all of the voices [of a composition]' ('vi si potriano spartire tutti i canti'). Also inserted is a *Regola Universale* showing the correlation of each note with the tablature equivalents in Italian, Neapolitan, and French tablature systems, along with their transposition up or down a tone. Tablature staves of more than six lines are said to be possible 'as pleases the player', which confirms the eight-line staff used by Cerreto, and implies that the number of lines can correspond to the number of courses on the lute. A practical example of Carrara's universal rule is given in five different versions of the well-known Psalm 150 for six, five, four, three, and two voices, transcribed in Italian, Neapolitan, and French tablature. The drawing of a lute now indicates eight rather than six courses, with a double top string (chanterelle) and without any sign of octave stringing on the lower courses. The remaining space on the broadside is taken up with elementary musical precepts which are called 'Introduttorio Musicale Maestrale'.

It is difficult to speculate about the possible intent, customers, or diffusion of these broadside sheets for the lute. The commercial value of including rules for reading tablature within lute publications was recognized in music publishing ever since Petrucci's earliest prints of 1507–8 for the purpose of attracting a wider public across the Alps, as we have seen. The broadsides, too, must have enjoyed a noteworthy commercial success that seems to answer a need for rules at a time when editions of Italian lute music cease to include them.[53] The facts that their present locations are distant from their place of publication, that they circulated for nearly a century, and that there was an attempt at a pirate edition in 1618 by Valesia, all attest to the popularity of these broadsides. We still do not know how much they sold for; we do

---

[52]   The first reprint (Rome, 1594) is classified as a unique copy located in Florence, Conservatorio di Musica Luigi Cherubini (see Brown, *Instrumental Music*, p. 394: 1594₄), and presumably corresponds to the example reproduced in Alberto Basso and Luciano Berio, *Sui sentieri della musica* (Milan, 1985), pp. 50–1, where it is cited without indication of provenance. The printer is indicated here as 'Ioan Antoni de Paulis' (instead of Ettore Ruberti).

[53]   The only instance of a broadside sheet listed in a music publisher's catalogue occurs in that of Giunta (Florence, 1604): *Liuto, e Modo d'accordarlo*. See Oscar Mischiati, *Indici, cataloghi e avvisi degli editori e librai musicali italiani dal 1591 al 1798* (Florence, 1984), p. 133: V, 891. It is not known if this corresponds to one of the known lute broadsides, but it might indicate one of the editions of Carrara or one of the pirate prints.

know, however, that a copy of Galilei's *Fronimo* sold for 3 lire and 10 soldi, a higher price than any other book of lute tablature in the Pigna catalogue of 1591.[54] We also know the sale price of the lost *Intavolatura di Lauto Libro Terzo* by Giovan Maria (Petrucci, 1508) was '110 quatrines'.[55] The number of printed lute books, manuals, and broadside sheets containing rules is also unknown. In general, the archives of the principal Italian cities that were once centres of music publishing have not been explored sufficiently or systematically for information contained in notarial deeds or documents of an economic nature.

Private instruction by *maestri di liuto* is another subject about which we know very little; we possess only a few casual citations in isolated studies. The type of payment, the social classes involved, and, above all, the pedagogical systems used in such private teaching still need to be investigated.[56] Iconographical evidence is perhaps

---

54 See Mischiati, *Indici . . .* II, 175 (*Catalogo Pigna,* Venice, 1591). Another copy of *Fronimo* is listed for sale in the Giunta catalogue (Florence, 1604): *ibid.*, p. 133: V, 837. We do not know in either case to which edition of *Fronimo* the catalogues refer, but it is probably the second if we are to believe what Galilei himself says about the first edition having been sold out. A copy of *Fronimo* was also in the possession of the renowned library of the king of Portugal, according to the catalogue of 1649, *Livraria de Música de El-Rei D. João IV* (facsimile edition of the Lisbon catalogue of 1649 edited by D. Peres (Lisbon, 1967), I, p. 432). In the same collection, among the numerous tablatures for lute and vihuela in print and manuscript, are found a number of rules that might be of Italian origin, but are not identifiable: the *la Doutrina famosa pella qual se insina a tanger no Laude* (*ibid.*, n. 438) might correspond to one of the editions of the rules of Carrara; and the *Carminum ad testudinis usum compositorum / Conthem introdução o necessaria para os tangedores de Laude, ou viola de 6.Libro I* (*ibid.*, n. 839) recalls instead one of the titles of the anthologies of Sixtus Kargel. It is interesting to note how this catalogue lists the 1623 edition of the first book for lute and chitarrone by Alessandro Piccinini: *Advertimentos para cum facilidade tanger os ditos instrumentos* (*ibid.*, n. 425). This might explain the enigmatic listing of a *Trattato sopra la Tabulatura* (Bologna, 1594) by Alessandro Piccinini in Brown, *Instrumental Music,* 1594[11].

55 'Costo en Roma 110 quatrines por Setiembre de 1512'. The description in the *Regestrum B* of the Biblioteca Colombina of Seville, where a copy of the book was housed, is given in Brown, *Instrumental Music,* p. 14, [1508][1], and allows us to establish that it contained two versions of the 'Regula pro illis qui canere nesciunt Italice et Latine'.

56 See the chapter by Victor Coelho in this volume, pp. 108–41 for an analysis of seventeenth-century pedagogy. A sample of studies that furnish interesting data on the activities of Italian lutenists is as follows: Remo Giazotto, *La musica a Genova* (Genoa, 1951), pp. 244ff. (lute 'schools' in Genoa from 1585 with at least six names of instructors); [A. Murano Putaturo], 'Napoli musicale alla fine del Cinquecento: gli stipendi dei maestri', *Napoli Nobilissima,* n.s., 3 (1922), p. 151 (notarial contracts of lute instructors in Naples); Dinko Fabris, 'Vita musicale a Bari dal Medioevo al Settecento', in *La musica a Bari. Dalle cantorie medievali al conservatorio 'Piccinni'* (Bari, 1993), pp. 19–108 (references to lute instructors and students, including young Polish students sent to study the lute at Bari by Queen Bona Sforza); William F. Prizer, 'Lutenists at the Court of Mantua in the Late Fifteenth and Early Sixteenth Centuries', *JLSA* 13 (1980), pp. 5–34; Helmuth Osthoff, *Der Lautenist Santino Garsi da Parma* (Leipzig, 1926) (lute instructors and students at Parma in the sixteenth and early seventeenth centuries); Jonathan Glixon, 'Lutenists in Renaissance Venice', *JLSA* 16 (1983), pp. 15–26; Elda Martellozzo Forin, *Il maestro di liuto Antonio Rotta (†1549) e studenti dell'Università di Padova suoi allievi* (Padua, 1968), pp. 425–43; Franco Pavan, 'Liutisti itineranti e rapporti culturali fra le corti italiane del primo Cinquecento', *Musica e Cultura* (Cremona, 1988), pp. 75–87; Alessandra Bollini, 'L'attività liutistica a Milano dal 1450 al 1550: nuovi documenti', *RIM* 21 (1986), pp. 31–60; David Nutter, 'Ippolito Tromboncino, "Cantore al Liuto" ', *I Tatti Studies. Essays in the Renaissance* 3 (Florence, 1989), pp. 127–74; Mirko Caffagni, 'L'autobiografia di Pietro Bertacchini', *Bollettino della Società Italiana del Liuto* 3 (1993), pp. 9–16 (the life and studies of a lutenist and theorbist in northern Italy in the second half of the seventeenth century); Victor Coelho, *The Manuscript Sources of Seventeenth-Century Italian Lute Music* (New York, 1995), pp. 19–26 (demographic and sociological profiles of lutenists, and their manuscripts), and Victor Coelho, 'Raffaello Cavalcanti's Lutebook (1591) and the Ideal of Singing and Playing', in *Le concert des voix et des instruments à la Renaissance,* ed. J.-M. Vaccaro (Paris, 1995), pp. 423–42 (for a study of the personal repertory of a young Florentine nobleman).

even more promising than the rare annotations found in manuscripts used by instructors or students of the lute.[57] This information can supplement and verify indications supplied by the rules, such as the position of the hands and of the instrument, the choice of lute over time, according to the social situation or, as seen in a few cases, in connection with the type of music being played. But it is evident that today, as in the past, instructions can only provide a somewhat meagre and enigmatic outline. No written instructions can ever substitute for experience, musical ability, and, when possible, a good teacher.[58]

Translated from the Italian by Paul Beier

[57]   For histories of manuscripts of the seventeenth century, and most of the Italian manuscripts containing brief and elementary instructions, the reader is referred to Coelho, *The Manuscript Sources*.

[58]   The author is indebted to Paul Beier for his many valuable suggestions during the preparation of this chapter.

3

THE PERFORMANCE CONTEXT OF THE ENGLISH LUTE SONG, 1596–1622

DANIEL FISCHLIN

I

What was the effect of a Dowland lute song on its audience? How did Thomas Campion conceive the relationship between his lyrics and his music? How did musicians prepare a performance? Were songs committed to memory? Did the audience listen quietly? Were comments made immediately after or during a performance about either the music or the text? How was a performance structured in terms of programming, use of gesture, instrumentation, choice of lyrics, and so forth? Were performances 'structured' at all? What were the relations between accompanist and singer, if they were in fact different people? What sort of performance space did they create? Did they face outwards, inwards, look towards the audience, turn away from the audience, look at each other, or a combination of all of these? Were these songs even intended for an audience beyond that of the singer and accompanist, and perhaps a few other people privy to the performance and its context? Since a performance involves both the performers and their audience, should not contemporary performances take into account the very different notions of audience particular to the Renaissance, and more particularly to the lute song?

Attempts to answer such questions will no doubt show that a vast range of possibilities existed in the performance and reception of the Elizabethan ayre. The paucity of information on the performance practices of lute ayres has been documented by Robert Spencer, who asserts that 'Elizabethan comment on singing itself is sparse, but even that tells us something. That writers equated learning to sing only with learning to sight-read indicates how little attention was paid to voice production'.[1] Even less documentation exists relating to techniques of lute accompaniment, and thus its performers are left to adduce performance practice from a wide spectrum of cultural sources that provide contextual information to that effect. Frequently that

---

[1] 'Singing English Lute Songs', *LSAQ* 29 (1993), p. 16.

information addresses matters relating to the performers' states of mind, their emotional preparedness to externalize sophisticated representations of an often inaccessible interiority. Admittedly the broad cultural dimensions that shape the metaphysics of performance are areas into which few dare to venture but they are omnipresent as factors that shape both the performance and its reception, whether in early modern or contemporary contexts.

The recent flurry of books on this topic[2] indicates the enormous diversity within the Elizabethan musico–poetic tradition, not to mention the often contentious 'nature' of different humanist aesthetics, perhaps best exemplified in Thomas Campion's and Samuel Daniel's debate on the relative value of rhyme.[3] The studies by Robert Toft and Anthony Rooley, in particular, purport to clarify issues of performance practice in the English ayre or lute song. They articulate Renaissance performance principles based on rhetorical analysis and on a putative mythographic context related to Orphic symbolism. But Toft's mastery of rhetorical analysis is undercut by his formulaic application of those analyses in a way that does not take into account broader cultural issues and how they affect the performer's self-presentation. And Rooley's reading of the degree to which Orphic self-representation was part of the general cultural context required to perform lute songs simplifies a much more complicated performance ethos, though in a way that provides some fascinating insights into the relations among Renaissance performance practice, literary and rhetorical conventions, and mythography.

In this essay I propose to revise these authors' findings through attention to the following: the literary contexts of the ayre, the iconography associated with the lute in paintings from the period, and Orphic mythography in so far as it is present in the *œuvre* of the lute song composers. I note that none of these matters – literary, iconographic, or mythographic – has received much scholarly attention from literary critics, musicologists, or performers of the lute song, especially in terms of performance practice. Rather than addressing technical questions, I shall examine instead some of the cultural contexts that contributed to the performance practices of singing lute ayres. My argument assumes an interconnectedness between the actual techniques of musical representation and the unspoken cultural realms that contribute to the aesthetics of its performance. Technique refracts aesthetic context, and since lute song performers have so little direct information on technique it is by

---

[2] See Robert Toft, *Tune Thy Musicke to Thy Hart: The Art of Eloquent Singing in England 1597–1622* (Toronto, 1993); Anthony Rooley, *Performance: Revealing the Orpheus Within* (Longmead, 1990); Erik S. Ryding, *In Harmony Framed: Musical Humanism, Thomas Campion, and the Two Daniels* (Kirksville, 1993); Robin Headlam Wells, *Elizabethan Mythologies: Studies in Poetry, Drama and Music* (Cambridge, 1994); Winifred Maynard, *Elizabethan Lyric Poetry and its Music* (Oxford, 1986).

[3] See Ryding, *In Harmony Framed*, especially pp. 85–92, for a useful summary of this debate. Ryding's book also presents a detailed analysis of the ongoing disputes about musical and poetic aesthetics that flourished in the late sixteenth century, disputes that had a profound impact on compositional and performance practices of the time.

means of a close examination of cultural context that some of the premises underlying the technical demands of its performance practice may come to be understood. Establishing the cultural context of performance practices relating to the lute song then becomes a reading of how early modern culture vested musico-poetic acts of representation with broader significances – ones that contemporary performers might seek to recuperate in order to produce the vestiges of an authentic performance.

Some of the rhetorical parameters for the performance of the lute song are proposed in Toft's *Tune Thy Musicke to Thy Hart*. In a close reading of the rhetoric in two Dowland ayres, Toft suggests that

> a successful performance of them depends upon the singer's ability to feign the affections in the texts and use the musical and rhetorical devices present in the songs to create the persuasive style of delivery they demand. In preparing to perform these songs, I suggest that singers follow the approach recommended in treatises of the period. First, consider the passions of the poem. Note the dominant affection and determine how the main parts of the text relate to this central passion. Then study individual sentences to discover the specific affections embodied in them. At the same time, observe the figurative language with which sentences have been decorated and decide which words require emphasis. Do not overlook the punctuation, for it is the vehicle through which the structure of the discourse is articulated, and the observance of it enables listeners to comprehend the thoughts and emotions of the texts easily. At this point the study of the structure of the text should be complete.[4]

Toft follows conventional rhetorical and oratorical procedure here, though in a manner that sublimates crucial performance issues relating to metrical structures at work in the poem and how those structures are reinforced or neglected by the musical setting. More importantly, Toft suggests an implicit analogy between oratory and singing, something he states more clearly in his introductory argument, which suggests that 'Singers today need to become musical orators who arouse passions in listeners through a manner of performance which is designed to approximate the intuitive understanding of delivery that early seventeenth-century singers would have had.'[5] To suggest that the suasive effects and ends of oratory are analogous to those of song is to skew unnecessarily two discursive forms with very different cultural contexts. Oratory had precise public functions – usually political, usually disputatious[6] – to which it was oriented. Song had a very different context,

---

[4] Toft, *Tune Thy Musicke to Thy Hart*, p. 128.

[5] *ibid.*, p. 12.

[6] See George Puttenham's comment to the effect that 'I am not ignorant that there be artes and methodes both to speake and to perswade and also to dispute' (*The Arte of English Poesie* [1589], ed. Gladys Doidge Willcock and Alice Walker (Folcroft, 1969), vol. III, p. 306). Puttenham, despite his frequent conflation of the poet and the orator, especially in terms of the suasive figures they share and the effects they produce, ends his book by suggesting that many orators (and poets) are guilty of the 'vnseasonable vsing' of their arts. The poet is to be 'more commended for his naturall eloquence then for his artificiall, and more for his artificiall well desembled, then for

lyric pronouncement being allied with the sublime, metaphysical effects that music was said to represent and induce. Oratory and song are thus distinctive forms of persuasion with cultural and aesthetic functions that are split along the general lines of the public associations of the former and the private, and very often metaphysical, significances of the latter. Thomas Campion's sarcastic description of the old style of theatrical declamation associated with comedy suggests a contrary performance practice for the ayre:

But there are some, who to appeare the more deepe and singular in their judgement, will admit no Musicke but that which is long, intricate, bated with fuge, chaind with sincopation, and where the nature of everie word is precisely exprest in the Note, like the old exploided action in Comedies, when if they did pronounce *Memini* ['I remember'], they would point to the hinder part of their heads, if *Video* ['I see'], put their finger in their eye. But such childish observing of words is altogether ridiculous, and we ought to maintaine as well in Notes, as in action, a manly cariage, gracing no word, but that which is eminent, and emphaticall.[7]

In the ayre the 'childish observing' of word-painting techniques is inappropriate, as is, by implication, the gestural and declamatory style of oratorical performance geared for public theatre.[8]

Oratory and rhetoric are outward-looking modes of expression whereas song establishes a very different vector of expressive orientation. The oratorical analogue with song is not sufficient, however useful it may be in establishing the suasive dimensions of a text, as a model for the declamatory and expressive features of lute song performance, which reject the public dimensions of performance in favour of private expression. Even if this small-proportioned aesthetic is itself only a rhetorical pose, the pose is significant for what it tells us about the imagined performance

the same ouermuch affected and grossely or vndiscretly bewrayed, as many makers and Oratours do' (vol. III, p. 307). In other words, the less constructed and artifical the performance, the better. The sentiment is echoed in Thomas Campion's remarks about the ayre made in his prefatory remarks to the reader of *Two Bookes of Ayres* (n.d.): 'Short Ayres, if they be skilfully framed, and naturally exprest, are like quicke and good Epigrammes in Poesie' (Walter R. Davis, ed., *The Works of Thomas Campion* (London, 1969), p. 55).

7 'To the Reader', *A Booke of Ayres* (1601); Davis, *The Works of Thomas Campion*, p. 15. For a satirical attack on oratory as well as on theatrical excess, see Thomas Nashe's *The Unfortunate Traveller*, pp. 292–5 (Thomas Nashe, *The Unfortunate Traveller and Other Works*, ed. J. B. Steane (Harmondsworth, 1971)). Nashe describes a comedy, *Acolastus, the Prodigal Child*, 'so filthily acted, so leathernly set forth, as would have moved laughter in Heraclitus. One, as if he had been planing a clay floor, stampingly trod the stage so hard with his feet that I thought verily he had resolved to do the carpenter that set it up some utter shame. Another flung his arms like cudgels at a pear tree, insomuch as it was mightily dreaded that he would strike the candles that hung above their heads out of their sockets and leave them all dark. Another did nothing but wink and make faces' (pp. 294–5). Though I do not mean to imply that all oratorical performance involved such ridiculous excesses, it is clear that the lute song represented a reaction to such egregious public displays of dramatic and oratorical bad taste.

8 Note that such theatrical expression had strong connotations of effeminacy in early modern England, and that Campion's comment regarding a 'manly cariage' suggests a rejection of such theatrical performativity. For further commentary on effeminacy and anti-theatricality see Laura Levine, *Men in Women's Clothing: Anti-Theatricality and Effeminization, 1579–1642* (Cambridge, 1994).

contexts of the ayre. Philip Rosseter's claim that the ayres he composed were 'made at his vacant houres, and privately emparted to his friends, whereby they grew both publicke, and (as coine crackt in exchange) corrupted',[9] is a significant indication of the performative context envisaged by lute song composers. Public performance corrupts the 'privately emparted' ayre thus making explicit the ayre's idealized private dimensions. A similar sentiment, expressed in more florid terms, occurs in John Dowland's prefatory comments 'To the courteous Reader', from *The First Booke of Songes or Ayres* (1597): 'How hard an enterprise it is in this skilfull and curious age to commit our priuate labours to the publike view, mine owne disabilitie, and others hard successe doe too well assure me: and were it not for that loue I beare to the true louers of musicke, I had concealde these my first fruits.'[10] Concealment of 'priuate labours' lies at the core of Dowland's concerns, and the implicit assumption seems to be that 'true louers of musicke' will share in a similar aesthetic.

The dedicatory comments to John Maynard's songbook, *The XII. Wonders of the World* (1611) also iterate a similar distinction between public and private display: '*Madame.* [Ioane Thynne] / What at first priuately was entended for you, is at last publickely commended to you.'[11] And Robert Jones, in the prefatory comments to the songbook he entitled *A Musicall Dreame* (1609), hints at an intimate aesthetic when he describes the songbook in the following terms: 'This my aduenture is no deed but a dreame, and what are dreames, but airie possessions, and seuerall ayres, breathing harmonious whisperings . . . set forth for pleasure.'[12] Based on these and other prefatory comments by the composers themselves there is clearly evidence to suggest that the lute song had an idealized private space as its performative context, one in which whispering, dreaming, pleasure, and intimacy were part of the aesthetic values reflected in both the lyrics and their musical settings. In sum, Toft's application of formulas and conventions of public rhetoric and oratory to such an idealized private context as the lute song superimposes the aesthetics of one medium on another with a very different cultural context in terms of intention and execution.

The degree to which the singer is capable of internalizing and then externalizing the metaphysical values of the lyric has as much to do with the song as with rhetorical structure. In other words, the singer could well be in full ignorance of rhetorical devices evident in a lyric and still produce a convincing performance because he or she is capable of representing other forms of cultural capital, other forms of the social energies that are made evident in performance. The question needs to be posed: how does the formulaic, literalized application of rhetorical

9   From the dedicatory address to Sir Thomas Mounson, *A Booke of Ayres* (1601); Davis, *The Works of Thomas Campion*, p. 14.
10   Edward Doughtie, ed., *Lyrics from English Airs, 1596–1622* (Cambridge, MA, 1970), p. 67.
11   *ibid.*, p. 380.
12   *ibid.*, p. 318.

analyses to a musical context guarantee an adequate performance practice, or allow the singer access to the sublime dimensions of the lyric he or she is delivering? Rhetoric is but one small part of a much larger cultural field, and singers and lutenists anxious to do the repertoire justice must negotiate more than the intricacies of rhetorical structure.

A brief look at one of Toft's musical examples will suffice to make my point. In a discussion of one of the acknowledged masterpieces of the lute song repertory, Dowland's *In darknesse let mee dwell,* which despite its less-than-inspired lyric content is a good example of a 'great' early modern art song, Toft makes a number of performance suggestions based on his understanding of rhetorical affect. Though useful as a general basis for argument about how to interpret the song, some specific suggestions beg additional commentary. For example, Toft argues that because the first phrase of the song, a statement of its conventional topos 'In darknesse let mee dwell', ends with the last note and word being set to a crotchet followed by a crotchet rest, 'Care should be taken to observe the abrupt termination' (see Ex. 3.1a).[13] For Toft, this is 'the musical counterpart of *aposiopesis',*[14] which Puttenham refers to as the 'figure of silence, or of interruption . . . fit for phantasticall heads and such as be sodaine or lacke memorie'.[15]

Here, two problems with Toft's analysis emerge. First, depending on the rhetorical treatise one is likely to get very different definitions, not to mention notions, of how to interpret a given figure. Henry Peacham's 1577 edition of *The Garden of Eloquence* suggests, for instance, that *aposiopesis* occurs 'when through some affection, as of feare, anger, sorrow, bashfulnesse, and such like, we breake of our speech, before it be all ended for feare . . . Thus there is a great suspition raysed by this kinde of speech, and yet nothing playnly tolde.'[16] The dilemmas facing a performer include not only which treatise to choose, but also – and here is the second problem that Toft faces – how to interpret what are, at best, vague performance indicators. How one ends the first phrase of 'In darknesse' is no doubt a crucial problem for a performer since it is the phrase that sets the tone for the song as well as the phrase that returns (epanaleptically) to close it, albeit with some significant rhythmic adjustments. Toft's recommendation that the phrase be ended abruptly so as to convey the impression that 'the singer's sorrow is almost too great for him to continue' is twinned with the suggestion that 'the torment of the singer can be demonstrated most vehemently if the last note is uttered as a sob' (Ex. 3.1b).[17]

Though there is no doubt that Dowland seems to have wanted a sort of rhythmic, if not substantive, caesura after the phrase, both the notions of abrupt ending

---

13   *ibid.,* p. 149.
14   *ibid.*
15   *The Arte of English Poesie,* vol. III, pp. 166–7.
16   Henry Peacham, *The Garden of Eloquence* (1577; rpt Menston, 1971), n.p.
17   Toft, *Tune Thy Musicke to Thy Hart,* p. 149.

Ex. 3.1a–b   John Dowland, *In darkness let mee dwell*, Song X from Robert Dowland, *A Musicall Banquet* (London, 1610)

and of sobbing are inappropriate. First, the song's *propositio* along with its musical setting do not call for any form of abruptness. The general tone of the song's musico-poetic content is spaciously contemplative in its breadth, the *propositio*, after all, being concerned with articulating the notion of 'dwell[ing]' in darkness. The song's musical structure reinforces its contemplative mode, it being one of the few through-composed, as opposed to strophic, ayres from the period. Furthermore, if we subscribe to either Puttenham's or Peacham's notions of *aposiopesis*, then there is no sense that abruptness is part of the rhetorical or oratorical flavour of the figure.

After all, there are different ways of falling into silence and of performing interruption, though the latter is clearly *not* what the song is doing. The song's initial phrase stages a contemplative topos for its auditors in a way that allows its due consideration from both musical and poetic vantage points. The notion of adding in a sob as an indication of the inexpressible emotions the singer will be grappling with, seems egregious in such a context, hinting more at the laboured word-painting that Campion is so caustic about than at the serious expression of melancholia.[18] In fact, if the song's textual context is clearly a statement of contemplative, melancholic introspection, neither abruptness nor sobbing are appropriate performative gestures, since the contemplative melancholic – and here I am thinking of Albrecht Dürer's depiction in 'Melencolia I' (1514) – is not given to the energies either one of these gestures requires.

Toft suggests that in performing the closing phrase of the song the singer reiterate the 'sob' as s/he 'simultaneously drives the hands out to either side in a violent motion designed to double the passion of abhorrence'.[19] The suggestion ignores the fact that there are different forms of performative silence, different ways of staging the movement towards silence, something that the song masterfully demonstrates since its compositional technique clearly manipulates the spaces between musical phrases as much as the musical phrases themselves. Furthermore, the driving out of the hands, a gesture more appropriate to the hyberbolic and affected rhetorical displays typical of French Baroque opera, clearly verges on the ridiculous, since it diminishes the particular effect of silence created at the song's end by virtue of a cumulative musical process.[20] Here, it is useful to remember Campion's imprecations against stage comedians who point at various parts of the anatomy to make obvious rhetorical points. Moreover, if the performer takes Peacham's comment on *aposiopesis* to heart – that it involves 'nothing playnly tolde' – then the *less* obvious the interpretation of the silence at the song's end the *more* accurate a rhetorical gesture the singer makes. Sobbing and driving the arms out at this moment would severely restrict the interpretative ambiguity implicit in not only the rhetorical gesture of *aposiopesis* but also in the literary and musical contexts of the line and its setting, the latter clearly verging till the last possible moment on a suspended cadence. The audience and reader do not know, after all, whether this is the darkness of the living death, of death imagined, or of melancholic self-absorption, to suggest but a few mutually inconclusive and suspended possibilities.

---

[18] Melancholy, to paraphrase Robert Burton's definition, is the 'character'of one's mortality (*The Anatomy of Melancholy*, ed. Holbrook Jackson (New York, 1977), I, p. 144).

[19] Toft, *Tune thy Musicke to thy Hart*, p. 153.

[20] Moreover, as a suggestion about performative gestures it fails to address those other physical dimensions that are so crucial to gestural discourse, particularly those relating to the angle of the head and the movement of the eyes.

The problems I have cited above indicate the perils of attending to but one of the myriad dimensions of the complex cultural field from which a performance emerges.[21] Another such dimension relates to what iconographical analyses reveal about the ayre's performance practices, which because of its intimate and introspective nature stages a quite unique alternative to the mass spectacles associated with the theatre, the masque, or even the performance of sacred music.[22] Iconographical representations of lute song and of the lute as a solo instrument invariably portray their performance as a theatre of intimacy, withdrawn from public spectacle the better to allow the performers their introspective concerns, or, in some cases, the better to allow the erotic undertones of such representations their full force. Here, the related problems of audience and iconographical interpretation come together in a productive way, though performers must be wary of simplistically adopting performance practices based on iconographical analyses. Musical performance and visual art are two very different media and one must be prudent in crossing the boundaries that separate them as acts of representation.

In Jan Brueghel's (1568–1625) fabulously allegorical painting in the Prado entitled 'Hearing', for example, a nude, female lutenist is featured in its foreground playing to a putto, who holds a music book (see Plate 1). In addition, the lutenist plays to various animals and birds and to a host of musical instruments and other allegorical objects which are largely dominated by the singular assortment of clocks and paintings observable in both foreground and background. The large chamber in which the performance takes place is virtually devoid of audience, the only other people in the painting being a small child in the background whose back is turned as he or she looks at a painting on the wall and a consort of musicians playing in a distant ante-chamber in the upper corner of the painting. The painting's composition takes pains to portray hearing as an experience of intimacy even in the vastest of internal domestic spaces. Brueghel's use of the lute as the instrumental focus of the scene suggests its potent significance as an emblem of the intimacy required to 'hear'. The performative space the painting imagines is characterized by the contrast between the vast expanses of pastoral countryside that lie in the background and the 'sound' imparted by the lutenist to the listening putto and stag who form the collective focus of the interior, domestic space.

The proximity to the lute of those who are 'hearing' in the painting is typical of the iconographic use of the lute as an emblem for the contiguity between performer and audience. The painting echoes, whether deliberately or not, Cesare Ripa's emblem of 'Udito' ('Hearing'), one of five 'Sentimenti' as described in his *Iconologia*

---

[21]   Note that despite my disagreement with Toft I do not intend my reading of the song's performance to be either prescriptive or proscriptive.

[22]   See Robert Spencer's comment that 'Most ayres were originally written for intimate domestic consumption' and that 'the original table-book format implied domestic self-entertainment' ('Singing English Lute Songs', p. 21).

Plate 1   Jan Brueghel ('Velvet Brueghel', 1568–1625), 'Hearing' (Madrid, Museo del Prado, no. 1395)

(1593): 'Donna che suoni vn Liuto, & a canto vi sarà vna Cerua'.[23] The stag has a conventional significance relating to hearing for 'it is charmed by music, and its hearing is very keen when it pricks up its ears'.[24] The attentiveness of both the putto and the stag highlights the harmonious relatedness of the natural, the symbolic, and the human worlds by way of music. The lute emblematizes values founded on the metaphysical connections between the natural and human worlds embodied in music's performative presence. Additionally, the presence of numerous exotic birds in proximity to the lutenist, but also off in the distance flying above the countryside, reinforces 'hearing' as an act that unifies the natural and the human as mediated by musical expression. The sound of the lute perhaps echoes the birdsong in the acts of mutual recognition and communal participation that 'hearing' signifies.

---

[23]   Cesare Ripa, *Iconologia* (1603), intro. Stephen Orgel (New York, 1976), p. 475; 'Woman who plays a lute, & on the side there will be a Hind'. The lute also figures in Ripa's emblem for 'Sanguigno per l'aria' (see Plate 2), which depicts a young man with a lute, a music stand, and a ram eating grapes. The iconography of the emblem associates the pleasing sounds of the lute with a sanguine temperament or humour whose element is air: 'Un giovane allegro, ridente, con vna ghirlanda di varij fiori in capo, di corpo carnoso, & oltre i capelli biondi hauerà il color della faccia rubicondo misto con bianco, & che sonando vn leuto dia segno con riuolgere gl' occhi al Cielo, che gli piaccia il suono, & il canto, da vna parte d'essa figura vi sarà vn montone, tenendo in bocca vn grappo d' vua, & dal' altra banda vi sarà vn librodi musica aperto' (*Iconologia*, p. 86). Musical, pastoral, and cosmic elements intermingle in the emblem as they do in Brueghel's 'Hearing'. The performance practice of the lute in this particular instance is clearly oriented towards the pleasure it gives the performer *as* the audience who hears and appreciates.

[24]   Michael Bath, *The Image of the Stag: Iconographic Themes in Western Art* (Baden-Baden, 1992), p. 207; see also pp. 219–20.

Plate 2   'Sanguigno per l'aria', Cesare Ripa, *Iconologia* (rpt Padua, 1611)

Even the painting's audience is provoked to imagine the sounds coming from the lute, for the lute is turned away from the gaze of the spectator, projecting its silent, imagined sound towards its proximate audience but also towards the empty, pastoral perspective that frames the background of the painting. As if to echo the enveloping silence symbolized by the pastoral distance, the numerous instruments foregrounded in the painting lie quiet, though the distant consort provides a kind of visual and aural counterpoint to the potential sound the silent instruments embody. The sympathetic correspondences between the consort playing in the background and the silent consort of instruments parallel the correspondences between the lutenist's sympathy with the natural environment and her domestic setting, a sympathy that echoes the correspondence between the civilized world within the room and the natural world without. The painting, then, emblematizes the links among *musica mundana, musica humana,* and *musica instrumentalis,* all of which contribute to *harmonia mundi.*[25] The sound of the lute instantiates that harmony, whereas the unplayed instruments that lie beside the lutenist remind the viewer of the importance of the human element in producing the *harmonia mundi.*[26]

[25]   See John Hollander, *The Untuning of the Sky: Ideas of Music in English Poetry, 1500–1700* (New York, 1970), pp. 20–51.

[26]   See also Victor Coelho's reading of the engraving by Giovanni Benedetto Castiglione (1609–64), *Melancolia,* which features an unplayed lute in its foreground. Coelho argues that the unplayed lute 'combined with the crumbling walls and sphere, represents the inaudibility of the harmony of the spheres, which also brings on melancholy' ('Musical Myth and Galilean Science in Giovanni Serodine's *Allegoria della Scienza',* in *Music and Science in the Age of Galileo,* ed. Victor Coelho (Dordrecht and Boston, 1992), p. 113). Silent as opposed to sounding instruments have significance in the iconographic depiction of both human and cosmic harmony, the sounding instrument

But the links are at best tenuous unless the appropriate performance context is in place, one in which the intimacy of the experience allows for the harmony that results from true hearing. What such allegorical representations had to do with the idealized performance contexts of the lute, whether in its capacity as a solo or an accompanying instrument, is a significant question. If secular Renaissance performers sought to recreate allegorical tableaux within the confines of their own performance practices, thus linking their performance with larger aesthetic, metaphysical, and even cosmic concerns and thereby increasing their cultural value in the eyes of their patrons and their audience, then contemporary performers have a great deal to absorb from such iconographical depictions, and a great deal to rethink in terms of their own performative presence.

Another early modern painting with similar implications for the performance practice of the lute song is 'Le Concert champêtre', attributed to Titian (painted *ca.* 1510 and formerly attributed to Giorgione) and now found in the Louvre. The *locus amoenus* that defines the cultural space portrayed by the painting is centred on the lute not only as an emblem of the harmonious ordering of the two couples, again brought into symbolic proximity to each other through the sound of the lute, but also as a signifier for the intimacies staged by the pastoral concert. In the latter case, the interwoven expressions of the two males and one of the women are focused on the lute as emblematic of the theatre of shared privacy that is this visual and allegorical concert. Even less overtly allegorical paintings in which the lute appears

having particular relevance as an emblem of the forms of human community established through 'hearing'. Note also the verses from 'The Argument of the Frontispiece' in Robert Burton's *The Anatomy of Melancholy* (1621), which anatomize the 'many features' of melancholy. The association of the lute with solitariness and self-love are explicit in verses three and four, which gloss the visual images in the frontispiece:

> The next of Solitariness,
> A portraiture doth well express,
> By sleeping dog, cat: buck and doe,
> Hare, conies in the desert go:
> Bats, owls the shady bowers over,
> In melancholy darkness hover.
> Mark well: if 't be not as 't should be,
> Blame the bad cutter, and not me.

> I' th'under column there doth stand
> *Inamorato* with folded hand;
> Down hangs his head, terse and polite,
> Some ditty sure he doth indite.
> His lute and books about him lie,
> As symptoms of his vanity.
> If this do not enough disclose,
> To paint him, take thyself by th' nose.

(Jackson edn, pp. 7–8). The symbology associated with the various forms of melancholy in these verses is clear enough, the lute signifying the solitary, self-interest of the melancholic *Inamorato*, the stag having associations with the solitariness of 'melancholy darkness'.

use similar and conventional visual tropes associated with the lute to stage an attentiveness to the sounds that harmonize social disposition. Gerard ter Borch's (1617–81) 'The Suitor's Visit' (National Gallery, Washington) portrays a moment of relative intimacy charged with erotic potential, in this case backgrounded by a woman playing the theorbo as a visual and aural accompaniment to the shared gaze of the lovers. Here, the iconographical performance context associated with the lute occurs within an intimate, domestic space to which the notion of a 'public', as defined by contemporary performance practice, would be completely foreign. Both the pastoral *locus amoenus* and the domestic chamber figure in standard early modern depictions of the lute in concert, confirming its idealized performance as one in which the values of physical closeness, privacy, and seclusion are fostered.

Both from the evidence in composers' prefatory remarks to the songbooks and from the iconographical evidence of contemporary representations of the lute in performance, then, it becomes evident that the lute song's performance context is neither geared towards a notion of audience as contemporary performance practice would have it nor possessed of the public dimensions of Renaissance entertainments. If anything, the radical newness of the lute song as an early modern manifestation of European secular art song lies in its marking out of a private, performative space apart from the public dimensions of theatre, courtly entertainment, or sacred music, all of which were intractably associated with public spectacle and function.[27] Not that the lute song did not have a social function. But my argument suggests that this function had more to do with the creation of an intimate and restricted performance space than it had to do with public display. Nor do I not mean to suggest that the lute song was a purely private experience. Rather, the lute song redirects social energies in a way that is not completely subject to the public gaze, not completely beholden to the contingencies of social function. This partially accounts, I think, for the virtual absence of early modern descriptions of the lute song's performance practices in anything but the most banal of details. The lute song defines a society apart by focusing on private expression that gains aesthetic value through its putative independence from the public sphere. In the ayre the emphasis is firmly on autology or self-apostrophe, in which the singer turns away from public expression to address the nature of private experience. Introspection is staged as a dialogue with one's self or at most with a real or an imagined other with whom one has an attachment, usually erotic or elegiac. Undoubtedly some of this has to do with the lute as an instrument whose discreet acoustic presence announces a corresponding discretion

---

[27] The masque, for example, serves to reinforce the consensual courtly values that authorize monarchic authority. The theatre provides an outlet for repressed social energies that are intrinsically subversive, even as it reinforces the diverse values of its audience. Sacred music publicly demonstrates the spiritual values that authorize sovereign investiture. Royal processions serve the function of embodying corporeally the symbolic dimensions of the monarch, thus publicly reinforcing the mythic dimensions of absolute rule.

on the part of the persona of the performer. By the very nature of its acoustic properties the lute limits its audience. Combine that with a performative context in which melancholy and self-apostrophe play significant roles in determining the personae of the lutenist and the singer, and the foundations of understanding the lute song's performance practice begin to fall into place.

Given such a context, it would be incorrect to attribute an homogeneous performance practice to the lute song, since within the larger genre of lute song there exist many sub-genres. Some of these sub-genres are demonstrably intended for more of an audience than others, some have no metaphysical import at all, and some reject melancholic or even erotic self-absorption in favour of more sprightly *carpe diem* material reflected in a more upbeat musical context. The public dimensions of a song like *His golden locks time hath to siluer turnde*,[28] celebrating Sir Henry Lee's retirement, are balanced against the melancholic *memento mori* and *tempus fugit* topoi that the persona of the singer transforms from public into personal expression. The emphasis, even in this public statement of Lee's loyalty to Elizabeth I – 'Blest be the harts that wish my soueraigne well / Curst be the soule that thinke her any wrong' – is firmly on the solitary nature of retirement, a state metonymically embodied in the very performance context of the song medium chosen for this lyric: 'But though from court to cotage he departe / His saint is sure of his vnspotted hart.' The song goes so far as to imagine Lee in his retirement cottage, teaching others the art of the song as if passing on the tradition of contemplative grace to which he has attained: 'And when he saddest sits in homely Cell / Hele teach his swaines this Caroll for a songe.' Attentive audiences that hear the song without knowing its specific occasional nature cannot help making the relation between song and the intimacy of contemplative experience, especially when that song acts as an indirect signifier for mortality. Even a more blatantly hedonistic song like *Come againe: sweet loue doth now enuite*[29] cannot but return to the context of apostrophe, the singer addressing, perhaps ironically, a beloved other in a familiar tone of erotic anxiety: 'I sit, I sigh, I weepe, I faint, I die, / In deadly paine, and endles miserie.' Again, whatever the public dimensions of the audience, the song reduces those dimensions to the interlocutor and the beloved, the very performative context of the song seeking to establish the intimacy that will lead to erotic 'com[ing]' and 'die[ing]'. In both songs there is a sense in which the performance context produces a spectacle that rejects the uncomplicated display of public sentiment for a much more sophisticated and nuanced private theatre of self to which few are admitted.

[28] Song 18, John Dowland, *The First Booke of Songes or Ayres* (1597); Doughtie, *Lyrics*, pp. 80–1. For further contextual commentary on this song, see Andrew Taylor, 'The Sounds of Chivalry: Lute Song and Harp Song for Sir Henry Lee', *JLSA* 25 (1992), pp. 1–23.
[29] Song 17, *ibid.*, pp. 79–80.

No doubt such a spectacle has its paradoxes. The public representation of interiority is rife with tensions between the conventions of external display and the hermetic dissimulation of private contemplation. How is a contemporary performance practice to recuperate and reproduce such a cultural context, especially when the lute song seemed to anticipate and reject many of the values that have come to be associated with contemporary performance practice? Is the contemporary staging of lute song performances in large performance venues (or in performance venues at all) true to the original cultural contexts in which the lute songs were conceived? And, if not, given the economic and aesthetic exigencies of contemporary performance practice, is it possible or desirable to convey in some small manner the flavour of an early modern context that is by its very nature self-effacing, opposed to conventions other than the ones it establishes for itself? Such questions, if they can be answered at all, need to be addressed by performers of the lute song, if only to acknowledge the explicit cultural differences that separate contemporary performance contexts from early modern contexts of which we have only a fragmentary knowledge.

The lute song marks the cultural space in which these contradictions are manifested in their full force, as if to suggest that in the public display of introspection there will always be a supplement to which no public can ever be privy. There always remains, in other words, a dimension of the performers' experience that is inaccessible to its audience. The cultural implications of such a pose, whether one agrees with its efficacy or not, are profound. Not only does the lute song come to signify a form of performative otherness, a rejection or revision of, or challenge to, mainstream performance values, it also creates the possibility for expressive subversion of conventional cultural values. The lute song's place in the cultural contexts of early modern English song merely serves to reinforce such a claim, for in the unique synergy created by amalgamating secular music and poetry in an experimental performance genre, composers and poets were able to experiment with those issues so contested by Renaissance humanists: monody and homophony versus polyphony, diatonicism versus chromaticism, consonance versus dissonance, and the struggle between the lyric texts and the musical scores for ascendancy in determining performative emphasis. These issues have important ramifications in terms of performance practice relating to the lute generally. To what degree was the lute foregrounded as an accompanying instrument, especially in those lute songs where chromaticism, dissonance, and polyphony figure as important expressive devices? To what extent was the lute intended to obscure the the lyric text, or to comment upon it? To what extent did the accompanist figure as part of the performance as opposed to the intended audience of the singer? And how were these interactions conceived of by the performers themselves, let alone by their putative audiences?

Such questions lead inevitably to broader questions: What states of mind are required to perform sixteenth- and early seventeenth-century music? What values, musical or otherwise, underlie the practice and ethos of early modern musicians? And, ultimately, can the study of things other than the music be explored productively in order to approximate the elusive imaginative and historical performance context of the lute song?

II

> From thence in saffron coloured robe flew Hymen through ye ayre,
> And into *Thracia* beeing calld by Orphy did repayre.
> He came in deede at *Orphyes* call: but neyther did he sing
> The woordes of that solemnitie, nor merry countnance bring,
> Nor any handsell of good lucke. His torch with drizling smoke
> Was dim: the same too burne out cleere, no stirring could provoke.
> The end was worser than the signe. For as the Bryde did rome
> Abrode accompanyde with a trayne of Nymphes too bring her home,
> A serpent lurking in the grasse did sting her in the ancle:
> Whereof she dyde incontinent, so swift the bane did rancle.
> Whom when the *Thracian* Poet had bewayld sufficiently
> On earth, the Ghostes departed hence he minding for too trie,
> Downe at the gate of *Tænarus* did go too *Limbo* Lake.
> And thence by gastly folk and soules late buried he did take
> His journey too *Persephonee* and too the king of Ghosts
> That like a Lordly tyran reignes in those unpleasant coasts.
> And playing on his tuned harp he thus began too sound.[30]

What could this passage, which opens the tenth book of Arthur Golding's mid sixteenth-century translation of Ovid's *Metamorphoses,* possibly have to do with the lute song? As a mythic figure Orpheus has been recognized to have a number of sometimes contradictory significances. John Hollander suggests that 'While Orpheus is traditionally associated with inducing activity in inanimate rocks, trees, and animals, and, finally, men, it is as a governor of feelings that he comes primarily to be used in English poetry of the seventeenth century.'[31] Robin Headlam Wells,

---

[30] Arthur Golding, *The XV. Bookes of P. Ouidius Naso, entytuled Metamorphosis translated oute of Latin into English meeter* . . . (London, 1567; rpt London, 1961), p. 201.

[31] *The Untuning of the Sky,* pp. 165–6. For a more complete discussion of Orphic poetic representations in the early modern period see Hollander, 162–76. Hollander associates Orpheus not only with 'abstract eloquence' but with 'the power of actual secular music' (*ibid.,* p. 163). In a discussion of the Renaissance Italian philosopher Pietro Pomponazzi (1462–1525), Gary Tomlinson cites a passage from *De incantationibus* in which Pomponazzi articulates a related theory about music's ability to alter both the mind and the body. Again Orpheus figures: 'What shall we say of musicians and singers to the lute, who with their songs and instruments lead even unwilling men now to anger, now to compassion, now to arms, now to worship, as the reports of Orpheus, Timotheus, and innumerable

building on Hollander's interpretation, argues that 'The humanist myth of the birth of civilization through song has its origins in classical poetics. In Horace's allegorization of the Orpheus story (*Ars poetica*) the Renaissance found a model that served as a basis for its own mythical account of the process by which authority persuades its subjects willingly to accept the rule of law.'[32] By contrast, a scholium on Virgil argues that 'there was an Orphic book about summoning the soul, called the *Lyre*. It is said that souls need the cithara in order to ascend.'[33] Roberto Calasso, besides asserting that 'Some even maintained that Orpheus was torn apart by women because he had been the first to declare the superiority of love with boys',[34] suggests that

Into the impervious history of Delphi, Orpheus and Musaeus arrive almost as parvenus, at least as compared with the Sibyls: 'They say that Orpheus put on such airs about his mysteries and was generally so presumptuous that both he and Musaeus, who imitated him in everything, refused to submit themselves to the test and take part in any musical competition' [Pausanias, *Description of Greece*, X, 7, 2]. This was when they were in Delphi. And perhaps Orpheus and Musaeus weren't avoiding that competition out of arrogance, nor for fear of being beaten, but because right there for all to see, as it still is today, was the rock where the Phemonoe [a priestess of Apollo supposed to have invented heroic verses] pronounced the very first hexameters.[35]

Orpheus, then. Index of the depth of human emotion. Founder of civilization. Player of the lyre. Mystic summoner of souls. Betrayer of women. Sibylline parvenu. The list is impressive in the scope of the mythic resonances associated with Orpheus and, meeting one of the crucial conditions of mythic narrative, it is incomplete, always subject to further interpretive interpolations and accretions.[36]

If we return to Golding's influential version of the myth, however, the crux of musical Orphism lies in the problem of communicating with the dead. Orpheus's mythic performance is pitched at Pluto in order to restore Eurydice's lost life through the persuasive musical powers that combine with Orpheus's narrative to move the 'bloodlesse ghostes' to tears.[37] Orphic performance is a staging of the encounter with death, a staging of the 'sound' that is life as it battles for some small

---

others show? Therefore it is not unreasonable or unnatural to alter and compel minds with sounds – which minds, once altered, clearly will alter their bodies' (*Music in Renaissance Magic: Toward a Historiography of Others* (Chicago, 1993), p. 202). The power of sound to alter and compel is a significant dimension of Orphic mythography and may have had as much to do with the general reception context of early modern music as it did with the actual performance practice.

[32] *Elizabethan Mythologies*, p. 8.

[33] Cited in M. L. West, *The Orphic Poems* (Oxford, 1983), p. 30.

[34] *The Marriage of Cadmus and Harmony*, trans. Tim Parks (New York, 1993), p. 81.

[35] *ibid.*, p. 144.

[36] For a useful summary of some of these in relation to the development of the Western musical tradition, see Wilfrid Mellers, *The Masks of Orpheus: Seven Stages in the Story of European Music* (Manchester, 1987).

[37] Golding, *The XV. Bookes of P. Ouidius Naso . . .* , p. 201.

victory against the mortality represented in Eurydice's 'incontinent' surrender to death. Performance takes place away from public spectacle, away from the hustle and bustle of daily life, and directs itself at the phantasms of death. The figurative resonances of such a reading in terms of early modern performance practices cannot be neglected in considering the larger cultural field to which the lute song belonged and upon which it commented.

Why this excursion into Orphic mythography and interpretation? Because in *Performance: Revealing the Orpheus Within,* Orpheus is the linchpin on which Anthony Rooley's reading of Renaissance performance practices depends.[38] Rooley, a devotee of Renaissance Neoplatonism as espoused by Marsilio Ficino and Pico della Mirandola, presents a number of ideas that form the basis of a quasi-speculative, quasi-pragmatic system applicable to performance generally, but specifically to the performance of the Elizabethan lute song, in which he is an acknowledged expert. In the context of Rooley's argument, Orpheus represents both the performer and sixteenth-century ideals of performance practice. The latter notion of Orphic performance will have particular resonances for lutenists familiar with the oft-cited reference to John Dowland in Robert Dowland's *A Varietie of Lute Lessons* (1610) as the 'English Orpheus', not to mention Henry Purcell's claim to being 'Orpheus Britannicus'. From these scanty and oftentimes clichéd appellations for great performer-composers, as well as from the related title of 'Il Divino' bestowed on Francesco da Milano, Rooley makes a case for Orpheus as a Renaissance embodiment of the power 'to move the soul' through 'divine inspiration'.[39]

However appealing such an idea is, and whatever it may mean to 'move the soul', it must be remembered that in the Renaissance such language – the language of 'ecstatic transport' into 'some divine frenzy'[40] – is a highly metaphorical language for the musical affects produced by great composers and performers. 'Ecstatic transport', as a literary trope, is firmly anchored in the conventional rhetoric of the time, one that in England, moreover, was the product of suspect Italianate influences.[41] Contemporary Renaissance scholarship has taught that students of the period must beware of over-investing too credulously in the import of such tropes. The experience of 'ecstatic transport' is difficult to quantify at the most lucid of times, and to suggest that ecstatic transport is Orphic in nature is to articulate a conventional literary rendering of highly stylized performance practices. The descriptions

---

[38] See my review of this book in *JLSA* 23 (1990), pp. 81–90.

[39] *Performance*, p. 9.

[40] *ibid.,* p. 8.

[41] For an extended attack on Italianate influences on England see Roger Ascham, *The Schoolmaster* (London, 1570), ed. Lawrence V. Ryan (Charlottesville, 1974), especially pp. 63–75. The following passage is representative of the more moderate of Ascham's comments on Italian culture: 'I was once in Italy myself, but, I thank God, my abode there was but nine days. And yet I saw in that little time, in one city, more liberty to sin than ever I heard tell of in our noble city of London in nine year' (p. 72).

of those practices made use of a very particular form of encomiastic and conventional rhetoric in keeping with the often overblown nature, however alluring, of Renaissance courtly discourse.

To accept such a reading of Orphic presence in the limited and all-too-infrequent descriptions of sixteenth-century performance practices is perhaps equivalent to accepting the standard clichés associated with Petrarchan love rhetoric – somewhat tantamount to believing that 'living deaths', 'freezing fires', and 'sweet despairs' represent anything but a conventional rhetoric associated with love. In other words, having called a love experience a 'living death' or a performance 'Orphic', are we really any closer to the spirit in which that 'love' is expressed – if it is ever 'love' and not a performative literary utterance made by the poet for the sake of a specific tradition or style – or that 'performance' created? The answer is a very qualified no. The problem involves a form of literary interpretation, an awareness of the complex rhetorical and tropological constructions that give ambiguous voice to the Renaissance.

In the case of 'reading' Orpheus, Rooley leaps from knowledge of the rhetoric of a few isolated cases that associate Orpheus with performance to several assumptions: '[I]t was recognised by men of their own age that these performers [Francesco, Dowland, Purcell] carried the fabled power of Orpheus to move the soul' and 'they ['these performers'] were able to communicate, fairly directly, the divine inspiration which had been symbolically granted to Orpheus'.[42] Such assumptions confuse rhetoric about performance with actual performance practices. It is one thing to call yourself Orphic or to be called as such by others, whereas it is quite another thing actually to be Orpheus, whatever 'being Orpheus' or having an 'Orpheus within' may have meant in a Renaissance context.[43]

Rooley affirms that '[t]he present contemplation focusses on music and the soul, and is a fusion of material presented by [John] Warden [*Orpheus: The Metamorphosis of a Myth*] from Ficino's work, with Plato [*sic*] and Orphic fragments, added to which is my own position as a performing artist. It is, in other words, a synthesis of some of the most exciting material ever set down as a guide for the performer.'[44] Such a fulsome claim begs some obvious questions. In what way do Neoplatonic philosophies aimed at transcending the sensual world to attain a mystico-spiritual union with the One of the immaterial world constitute a 'guide for the performer', especially if the performer does not share in the far-from-homogeneous belief systems of the Neoplatonists? How is music an expression of the soul? What constitutes the soul? Who has one? And what if 'soul', when used figuratively in describing Renaissance performance practices, is merely a trope for the bodily

---

[42] *Performance*, p. 9.
[43] It may be noted that Rooley does not present a single Renaissance text in which either of these two phrases occurs.
[44] *Performance*, p. 82.

experience of performance – its stresses, its moments of *ekstasis,* its failures, not to mention its social and its spatio-temporal contexts? In other words, what if 'soul' is merely an effect of language, or a by-product of the effects of performance on the body?

The complicated relationship between sacred and secular performance practice is elided in Rooley's Orphic analysis, a situation that also potentially misrepresents the way in which Renaissance performance practices actually evolved and were conceived. The notion, for example, of an analogy to be made between Orpheus and the contemporary performer, though useful in the limited context of those who wish to adopt the same beliefs as Rooley/Orpheus, is, in this context, somewhat disturbing. Rooley presents a classic (mis)reading or idealization of the myth, a revisionary understanding that suits the purposes of his notion of performance as a ritual expression of the classical values of clarity, reverie, sublimity, beauty, love, respect, and harmony. He states, for instance, that '[w]hen Orpheus steps forward singing new songs of divine inspiration, then Euridice is enticed from out of the audience and the oldest reactions of the myth are re-enacted – Orpheus and Euridice are united in love and harmony'.[45] Besides wondering how the 'oldest [unsubstantiated] reactions' to the myth are re-enacted – as if contemporary readers can ever be privy to the exact historical resonances of the myth in its past contexts – one must also wonder when and if such an enticement is effected between the audience and the performer. The lines seem to read the myth as leading to an aggregate harmony, a fulfilment of a binding love in the act of performance that is the simulacrum of the imagined unity to be read into Orpheus and Eurydice's pairing.

This reading is in contradiction to the myth itself, which proposes as its central experiences disjunction, fragmentation, dismemberment *(sparagmos)*, and the creative power of melancholy through separation. Such a reading also ignores how the myth was treated in a Platonic context. Phaedrus, for instance, in an extended passage on love in the *Symposium*, argues that

heaven itself has a peculiar regard for ardor and resolution in the cause of Love. And yet the gods sent Orpheus away from Hades empty-handed, and showed him the mere shadow of the woman he had come to seek. Eurydice herself they would not let him take, because he seemed, like the mere minstrel he was, to be a lukewarm lover, lacking the courage to die as Alcestis died for love, and choosing rather to scheme his way, living, into Hades. And it was for this that the gods doomed him, and doomed him justly, to meet his death at the hands of women.[46]

The passage is instructive in what it reveals about Orpheus in so far as he figures in some Platonic and Neoplatonic versions of the myth: an incomplete lover who lacks

---

[45]   *ibid.,* p. 115.
[46]   Plato, *Collected Dialogues*, ed. Edith Hamilton and Huntington Cairns (Princeton, 1980), pp. 533–4, 179d.

passion and courage, scheming his way into Hades while alive, not having the capacity to die for his passion – someone who must die, ultimately, at the hands of the very forces he has failed in order to understand the nature of ardent love.

Such a reading, still compelling in a contemporary context, is distant from Rooley's own speculative (mis)reading of Orpheus as a signifier of harmony and spiritual fulfilment: 'If every performer has an Orpheus within, then it seems fruitful to consider that every audience contains Euridice. The performance is itself the descent [to the underworld], where lovers meet and recognise each other, take hands and ascend, united, together. The culmination, the distilled silence at the end of the work, or recital, is heaven.'[47] Again, Rooley makes an interpretive leap from Orpheus as signifying the performer to Eurydice as signifying the audience, when, in fact, it may be more useful to consider the performer as a symbolic embodiment of the play between the descent and ascent represented by Orpheus and Eurydice – whatever such an interpretation ultimately contributes to the understanding of sixteenth-century performance practices. What if the performer must descend into his or her own underworld, rather than the underworld of the audience, in order to create? What if the lesson of the Orpheus myth for performers is one that has to do with confronting loss from within rather than projecting that loss onto the audience as symbolic of Eurydice? What if, to borrow from Maurice Blanchot, 'for Orpheus everything collapses into the certainty of failure where there remains only, as compensation, the work's uncertainty, for is there ever a work?'[48]

In the context of the Phaedric/Platonic reading given above, one wonders if Rooley would still wish to maintain his notion of Orpheus as the 'archetypal performer',[49] that is, one who lacks the courage to confront the compelling passions of love instantiated in musical expression? And yet the Phaedric/Platonic reading of the myth has, perhaps, significant lessons for the performer. Rather than attempting to attain the illusion of unity with the 'shadow' of the audience (as a type of

---

[47] *Performance*, p. 78.

[48] 'Orpheus's Gaze', in *The Space of Literature*, trans. Ann Smock (Lincoln, NB, 1982), p. 174. Blanchot's suggestive reading of the Orpheus myth is also not taken into account by Rooley, even though Blanchot makes direct connections with one of the important themes evident in Rooley's book, that of inspiration. Blanchot suggests that '[t]o look at Eurydice, without regard for the song, in the impatience and imprudence of desire which forgets the law: *that is inspiration*' (*The Space of Literature*, p. 173). Here impatient and imprudent desire that overturns the law is at the crux of the myth – just as it was for Monteverdi and his librettist Striggio in *Orfeo* (1607): their Orpheus, 'conquered by his own emotions', loses Eurydice 'through too much love'. Such a reading (originating perhaps as a Christian gloss on the pagan myth) would have interesting applications to a performance practice that enacted such desire. Blanchot also has interesting things to say about Orpheus's relation to song: 'only in the song does Orpheus have power over Eurydice. But in the song too, Eurydice is already lost, and Orpheus himself is the dispersed Orpheus; the song immediately makes him "infinitely dead". He loses Eurydice because he desires her beyond the measured limits of the song, and he loses himself, but this desire, and Eurydice lost, and Orpheus dispersed are necessary to the song, just as the ordeal of eternal inertia is necessary to the work' (*The Space of Literature*, p. 173). Again, dispersal, loss, and desire beyond the aesthetic limits of song figure in the myth, all of which contradict Rooley's reading of Orpheus as symbolic of the performer's harmonious union with the audience.

[49] *Performance*, p. 3.

Eurydice), the performer's energies are perhaps better expended in avoiding the vainglory and lukewarm passions that vitiate the affective powers of music – powers that are, after all, as much the result of the performer's ability to express disjunction, dissonance, fragmentation, and the pervasive melancholy of memory, as they are the result of the expression of harmony, love and other so-called 'positive' values.

There is a further troubling notion evident in the comments from Rooley that I have already cited, namely, that it is the performer's duty as Orpheus to generate experiences of unity and harmony, a duty that in any context implies an aesthetics of homogeneity that is not without its problems. How to explain this to a Gesualdo, a Bach, or an Ives or any other innovator who dares to question assumptions about the homogeneity of the creative process, its structures, and its affects? The presumption of such an aesthetics of homogeneity when read in the context of Orpheus as a myth of dismemberment and failed union is problematic, to say the least. In this light, the reading of the Orpheus myth that Rooley offers is not fully developed or considered in terms of its relation to performance practice. The practical implications of such mythographic considerations are significant for performance practice in so far as the very diversity (and contradictoriness) of mythographic contexts for Orpheus would seem to point to an analogous diversity in actual performance practices. The lesson to be learned is that imposing rigid readings on mythography or performance practice is contrary to the early modern cultural context, a context that encouraged aesthetic pluralism within conventional signifying systems.

The actual instances in which lute song composers refer to Orpheus are, in fact, few, and always occur in prefatory remarks common to the songbooks. The dedication to Sir George Carey that prefaces Dowland's 1597 book of songs, for example, cites Orpheus as part of a conventional genealogy. Harmony results from the 'swetnes of instrument' combined with the 'liuely voice of man, expressing some worthy sentence or excellent Poeme'.[50] For Dowland, the art of music is an outgrowth of poetic expression, 'for *Linus Orpheus* and the rest, according to the number and time of their Poemes, first framed the numbers and times of musicke'.[51] The prefatory Latin epigram to the same book, contributed by Thomas Campion, also mentions Orpheus in an encomiastic comparison with Dowland: 'Famam, posteritas quam dedit Orpheo, / Dolandi melius Musica dat sibi' ('The fame which posterity gave to Orpheus, the music of Dowland gives to him').[52]

The dedicatory address to William Earl of Derby in Francis Pilkington's *The First Booke of Songs or Ayres* (1605) briefly mentions Orpheus in a different context, suggesting that the audience capable of understanding the aesthetic values of the lute song is limited. Pilkington asks 'For who regardeth the melodius charmes of

[50] Doughtie, *Lyrics*, p. 66.
[51] *ibid.*
[52] *ibid.*, p. 69; translation in Davis, *The Works of Thomas Campion*, p. 195.

Orpheus, or enchanting melodie of *Arion?*' and answers 'surely but a few', thus indicating that the musical values associated with the lute song are understood by the 'few' who are initiated into the Aristoxenian and Pythagorean notions that 'the Soule of man was Musicke' and that the 'being thereof was framed of numbers'.[53] The commendatory Latin poem to Robert Dowland's *A Musicall Banquet* (1610), by Henry Peacham, also makes conventional mention of Orpheus and Linus,[54] and Ben Jonson's dedicatory poem to Alfonso Ferrabosco's *Ayres* (1609) makes an oblique reference to the power of Orpheus's and Amphion's music in 'building Townes, and making wilde Beasts tame'.[55] Orpheus, then, was seen as part of the aesthetic and mythographic lineage of music, a lineage in which the lute song composers sought their place, if these scattered indices can be taken at their face value. Pilkington's comment is perhaps the most revealing for what it says about how lute song composers thought about the reception of their work. The transcendental values of music as an expression of soul are held by a 'few', though Pilkington's own way of putting it ('surely but a few') suggests that this is conjecture on his part. Thus, to discuss lute song performance practice in generalized Orphic terms seems hardly accurate, without understanding the larger cultural dimensions of Orphic mythography, not to mention the specific and limited usage of Orphic symbology by the lute song composers and poets.

As a last perspective that may be brought to bear on the connections between Orphic mythography and the lute song composers, I turn to Thomas Campion's *The Lords' Masque* (performed on 14 February 1613 for the wedding of Princess Elizabeth), which features Orpheus in a prominent role. A brief look at Campion's use of Orpheus in the masque will make my point regarding the wariness with which the performance context of the lute song may be termed Orphic. Early in the masque Mania, the goddess of madness, appears 'wildly out of her cave'[56] demanding to know 'What powerfull noise is this importunes me, / T'abandon darkenesse which my humour fits'.[57] The mad humour associated with darkness is disturbed by Orpheus's 'powerfull noise' or musical summons. Orpheus demands that Mania release Entheus, who has been imprisoned in a cave full of 'Franticks', and Mania expresses her fear that the frantics will 'disturbe / The peace of *Jove*'.[58] Orpheus quells her fears stating that '*Jove* into our musick will inspire / The power of passion, that their [the frantics'] thoughts shall bend / To any forme or motion we intend.'[59]

---

[53] Doughtie, *Lyrics*, p. 221.
[54] *ibid.*, p. 343.
[55] *ibid.*, p. 291.
[56] Davis, *The Works of Thomas Campion*, p. 249.
[57] *ibid.*
[58] *ibid.*, p. 250.
[59] *ibid.*

Orpheus invokes music to aid him ('Let Musicke put on *Protean* changes now'[60]) once the frantics have been released, whereupon the following stage directions occur:

At the sound of a strange musicke twelve Franticks enter, six men and six women, all presented in sundry habits and humours: there was the Lover, the Selfe-lover, the melancholike-man full of feare, the Schoole-man over-come with phantasie, the over-watched Usurer, with others that made an absolute medly of madnesse; in middest of whom Entheus *(or Poeticke furie) was hurried forth, and tost up and downe, the Lunatickes fell into a madde measure, fitted to a loud phantasticke tune; but in the end thereof the musicke changed into a very solemne ayre, which they played softly, while* Orpheus *spake.*[61]

The sequence of events along with the stage directions are instructive in what they say indirectly about performance practice, though again Orpheus is used in a manner that is broadly symbolic, part of the humanist exposition of the harmonizing or civilizing power of music. The solemnity of the 'ayre' that accompanies Orpheus's speech is an index of the self-possession that empowers the performer over his or her audience.

At this crucial juncture in the masque Orpheus expels Mania and the 'Phantasticks': 'Through these soft and calme sounds, *Mania,* passe / With thy Phantasticks hence; heere is no place / Longer for them or thee'.[62] The lines denote the cathartic, purgative effect of music in its ability to banish madness and fantastic behaviour, performance being the magical empowerment of sounds that dispel the disruptive social forces represented by the frantics. The music of the 'solemne ayre' when combined with Orphic speech resists the frantic behaviour of the lover, the egotist, the melancholic, the scholar, the usurer, and others, producing an alternative to the social dementias they represent. From the perspective of the lute song's performance practice, the 'ayre' metonymizes the social value of performance and its paradoxical ability to resist the chaotic social forces that produce the various forms of manic behaviour articulated by the masque. Again, where the 'ayre' is invoked there is a turn away from the public, as if to suggest that the power embodied in musico-poetic performance is the power to assert the salutary and solitary dimensions of self. Self, embodied in the masque in Orphic terms, is opposed to the 'sundry habits and humours', the 'absolute medley of madnesse' that require expulsion. The social function of Orphism, in this particular instance, is clearly a symbolic aspect of a larger concept of performance practice in which the value of personal expression is opposed to a broader social context while nonetheless contributing to the harmonious fabric of that context.

---

[60] *ibid.*

[61] *ibid.*, pp. 250–1.

[62] *ibid.*, p. 251.

Thus, though contemporary performers must be extremely wary of generalizations about the Orphic dimensions of early modern performance practice, there are, in a few, isolated texts, helpful indicators regarding the cultural values and aesthetic contexts they may attempt to instil in a contemporary performance. The evidence brought forward in this essay in specific relation to the lute song would suggest that those values and contexts must emphasize the intimacy of the performers' relations with their audience, the latter being of necessity limited in number; they must reject the notion of public, oratorical space for a very different context governed by the symbolic values of pastoral and domestic space; and they must abjure the overly simplistic application of any one dimension of early modern culture, whether literary, visual, or musical, as the sole determinant of an informed performance practice. In opposition to contemporary practice in which the public too frequently imposes its aesthetic demands on the performer as a product to be consumed, the aesthetics of lute song performance invert and reject such a structure, invoking the ideal of a performance geared to the performer's ability to fashion the private space in which an economy of intimate exchange is enacted. Music, as Campion suggests in *The Lords' Masque,* is a work of 'passion'.[63] Like the lover, the performer enacts and facilitates the intimacies of exchange, the invisible and sometimes barely audible intercourse that gives the performative expression of the lute song its elusive affect.

[63]   *ibid.,* p. 257.

4

PER CANTARE E SONARE: ACCOMPANYING ITALIAN LUTE SONG OF THE LATE SIXTEENTH CENTURY

KEVIN MASON

While modern lute players occasionally perform Italian lute songs from pre-existing intabulated accompaniments, they are usually required to create their own realizations. To effect a convincing realized accompaniment, the lutenist needs to consider many issues, among them the poetic structure of the text, the composer's intentions, the original performing context, the vocal styles and voice-types of lute song, whether the overall style of the music is appropriate for lute accompaniment, and what the original notational or printing format can reveal about performance. The lutenist must then confront the question of style, which is without a doubt the most elusive issue in lute accompaniment; for how can anyone today make a personal assessment about something so ephemeral as a 400-year-old lute tablature that is in itself a personal assessment? Thus, in writing about accompanimental style one risks pedantry and systematization; this is why so few lutenists of the past attempted to codify their knowledge.

Given our present need for this kind of information, my original intention for this chapter was to write about the accompaniment of early seventeenth-century Italian music on the lute and theorbo, a topic that has been central to my activities as both a player and a scholar for many years. Some historical information on this topic survives in the form of written-out tablature accompaniments published by Rossi, Kapsberger, Corradi, and Castaldi, as well as in the numerous Italian lute manuscripts that include continuo parts realized in tablature. These sources are central to our understanding of basso continuo playing in the early Baroque, but at the same time many features of these tablatures contradict what we know about historical accompaniment from other sources. For instance, Rossi's arrangements of five-part madrigals ignore the re-entrant tuning of the theorbo by including inner parts that cross the tuning break and suddenly leap up or down a seventh rather than a second.[1] Also, a comparison of the tablature with the vocal parts suggests not only

---

[1] Salamone Rossi, *Il primo libro de madrigali* (Venice, 1600).

72

the usual nominal theorbo tuning in A, but a second tuning a fourth higher in D, a pitch level unsupported by any other evidence from seventeenth-century Italian sources. In *Brussels 704,* one of the largest and earliest sources of monody, the intabulated lute accompaniments are written in an amateurish manner in which virtually every bass note is realized with four-note chords, and with little to no concern for proper voice-leading.[2] In addition, many of the solo songs with theorbo accompaniment that appear in the collections of Kapsberger, Corradi, and Castaldi consciously double the singer's part – a practice that would seem to go against period aesthetics as well as our own.[3]

It soon becomes clear that in all of these sources the problems and contradictions reside not with the tablatures, but with our own perspective. In other words, we have interpreted these early sources from our modern performing experiences and through a filter of various treatises, most of them designed primarily for keyboard players and largely dating from later in the century. As modern musicians, we tend to look at the past backwards in a straight line, using whatever is closer in time, and therefore more familiar, in order to explain something further removed. However, a reasonable understanding of Italian lute and theorbo accompaniment in the early seventeenth century is impossible to achieve without a more *forward*-looking perspective – that is, through the investigation of Italian lute accompaniment from the end of the sixteenth century. Therefore, in this article I shall examine the arrangement of secular vocal polyphony for one or more voices with lute,[4] which constitutes the written tradition of Italian lute song that immediately precedes (but also overlaps with) continuo song of the seventeenth century.

One of the richest and most enduring performance conventions in Renaissance Italy was that of singing to the lute. Throughout the *cinquecento,* two separate Italian lute song traditions can be distinguished. The first, an unwritten one, began at least as early as the mid fifteenth century, and is defined by poetry that was sung to an improvised melody over an accompaniment consisting of a simple chordal formula.[5] Though little tangible evidence of the unwritten tradition survives, its importance

---

2   Brussels, Bibliothèque du Conservatoire Royale de Musique, Ms. Littera F. No. 704 (undated, *ca.* 1590–1600); 45 of the 140 continuo songs in this collection include accompaniments for lute.

3   Giovanni Girolamo Kapsberger, *Libro primo di villanelle* (Rome, 1610; rpt Florence, 1979) and *Libro terzo di villanelle* (Rome, 1619; rpt Florence, 1979); Flamminio Corradi, *Le Stravaganze d'Amore* (Venice, 1616); and Bellerofonte Castaldi, *Capricci a due stromenti* (Modena, 1622; rpt Geneva, 1981).

4   For the purposes of this study, the tablature source must include a song text, either with or without a mensural part, to be considered as an accompaniment.

5   Important contributions on this topic include: Nino Pirrotta, 'The Oral and Written Traditions of Music', and 'Music and Cultural Tendencies in Fifteenth-Century Italy', both included in his *Music and Culture in Italy from the Middle Ages to the Baroque* (Cambridge, MA, 1984), pp. 72–79 and 80–112; see also James Haar, 'Monophony and the Unwritten Traditions', in *Performance Practice: Music Before 1600,* ed. Howard Mayer Brown and Stanley Sadie (New York, 1989); pp. 240–66, and David Nutter, 'Ippolito Tromboncino, "Cantore al Liuto" ', *I Tatti Studies. Essays in the Renaissance* 3 (1989), pp. 127–74.

should not be underestimated since it continued well into the seventeenth century, and its influence can be seen in many notated repertories of Italian vocal music. The other tradition of Italian lute song is characterized by written-out arrangements of polyphony. Its first great flowering coincides with the beginnings of music publishing in the early years of the sixteenth century. During those years, many polyphonic frottole were arranged for solo voice and lute – a practice aided by the invention of lute tablature, to facilitate the notation of polyphony – and by the change from plectrum to finger technique, which made it easier to play polyphony on the lute.[6] The largely chordal, melody-dominated nature of the frottola made it ideal for arrangement as lute song. By the middle years of the century, the madrigal, with its equal-voiced polyphonic texture, rose to prominence, but few Italian sources document the arrangement of such music for voice and lute.[7] If the scarcity of sources of lute song between 1530 and 1570 suggests low consumer interest, then the abundance of sources from 1570 to around 1600 reveals just the opposite. During these years, many collections of polyphonic vocal music were printed for the use of singers and lutenists alike, and Italian lute manuscripts began to include lute songs alongside the solo repertory.[8] Madrigals and canzonettas by many of the greatest Italian composers were selected for arrangement, though there seems to have been a distinct preference for light strophic poetry set in a mostly homophonic style. In the Italian lute song tablatures of the late sixteenth century, one can see a stylistic bridge between the literal arrangement of polyphony, which is characteristic of most of the sixteenth century, and a chordal style composed freely above the bass

[6]   Those sources include: Franciscus Bossinensis, *Tenori e contrabassi . . . Libro primo [& secondo]* (Venice, 1509 and 1511); *Frottole . . . per cantar et sonar col lauto* ([Venice,1520]); and Paris, Bibliothèque Nationale, Rés. Vmd. ms. 27 (dated *ca.* 1505). These early sources are discussed in Howard Mayer Brown, 'Bossinensis, Willaert and Verdelot: Pitch and the Conventions of Transcribing Music for Lute and Voice in Italy in the Early Sixteenth Century', *RdM* 75 (1989), pp. 25–46; Francesco Luisi, ed., *Frottole di B. Tromboncino e M. Cara* (Rome, 1987); Lewis Jones, 'The Thibault Lute Manuscript: An Introduction', *The Lute* 22 (1982), pp. 69–87 and *The Lute* 23 (1983), pp. 21–6; Benvenuto Disertori, ed., *Le frottole per canto e liuto intabulate da Franciscus Bossinensis* (Milan, 1964); Geneviève Thibault, 'Un manuscrit italien pour luth des premières années du XVI siècle', in *Le luth et sa musique,* ed. Jean Jacquot (Paris, 1957), pp. 43–76; and Claudio Sartori, 'A Little Known Petrucci Publication: The Second Book of Lute Tablatures of Francesco Bossinensis', *MQ* 34 (1948), pp. 234–45.

[7]   Surviving sources include: Adrian Willaert, *Intavolatura de li Madrigali di Verdelotto da cantare et sonare nel lauto, intavolati per Messer Adriano* (Venice, 1536; rpt Florence, 1981); Uppsala, Universitetsbiblioteket, Vocalmusik i handskrift 87 (*ca.* 1557); and Verona, Accademia Filarmonica, Ms. 223 (*ca.* 1548–60). The Willaert print is discussed in Brown, 'Bossinensis, Willaert and Verdelot'. The Uppsala manuscript is described in Bengt Hambraeus, *Codex Carminum Gallicorum,* Studia Musicologica Upsaliensia 6 (Uppsala, 1961). A study by David Nutter of the Verona manuscript is in progress. The Italian *viola a mano,* known in Spain as the *vihuela,* was a symbolic and practical equivalent of the lute. Polyphony by Italian composers arranged for voice with vihuela accompaniment can be found in the following mid sixteenth-century Spanish sources: Enriquez de Valderrábano, *Libro de musica de vihuela intitulado Silva de sirenas* (Valladolid, 1547); Diego Pisador, *Libro de musica de vihuela* (Salamanca, 1552); and Miguel de Fuenllana, *Libro de musica para vihuela intitulado Orphenica lyra* (Seville, 1554). The contents of these and all other sixteenth-century printed sources cited in this study are listed in Howard Mayer Brown, *Instrumental Music Printed before 1600* (Cambridge, MA, 1980).

[8]   See Victor Coelho, 'Raffaello Cavalcanti's Lutebook (1590) and the Ideal of Singing and Playing', in *Le concert des voix et des instruments à la Renaissance,* ed. Jean-Michel Vaccaro (Paris, 1995), pp. 423–42.

line of the vocal model. This change in style parallels the emergence of Italian monody and the origins of basso continuo accompaniment.

The lute was the most popular instrument for accompanying Italian song in the sixteenth century, and the combination of voice and lute can be seen as a manifestation of humanism in which performers sought to imitate the musical recitation of ancient Greek poets who accompanied themselves on the kithara. Throughout sixteenth-century art, literature, music, and especially theatre, where characters and situations *all'antica* abound, descriptive sources document the lute as a symbol of humanist ideals and, more practically, as accompaniment to both solo and ensemble voices.[9] One might expect the frequent use of other symbolic instruments like the guitar (*chitarra*) or the cittern (*cithara,* or *cetra),* since both share the word 'kithara' as their etymological root, but few surviving sources of any provenance document their use in vocal accompaniment.[10] Clearly, practical considerations often outweighed symbolic ones. Given the polyphonic nature of sixteenth-century vocal music, arranging polyphony for 'imperfect' chordal instruments – those with a narrow compass like the guitar and cittern (both usually with four or five courses) – would be possible but difficult for pieces in three or four parts and next to impossible for five- and six-part music without significant editing.[11] In this light, it makes sense that the more 'perfect' chordal instruments, that is to say those with sufficiently wide compasses like lutes and keyboards, were most often chosen to accompany polyphonic song.[12]

Beyond this, there was a clear preference for lutes rather than keyboard instruments, in spite of the latter's superiority in reproducing thick, polyphonic textures. This bias against keyboards is expressed in both symbolic and practical terms by the Florentine lutenist and theorist Vincenzo Galilei, one of the key participants in the development of accompanied song. In the *Fronimo Dialogo,* his well-known treatise

---

[9] See Howard Mayer Brown, *Sixteenth-Century Instrumentation: The Music for the Florentine Intermedii.* Musicological Studies and Documents 30 (American Institute of Musicology, 1974), *passim.*

[10] Only one Spanish and two French prints from the sixteenth century include songs with Renaissance guitar. None of the sixteenth-century Italian guitar tablatures include texts or mensural parts, although the guitar became one of the most popular instruments for accompanying strophic song in the seventeenth century. The only surviving Italian collections for cittern that include song accompaniments are Paolo Virchi's *Primo libro di tabulatura di citthara* (Venice, 1574), which includes seven texted intabulations of *canzoni napolitane,* and the seventeenth-century manuscript, Naples, Biblioteca del Conservatorio 'San Pietro a Majella', Ms 7664, which likewise includes a few texted intabulations for cittern; see Dinko Fabris, 'Composizioni per "cetra" in uno sconosciuto manoscritto per liuto del primo seicento', *RIM* 16 (1981), pp. 185–206, and Victor Coelho, *The Manuscript Sources of Seventeenth-Century Italian Lute Music* (New York, 1995), pp. 107–10. Arrangements of Italian vocal polyphony for solo cittern are somewhat more common, but except for Virchi, are found only in non-Italian sources. See Brown, *Instrumental Music, passim,* and Donna Cardamone, ed., *Orlando di Lasso et al.; Canzoni Villanesche and Villanelle,* Recent Researches in the Music of the Renaissance 82–3 (Madison, WI, 1991).

[11] Virchi's collection, however, is for six-course cittern and does include solo intabulations of madrigals in four, five and six parts, one of them 'Per sonar con la citthara da quattordeci corde'.

[12] The harp would also seem to be appropriate, but no sixteenth-century sources with harp accompaniments have come to light.

on intabulating vocal music for solo lute, Galilei first cites a symbolic example – the ancient Greek poet and musician Timotheus, who would accompany his voice only with the lute or some similar instrument.[13] Renaissance pictorial representations of other ancient poets, like Orpheus, Ovid, Arion, and Apollo, commonly include lutes, lire da braccio, vihuelas, and other chordal instruments, but rarely (if ever) include the harpsichord as an appropriate symbol. Galilei then goes on to point out practical advantages of the lute, citing its ability to play unisons on different strings, the use of equal temperament, portability, and the lute's relative ease of maintenance, in contrast to the complicated mechanics of harpsichord quills, jacks, and strings that need constant adjustment. Although Galilei does not mention the lute's dynamic capabilities and variety of tone colours, these qualities must have been considered advantages as well. The only deficiency he allows the lute is that it does not sustain sound as long as the harpsichord. In spite of Galilei's criticisms, a modest number of keyboard accompaniments to Italian vocal polyphony do survive.[14] Italian keyboard arrangements of polyphony generally are notated in either *partitura* (open score) or *intavolatura* (closed score). The latter notation is the keyboard equivalent of lute tablature, which became the most efficient method of notating polyphony for stringed instruments with frets.

Italian lute tablature accompaniments from the late sixteenth-century fall into two categories: (1) those with separate vocal parts, and (2) those without, commonly known as 'texted intabulations'. Table 4.1 lists sources in the first category consisting of prints and manuscripts from *ca*. 1570 to 1603 that provide one or more vocal parts in mensural notation along with Italian tablature for the lute.[15]

---

[13] *Fronimo Dialogo* . . . (Venice, 1584; facsimile rpt Bologna, 1969), pp. 51–2. See also the English translation by Carol MacClintock in Musicological Studies and Documents 38 (American Institute of Musicology, 1985), pp. 88–9.

[14] See, for instance: Marco Facoli, *Il secondo libro . . . d'arpicordo* (Venice, 1588); Simone Verovio, ed., *Diletto spirituale* (Rome, 1586); Verovio, *Ghirlanda di fioretti* (Rome, 1589); Verovio, *Canzonette a quattro voci* (Rome, 1591); Verovio, *Lodi della musica* (Rome, 1595); G. F. Anerio, *Dialogo pastorale* (1600); and Luzzasco Luzzaschi, *Madrigali . . . per cantare et sonare* (Venice, 1601). In addition, fascicles IVb and VI (dating from the late sixteenth century) of a manuscript without shelf mark in Castell'Arquato, Chiesa Collegiata, include texted keyboard scores of sixteenth-century madrigals. Keyboard score accompaniments to sacred music, on the other hand, are plentiful. Imogene Horsley covers in depth the sacred repertory from around 1590 in 'Full and Short Scores in the Accompaniment of Italian Church Music in the Early Baroque', *JAMS* 30 (1977), pp. 466–99.

[15] The contents of all the prints listed in Table 4.1 that date from before 1600 are listed in Brown, *Instrumental Music*. The contents of Anerio (1600) are listed in Emil Vogel, et al., *Bibliografia della musica italiana vocale profana* (Rome, 1977), and the contents of Ferrari (1600), Giancarli (1602), and Barbetta (1603) are listed in Franco Rossi, *Il liuto a Venezia dal rinascimento al barocco* (Venice, 1983). Many of the sources in Table 1 are described by Leslie Chapman Hubbell, 'Sixteenth-Century Italian Songs for Solo Voice and Lute', Ph.D. diss., Northwestern University, 1982. Studies of individual sources include: Claude Palisca, 'Vincenzo Galilei's Arrangements for Voice and Lute', in *Essays in Musicology in Honor of Dragon Plamenac on his 70th Birthday,* ed. Gustave Reese and Robert Snow (Pittsburgh, 1969), pp. 207–32; Carol MacClintock, 'A Court Musician's Songbook: Modena MS C311', *JAMS* 9 (1956), pp. 177–92; and Joel Newman, 'A Gentleman's Lute Book: The Tablature of Gabriello Fallamero', *CM* 2 (1965), pp. 175–90.

Table 4.1 *Polyphonic music with mensural voice parts and Italian tablature accompaniments for lute*

Prints

1570	Antonelli, Cornelio	*Il primo libro delle napolitane ariose . . .* (Venice, 1570). 33 *napolitane;* solo voice of 3-part pieces in score with lute tab.
1570	Gorzanis, Giacomo de	*Il primo libro di napolitane . . .* (Venice, 1570). 25 *napolitane;* solo voice of 3-part pieces in score with lute tab.
1571	Fiorino, Gasparo	*La nobilità di Roma . . . vilanelle à tre voci . . . intavolate dal magnifico M. Francesco di Parise, musico eccellentissimo in Roma* (Venice, 1571; rpt 1573; facs. rpt Bologna, 1970). 32 villanellas; 3 voice parts & lute tab. in choirbook format.
1584	Fallamero, Gabriel	*Il primo libro de intavolatura da liuto . . .* (Venice, 1584). includes 21 canzonettas; solo voice of 3- & 4-part pieces in score with lute tab. & 1 texted intabulation.
1584	Galilei, Vincenzo	*Fronimo dialogo . . .* (Venice, 1584; facs. rpt Bologna, 1969). pp. 14–23, two songs in *partitura* scored with lute tablature.
1586	Verovio, Simone, ed.	*Diletto spirituale canzonette a tre et a quattro voci . . .* (Rome, 1586; rpt [1590] & 1592; facs. rpt Bologna, 1971). 21 canzonettas in Latin; 3 & 4 voice parts with lute tab. and kybd score in choirbook format.
1589	Verovio, Simone, ed.	*Ghirlanda di fioretti musicale . . .* (Rome, 1589 [rpt in 1591 by Vincenti in 3 vols. with 5 new pieces and without the keyboard score]). 25 canzonettas; 3 voice parts with lute tab. and kybd score in choirbook format.
1590	Vecchi, Orazio	*Selva di varia ricreatione . . .* (Venice, 1590; rpt 1595). Mod. edn of lute songs only by Oscar Chilesotti in *Arie, Canzonette e Balli a Tre, a Quattro e a Cinque voci con liuto di Horatio Vecchi* (Bologna, 1968) 11 of 37 pieces have tab.; 4 *arie* à 3, 4 canzonettas à 4, & 3 vocal *balli* à 5, with lute tab. in partbook format.
1591	Verovio, Simone, ed.	*Canzonette a quattro voci . . .* (Rome, 1591; rpt 1597 without intabulations). 19 canzonettas; 4 voice parts with lute tab. & kybd score in choirbook format.

1591	Vincenti, Giacomo, ed.	*Canzonette per cantar et sonar* . . . *Libro primo [secondo]* *[terzo]* (Venice, 1591 [=*Ghirlanda* (1589) with 5 new pieces added to bk 3]; rpt & rev. 1601, 1607, & 1608). 25 canzonettas; 3 voice parts & lute tab. in choirbook format.
1592	Bellasio, Paolo	*Villanelle a tre voci* . . . (Venice, 1592). 16 villanellas; 3 voice parts & lute tab. in partbook format.
1594	Gastoldi, Giovanni	*Balletti a tre voci* . . . (Venice, 1594; rpt 1598, 1604, 1611). Mod. edn by Giuseppe Vecchi (Bologna, 1970). 16 *balletti;* 3 voice parts & lute tab. in partbook format.
1595	Verovio, Simone, ed.	*Lodi della musica* . . . (Rome, 1595; facs. rpt Bologna, 1971). 18 canzonettas; 3 voice parts with lute tab. & kybd score in choirbook format.
1596	Orologio, Alessandro	*Canzonette a tre voci* . . . (Venice, 1596). 14 canzonettas; 3 voice parts & lute tab. in choirbook format.
1597	Vecchi, Orazio	*Canzonette a tre voci* . . . (Venice, 1597). 34 canzonettas; 3 voice parts & lute tab. in partbook format.
1600	Anerio, Giovanni F.	*Dialogo pastorale* . . . (Rome, 1600). Mod. edn with tablature facs. by Arnaldo Morelli, in *Studi Musicali Romani* 2 (Rome, 1983). 15 spiritual canzonettas; 3 voice parts with lute tab. & score in choirbook format.
1600	Ferrari, Alfonso	*Canzonette a tre voci* . . . *libro secondo* (Venice, 1600). 12 canzonettas; 3 voice parts & lute tab. in choirbook format.
1602	Giancarli, Heteroclito	*Compositioni musicali intavolate per cantare et sonare nel liuto* (Venice, 1602). 19 vocal pieces arranged for lute with canto line in mensural notation. This print survives only in a private library in Regensburg and was not examined for this study.
1603	Barbetta, Giulio Cesare	*Intavolatura di liuto delle canzonette a tre voci* . . . (Venice, 1603). 14 canzonettas in three voices arranged for lute. There is no vocal part, but this type of publication is consistent with sources whose tablatures double as solos and accompaniments.

Manuscripts

Landau–Finaly	Florence, Biblioteca Nazionale: Landau–Finaly Mus. Ms. 2. Manuscript additions to Galilei's *Fronimo dialogo* (1568). Dated *ca.* 1570.
	fols. 1r–6v, 12v–13v, & 14v–19r. 10 pieces (9 madrigals & 1 *napolitana*) with bass voice part in mensural notation and lute tablature in choir-book format.
Lucca	Lucca, Biblioteca statale: Mus. Ms. 774. 'Intavolatura di leuto da sonare e cantare'. Undated, *ca.* 1595.
	fols. 32r, 41v–44r, 45r & 47r. 7 intabulations of canzonettas with texts in block form, 3 of which have mensural lines for bass voice on non-adjacent folios.
Bottegari	Modena, Biblioteca Estense: Ms C 311. 'Arie e canzoni in musica di Cosimo Bottegari'. Dated 1574.
	30 madrigals, 13 *arie,* 57 *napolitane* along with 19 Latin-texted pieces, 1 chanson, 1 *lied* and 4 untexted *arie da cantar* for solo voice with lute in score. Modern edition by Carol MacClintock, *The Bottegari Lutebook,* The Wellesley Edition 8 (Wellesley, MA., 1965).
Modena	Modena, Biblioteca Estense: Ms. x.k.6.31. 'Libro di Villanelle'. Undated, *ca.* 1590–1600.
	fols. 6v–8r. 24 villanellas in 3 parts with lute tablature staves in choir-book format. Only 2 pieces have tablature written in; similar to Verovio publications.

The twenty-three sources listed in Table 4.1 include a sizable repertoire of more than 480 different pieces.[16] A few of these, such as Antonelli, Gorzanis, Fallamero, Galilei, and *Bottegari,* are notated in score and intended for performance by a solo voice with lute accompaniment (see Plate 3).

---

[16] Italian music publishers' catalogues from around 1590 until as late as 1662 list other sources whose survival is uncertain. All are edited by Oscar Mischiati, *Indici, cataloghi e avvisi degli editori e librai musicali italiani dal 1591 al 1798* (Florence, 1984). Catalogues of the Venetian publisher Vincenti dated 1591, 1621, 1649, and 1662 all list a collection entitled 'Canzonette Giovanelli con la intavolatura di liuto'. Brown, *Instrumental Music,* includes the Giovanelli print (probably Ruggiero) as [1592]$_4$. The three later Vincenti catalogues also list a collection by Luca Marenzio entitled 'Canzonette Marenzio per il liuto'. Brown lists what may be the same print as [159?]$_3$ with the title *Villanelle a 3, para tanger no laude* according to an inventory of the library of King John IV of Portugal. The 1591 catalogue of the Gardano publishing firm in Venice includes a print entitled *Intabolatura del Tromboncino da cantar in liuto.* Brown suggests that Ippolito Tromboncino is the composer and that the collection probably appeared in the 1570s – a dating consistent with information presented by Nutter, 'Ippolito Tromboncino'.

Ernst Pohlmann, *Laute, Theorbe, Chitarrone: Die Lauten-Instrumente ihre Musik und Literatur von 1500 bis zur Gegenwart,* 3rd edn (Bremen, 1971), p. 51 cites the following spurious source by Fabritio Dentice: 'Canzonen mit Lauten-Begleitung im Ms. Modena F. 1367'. Although a manuscript with that call number is listed in the catalogue of the Biblioteca Estense, Modena, it is described as containing Italian cantatas from the late seventeenth century. Furthermore, no mention is made of the manuscript or of any similar manuscript in Dinko Fabris's thorough biographical study of Dentice: 'Vita e opere di Fabrizio Dentice, nobile napoletano, compositore del secondo cinquecento', *Sm* 21 (1992), pp. 61–113.

Plate 3   Score format, *Se scior si ved'il laccio* [Pitio Santucci] Antonelli, *Il primo libro delle napolitane ariose* (Venice, 1570), p. 3

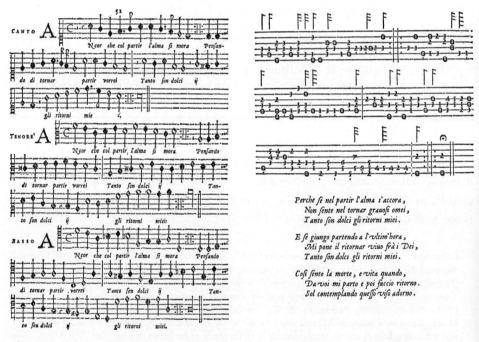

Perche se nel partir l'alma s'accora,
Non sente nel tornar grauosi omei,
Tanto son dolci gli ritorni miei.

E se giungo partendo a l'ultim'hora,
Mi pone il ritornar viuo frà i Dei,
Tanto son dolci gli ritorni miei.

Cosi sento la morte, e vita quando,
Da voi mi parto e poi faccio ritorno.
Sol contemplando quesso viso adorno.

Plate 4   Choirbook format, *Ancor che col partir*, Gasparo Fiorino, *La nobiltà di Roma* (Venice, 1571), pp. 52–3

The remaining sources, however, adopt either a choirbook or partbook format. In the former, one or more of the voice parts and the tablature are included in a single book, the parts usually appearing on facing pages, as seen in Plate 4.
Partbook format is similar to choirbook, except that each voice part is included in its own separate book. The lute tablature usually appears with the superius part either

Table 4.2 *Texted intabulations of polyphonic Italian vocal music*

Prints	
1584	Fallamero, Gabriel. *Il primo libro de intavolatura da liuto* (Venice, 1584). p. 79. One texted intabulation, a canzonetta, at the end of the final section of lute solos.
1599	Terzi, Giovanni A. *Il secondo libro de intavolatura di liuto* . . . (Venice, 1599; facs. rpt Florence, 1981). pp. 8–9, 52–3, 74, 77–8, and 114–15. 13 texted lute intabulations described in table of contents as 'Canzonette a 3 4 and 5 voci, con le sue parole'.
1603	Besard, J. B. *Thesaurus harmonicus* . . . (Cologne, 1603; facs. rpt Geneva, 1975). fol. 50v. A single texted intabulation of a villanella amid the section of villanellas for solo voice with lute (mensural notation and French lute tablature).
Manuscripts	
Chilesotti	Bassano del Grappa, Biblioteca civica: Ms. without number, 'Lautenbuch' (formerly in the private library of Oscar Chilesotti, otherwise, the survival of the manuscript is unconfirmed). Undated, *ca.* 1595–1600. Copied in Bavaria, but contents reflect Italianate tastes. pp. 37, 84–5, 139, 168–9. 5 canzonettas with text in block form and 1 *ottava rima* with text underlaid. Mod. edn. by Oscar Chilesotti in *Da un codice 'Lautenbuch' des Cinquecento* (Leipzig, 1890/1926; rpt Bologna, 1968).
Cavalcanti	Brussels, Bibliothèque Royale de Belgique: Ms. II, 275 D. 'Questo libro e di Raffaello Cavalcanti . . .', dated 1590. fols. 50r–62v, 74r–87r, 89v, 90v, 92v–93v. 71 pieces (*arie, napolitane,* and madrigals) in texted lute tablature.
Florence 62	Florence, Biblioteca Nazionale: Ms. B. R. 62. Undated, *ca.*1585. fols. 2r–v. Two song intabulations with text.
Florence 109	Florence, Biblioteca Nazionale: Ms. Magl. XIX 109. Undated, *ca.* 1570–80. fols. 1r–9r. 17 intabulations with block texts, all but 1 (a madrigal) are villanellas.
Florence 168	Florence, Biblioteca Nazionale: Ms. Magl. XIX 168. Dated 1582. fols. 1v, 10v–11r, and 17v–18r. 3 texted vocal intabulations of villanellas.
Genoa	Genoa, Biblioteca Universitaria: Ms. F.VII.I, 'Giardino de intavolatura per il leuto delle piu rare . . . che il Principe Il Signore Marchese di San Sorlino fratello del Signore Duca di Nemours mi ha fatto favore di lasciarmeli copiare sopra tutte le sue piu rare Intavolature'. Undated, *ca.* 1580–95. fols. 33r and 34r 2 texted intabulations (one in Latin and the other in French).

Haslemere	Haslemere, Dolmetsch Library: Ms. II.C.23. Undated, *ca.* 1600. Includes intabulations of madrigals, some with text underlaid. This important source was unavailable for study except for a single page with a texted intabulation of Lasso's madrigal *Vivo sol di speranza* included as a facsimile in Uta Henning-Supper, 'Treasures of the Dolmetsch Library Unveiled', *The Consort* 26 (1970), 437.
Lucca	Lucca, Biblioteca statale: Mus. Ms. 774. 'Intavolatura di leuto da sonare e cantare'. Undated, *ca.* 1595. fols. 32r, 41v–44r, 45r and 47r. 7 intabulations of canzonettas with texts in block form, 3 of which have mensural lines for bass voice on non-adjacent folios.
Montreal	Montreal, Bibliothèque du Conservatoire de Musique: Ms. without call number. 'Intavolatura di liuto: Orazio Vecchi e discepoli', undated, *ca.* 1580–90. ff. 3v, 4v–6r, 58v–59v, 69r–70r, and 74v. 13 texted intabulations of canzonettas.
San Gimignano	San Gimignano, Biblioteca Comunale: Fondo San Martino, Ms. 31. Undated, *ca.* 1584–90. fols. 7v, 13v, 25r, and 29v. 4 texted intabulations of villanellas.
Vienna	Vienna, Österreichische Nationalbibliothek: Ms. codex 18821, 'Das ist mein altt lauttenbuch alss ich [Octavianus Secundus Fugger] in Bononia [Bologna] A° 1562 gestudiert hab'. Dated 1562. f. 24r 1 intabulation of a villanesca with a single stanza of text in block form.
Wolfenbüttel	Wolfenbüttel, Herzog-August-Bibliothek: Ms. Guelf. 18.7 Aug. 2°; 18.8 Aug 2°, 'Philippi Hainhoferi Lautenbuecher', dated 1603 and 1604. South German provenance compiled for Augsburg patrician and diplomat Philipp Hainhofer. Part II includes 32 texted intabulations of madrigals, canzonas, canzonettas, and *napolitane*.

on the same page or on the opposite one, choirbook style. Both formats allow for either a purely vocal performance, or for a lute player to accompany one or more of the voices. Although most of these sources state that their contents are 'for singing and playing' ('per cantare e sonare'), they provide no specific information on the possible combinations of voices and instruments.

The second type of accompaniment, the texted intabulation, is found exclusively in manuscripts and prints of solo lute music. These works, numbering over 160 pieces, include complete song texts with the tablature but without a separate mensural part. Because of their close association with solo arrangements, texted intabulations are sometimes overlooked as an important body of accompaniments.[17] These sources are listed in Table 4.2.[18]

In almost all of the sources, a small number of texted intabulations (from just a single piece to as many as seventeen) are sprinkled in amongst pieces for solo lute; *Cavalcanti* is an exception with close to a third of its contents (71 out of 248 pieces) having texts. The arrangements are for the most part literal, allowing for dual functions as both accompaniments and solos; but the careful underlay of text in many sources suggests that the tablatures are primarily accompaniments in which the lutenist might either sing to his own accompaniment or use the words as cues while accompanying a vocal ensemble.

The song texts are presented in two ways. In four of the manuscripts, *Chilesotti*, *Florence 109*, *Lucca*, and *Vienna*, the text is inscribed in verse form beneath the intabulation. In the remainder of the sources, the text of the first stanza is underlaid beneath the tablature, while the remaining stanzas are inscribed in block form wherever space allows (see Plate 5).

Intabulations with underlaid text may be equivalent to pieces in score, only without the mensural part. For instance, Besard (1603) includes, amid pieces in score format, one texted intabulation that seems to fill left-over space too small to accommodate the mensural part. In addition, a single canzonetta is added at the end of Fallamero's print as a texted intabulation while all of the other canzonettas are in score format. If one accepts that these are solo songs, then it follows that such a shorthand procedure assumes sufficient familiarity with the vocal model for the singer to distinguish the melody, or whichever part is to be sung, from the other notes of the tablature.[19] The only clue for determining which note is to be sung is the text setting, which in many cases is less than careful.

The most distinctive feature of the Italian lute song repertory is that it is dominated by settings of light strophic poetry: villanellas or *napolitane*, canzonettas, *arie*, and *balletti*.[20] Except for a single piece (a motet) published by Galilei, every

---

[17]   The significance of texted intabulation practice is strengthened by a small number of parallel sources for keyboard. Texted keyboard scores from the sixteenth-century include Facoli's *Il secondo libro d'intavolatura* (1588) and a manuscript without shelf mark in Castell'Arquato, Chiesa Collegiata, fascicles IVb and VI. The practice continued into the seventeenth century as evidenced by a number of continuo realizations that survive as texted lute tablatures and keyboard scores.

[18]   For a description and thematic catalogue of seventeenth-century Italian lute manuscripts, including descriptions of the Montreal and San Gimignano sources listed in Table 2, see Coelho, *The Manuscript Sources*. The contents of *Cavalcanti*, along with *Florence 109*, *Florence 168*, *Lucca*, and *Vienna*, are described in Hubbell, 'Sixteenth-Century Italian Songs', pp. 461–535.

[19]   Texted intabulations of Spanish song for voice and vihuela are included in the collections of Milan (Valencia, 1536), Narvaez (Valladolid, 1538), Mudarra (Seville, 1546), Valderrábano (Valladolid, 1547), Pisador (Salamanca, 1552), Fuenllana (Seville, 1554), and Daza (Valladolid, 1576). In all but two of the seven prints (Mudarra and Daza), the ciphers of the sung part are highlighted in red ink.

[20]   These strophic forms are discussed in Ruth I. DeFord, 'Musical Relationships between the Italian Madrigal and Light Genres in the Sixteenth Century', *MD* 39 (1985), 107–68. The strong association of the lute with strophic

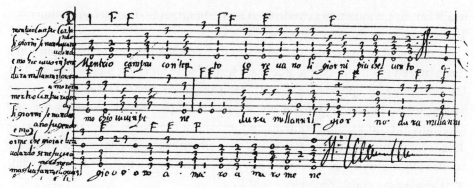

Plate 5   Texted intabulation, *Mentre io campai (Napolitana di Orazio Vecchi) Cavalcanti*, fol. 50v

printed source and about half of the manuscript sources are devoted entirely to strophic song. It is clear not only that strophic forms were favoured, but also that only certain vocal textures were suitable for Italian lute song – an opinion that is supported by the contents of Orazio Vecchi's *Selva di varia ricreatione* (Venice, 1590). This virtual 'encyclopedia' of musical and poetic forms lists on its title-page madrigals, *capricci, balli,* arias, *justiniane,* canzonettas, fantasias, serenatas, dialogues, a *lotto amoroso,* and a *battaglia,* all for between three and ten voices. As the title-page further specifies, only the arias *(a 3),* the canzonettas *(a 4)* and the *balli (a 5)* contain lute accompaniments. Among the sources listed in Tables 4.1 and 4.2, only Vecchi's print, along with Fallamero, Verovio (1586 and 1591), Terzi, *Cavalcanti, Montreal,* and *Lucca,* include lute accompaniments to four-part strophic songs. The prints by Vecchi and Terzi include the only four examples of five-part strophic songs with lute. The remainder – the overwhelming majority of the lute song sources – contain songs for three voices. These three-part songs are typically scored for two close- or equal-voiced upper parts that move in parallel thirds above a bass. Less commonly, the second part is for alto or tenor, and moves independently of the top part. Although short passages of imitative polyphony do appear, the style is predominantly homophonic. The arrangement of such music for the lute is a fairly simple matter.

Surprisingly few of the late sixteenth-century Italian lute song sources include arrangements of madrigals, which amount to only about sixty pieces contained in *Landau-Finaly, Bottegari, Cavalcanti, Florence 109, Haslemere,* and *Wolfenbüttel.* In the first two, the arrangements present a single vocal line of the original work (in four to six voices) with the tablature; the remaining four manuscripts include texted intabulations. While a few Italian prints of solo lute music do include both madrigals and strophic pieces, a clear distinction is made between the two. Terzi, for example,

poetry in the late sixteenth century derives from performance traditions of the earlier *canzone villanesca alla napolitana.* Numerous descriptions of villanesca performances with lute are cited in Donna Cardamone, *The 'canzone villanesca alla napolitana' and Related Forms, 1537–1570* (Ann Arbor, 1981), pp. 161–75.

includes intabulations of canzonettas, all of which have texts, and madrigals, none of which are texted. Likewise, Fallamero includes solo intabulations of madrigals, as well as *napolitane* arranged for solo voice (in mensural notation) and lute. Furthermore, at the end of his collection, following a section of madrigals for solo lute, Fallamero adds one extra piece: a texted intabulation of Fiorino's canzonetta *Anchor che col partire*. One can easily imagine Fallamero wanting to include such a charming piece after the rest of the collection had been typeset, even if it had to be placed in the wrong section. However, the question here is why, in this situation, would Fallamero bother adding text to the intabulation? Perhaps the most plausible reason becomes clear after one has played many madrigal and canzonetta intabulations on the lute. While the polyphonic complexities of the madrigal are more difficult to realize on the lute than the more chordal settings given to strophic poetry, madrigals are far more interesting to play because of their sophisticated counterpoint and varying textures. This could explain why untexted, solo lute arrangements of madrigals throughout the sixteenth century far outnumber arrangements of strophic songs, or why barely a handful of strophic song intabulations from 1570 to 1600 include no texts.[21] For musicians in the late Renaissance, it would seem that the most interesting feature of a strophic song lay in its text rather than in its musical composition. For Fallamero, it may have been unthinkable to include a canzonetta intabulation without at least including its text.

The relatively small number of madrigals that survive in lute song arrangements might not be, however, an accurate barometer of the popularity of singing madrigals to the lute. In Girolamo dalla Casa's *Il vero modo di diminuir* (1584), for instance, it is mentioned that the vocal diminutions are not only for singing in ensemble, but also 'for those who delight in singing to the lute' ('quelli, che si dilettano di cantar nel Liuto'). Moreover, in the table of contents, dalla Casa labels the entire section of pieces in question as 'Madrigali da Cantar in compagnia, & anco co'l Liuto solo'.[22] Madrigals with lute figure prominently in the international lute anthologies of non-Italian musicians like Emanuel Adriaensen, Joachim van den Hove, and Adrian Denss.[23] These sources, presented in Table 4.3, include well over 150 different madrigals.

In these sources, only two mensural voice parts of the vocal model, the superius and bassus, are given usually in choirbook format along with French tablature for

[21]   While it is possible that solo lute intabulations also served as accompaniments, the only evidence to support this practice is that the converse is true: many lute accompaniments are complete arrangements of their vocal models and can be played as lute solos.

[22]   *Il vero modo di diminuir . . . libro secondo* (Venice, 1584; facsimile rpt Bologna, 1980), 'Alli Lettori' and p. 50, 'Tavola'.

[23]   These sources of non-Italian provenance include accompaniments in French tablature and technically fall outside the parameters of this study. Nevertheless, they will be considered here because they constitute an important body of literature that may reflect Italian practices, especially the intabulations of Adriaensen, who studied in Rome as a youth.

Table 4.3 *French tablature accompaniments of Italian polyphony*

1584	Adriaensen, Emanuel	*Pratum musicum* . . . (Antwerp, 1584; facs. edn Buren, 1977). Includes 16 madrigals in French tablature with SB voice parts in choirbook format, 3 madrigals for two lutes with SSB voice parts, 1 *napolitana* for four lutes with SATB voices, and 15 *napolitane* – 12 for lute with STB voices, 1 with SATB voices, and 2 with SB voices.
1592	Adriaensen, Emanuel	*Novum pratum musicum* . . . (Antwerp, 1592; facs. rpt Geneva, 1977). Includes 25 madrigals in French tablature with SB voice parts in choirbook format, and 4 villanellas for lute with SB & STB voice parts.
1594	Denss, Adrian	*Florilegium omnis fere generis* . . . (Cologne, 1594). Includes 71 madrigals and canzonettas for 3 to 6 voices for lute in French tablature with SB & STB voice parts.
1600	Adriaensen, Emanuel	*Pratum musicum* . . . (Antwerp, 1600). A modified reprint of 1584 with some new pieces. Includes an extra 10 madrigals, 9 *balletti* & 2 villanellas in French tablature with SB voice parts.
1601	Hove, Joachim van den	*Florida, sive cantiones* (Utrecht, 1601). Includes 43 madrigals in French tablature for lute with SB voice parts.
1603	Besard, Jean-Baptiste	*Thesaurus harmonicus* . . . (Cologne, 1603; facs. rpt Geneva, 1975). Includes 10 villanellas for solo voice and lute in French tablature in score (one piece is a texted intabulation) and 10 villanellas by Luca Marenzio for SAB voices and lute in choirbook format.

lute. Adriaensen (1584), however, provides a lute–duo accompaniment for three of the madrigals (which, incidentally, include SSB voice parts), and although his three arrangements of madrigals for three lutes include no mensural parts on any adjacent folio, they also could be used as accompaniments since the SB voices of all three vocal models appear elsewhere in the collection. The formal consistency in these northern anthologies can be explained in part by Adriaensen's reputation as a virtuoso lute player and arranger of vocal music, as well as by the success of his

Pratum musicum, whose format seems to have been consciously emulated by Denss and van den Hove. It is difficult to speculate about the performance practice implications of the format other than to say that the lute arrangements are complete as lute solos with soloistic ornamentation. Either or both of the vocal parts could be accompanied by the intabulation with convincing results.

It is worth noting that the repertory we have examined so far is secular. Again, surviving sources do not always reflect an accurate image of performance practice, but it would seem from the sixteenth-century Italian lute song repertory that the instrument's use in sacred music was limited largely to accompanying devotional songs. Spiritual canzonettas with Latin texts make up the entire contents of Verovio (1586), and similar pieces with Italian texts appear in Anerio (1600). *Bottegari* includes several devotional songs with both Latin and Italian texts. In addition, Latin motet arrangements for voice and lute can be found in publications by Bottegari, Galilei, Adriaensen (1584) and van den Hove.

About three-fourths of the late sixteenth-century Italian lute song repertory was originally composed by some of the best-known composers of the period, including Vecchi, Gastoldi, Marenzio, Ferrabosco, Giovanelli, Lasso, Palestrina, Rore, Striggio, and Wert, as well as many less familiar composers, such as Felice Anerio, Giovanni Francesco Anerio, Paolo Bellasio, Cosimo Bottegari, Girolamo Conversi, Gasparo Costa, Giovanni Ferretti, Gasparo Fiorino, Giacomo Gorzanis, Giovanni Maria Nanino, and Ippolito Tromboncino. The task of arranging vocal polyphony was far more mundane than composing, however, and we know frustratingly little about arrangers other than the fact that they must have been players themselves. None of the most prominent composers named in these sources were particularly known as lute players, and they probably had nothing to do with the arrangement of their music. An exception was Vincenzo Galilei. Besides the two polyphonic song arrangements for solo voice and lute contained in his *Fronimo,* a manuscript addition written by Vincenzo and added to the 1568 edition contains madrigals he arranged for lute by Lasso, Palestrina, Ferretti, and Striggio, along with unattributed madrigals that may be Galilei's own compositions. Likewise, Cosimo Bottegari, who served as a court musician in Bavaria and Florence, composed and arranged both madrigals and strophic songs, and most likely arranged all of the other pieces in *Bottegari.*

Composers of *napolitane* and canzonettas, like Bottegari, seem to have taken an active role in arranging their music for voice and lute. The prolific Modenese composer and *maestro di cappella* Orazio Vecchi made a special trip to Venice from Modena to supervise the publication of his *Canzonette a tre voci* (1597).[24] One might reasonably assume that the blind lute virtuoso Giacomo Gorzanis, who published

---

[24] *New Grove Dictionary of Music and Musicians,* ed. Stanley Sadie (London, 1980), vol. 19, s.v. 'Vecchi, Orazio', p. 584.

two collections of *napolitane* (the first in 1570 with lute, and the second in 1571 without), was responsible for his own lute accompaniments. Although the title page of Fallamero's *Primo libro de intavolatura* (1584) suggests that he composed the music in that collection, the table of contents clarifies Fallamero's primary role as arranger ('intavolate nel liuto da Gabriel Fallamero'), though he still may have been the composer of the unattributed *napolitane*. Likewise, Cornelio Antonelli acknowledges on the title page of his *Primo libro delle napolitane ariose* (1570) that he did not write the music contained in his collection but was responsible for the lute arrangements. The title page of the Venetian singer and composer Gasparo Fiorino's first collection of villanellas, *La nobilità di Roma* (1571), states that the Roman lutenist Francesco di Parise arranged the lute parts. We can also be fairly certain that the two Dutch lute virtuosi Emanuel Adriaensen and Joachim van den Hove intabulated all of the vocal arrangements in their anthologies. As for the remainder of the lute accompaniments, one can only speculate whether the composer, the anthologist, or another party was responsible.

While most Italian lute song collections were published in Venice, and the majority of the manuscripts that contain such pieces are either Florentine in origin or connected with some other northern Italian city, a significant number of sources suggest Rome as a centre for strophic lute song. Writing about his musical education as a youth in the 1570s, Vincenzo Giustiniani makes a clear connection between accompanied strophic song and Rome.[25]

And in solo singing to some instrument, the taste for *Villanelle napoletane* prevailed, in imitation of those composed also in Rome, and particularly by a certain Pizio, an excellent musician and eminent jester. In the course of time, musical tastes changed and the compositions of Luca Marenzio and Ruggiero Giovanelli appeared with inventions of new delight, as much for those to sing with a few voices, as for a solo voice to some instrument, the excellence of which consisted of a new *aria*, pleasant to the ear, [and] with a few easy imitative passages [made] without extraordinary artifice.[26]

The 'certain Pizio' may be Pitio Santucci whose villanella *Se scior si vedra il laccio* can be found in five lute song sources, almost all dating from the 1570s.[27] Giovanelli and

---

[25] *Discorso sopra la musica,* included in Vincenzo Giustiniani, *Discorsi sulle arti e sui mestieri,* ed. Anna Banti (Florence, 1981), pp. 17–36. For a complete English translation, see *Discorso sopra la musica,* trans. Carol MacClintock, Musicological Studies and Documents 9 (American Institute of Musicology, 1972).

[26] *Discorsi sulle arti,* pp. 20–1: 'E per cantare con una voce sola sopra alcuno stromento prevalesse il gusto delle Villanelle napoletane, ad imitazione delle quali se ne componevano anchi in Roma, e particolarmente da un tal Pizio musico bravo e buffone nobile. In poco progresso di tempo s'alterò il gusto della musica e comparver le composizioni di Luca Marenzio e di Ruggero Giovanelli, con invenzione di nuovo diletto, tanto quelle da cantarsi a più voci, quanto ad una sola sopra alcuno stromento, l'eccellenza delle quali consisteva in una nuova aria e grata all'orecchie, con alcune fughe facili e senza straordinario arteficio.' The English translation is my own.

[27] Antonelli (1570), p. 33; Gorzanis (1570), p. 26; *Florence 109,* fol. 2r; *Bottegari,* fol. 1v; and *San Gimignano* (1584–90), fol. 29v.

Marenzio are well-known Roman composers who began publishing collections of *villanelle alla napolitana* in the 1580s. The first Roman edition of Marenzio's *Terzo libro delle villanelle et arie alla napolitana a tre voci* (1585) even includes a title-page addition further describing the music as being 'in the manner that is used today for singing in Rome' ('nel modo che hoggidì si usa cantare in Roma'). Both Giovanelli and Marenzio are commonly represented in anthologies of Italian lute song, and each might also have published their own collections of villanellas with lute.[28]

Works by other Roman composers can be found in the anthologies of the Dutch calligrapher Simone Verovio, who was active in Rome as an engraver, publisher, and composer during the last quarter of the sixteenth century. Among his collections are four beautifully engraved anthologies of canzonettas with lute tablature (and keyboard score arrangements) that reflect the Roman enthusiasm for strophic song with lute. His anthology *Ghirlanda di fioretti musicale* (1589) achieved such popularity that the Venetian publisher Giacomo Vincenti reissued it as a three-volume set in 1591, without the keyboard score but with five new pieces by Orazio Scaletta, and again in 1601, 1607, and 1608. The Roman taste for strophic songs with lute even crossed boundaries between secular and sacred repertories. The composers who contributed works to Verovio's 1586 collection of Latin-texted spiritual canzonettas with lute and his secular canzonetta collections with lute of 1589, 1591, and 1595 were some of the most prominent church musicians in Rome – Palestrina, Giovanelli, Marenzio, Felice Anerio, Paolo Quagliati, Rinaldo del Mel, Francesco Soriano, Scaletta, and Giovanni Maria Nanino. Verovio also published G. F. Anerio's *Dialogo pastorale* (1600) – a Christmas collection of Italian-texted spiritual canzonettas in three voices with lute or keyboard.

While vocal polyphony presented in choirbook and partbook formats was certainly performed by a solo voice with lute, and texted intabulations imply the same, the only songs clearly intended to be performed this way are those notated in score. Yet, even in the few sources using score format (just four prints and one manuscript), the songs are in all probability arrangements of polyphony. Of the more than 120 solo songs in *Bottegari*, about half of their vocal models remain unknown. Nevertheless, the style of accompaniment is strictly polyphonic with a consistency of texture and voice-leading that suggests arranged accompaniments rather than ones idiomatically composed for lute. Some of the songs by Ippolito Tromboncino, for example, commonly thought to be idiomatic songs for voice and lute, have recently been shown to be arrangements of polyphony.[29]

The Bottegari manuscript also includes two songs, one of them by Giulio Caccini, which have concordances in later sources of monody, and in each song, the

28   Neither print survives; see n. 16 above.
29   See Nutter, 'Ippolito Tromboncino', pp. 127–74.

accompaniments are written in a polyphonic style.[30] The song in *Bottegari* is not the only polyphonic composition by Caccini to survive in a later continuo version.[31] Like many early composers of Italian monody, Caccini embraced the ideas of theorists like Galilei, who was among the first to experiment with monodic composition.[32] Although Galilei could accept the idea of monody, he could not reject polyphony so easily, believing that a denial of harmony was the same as depriving a painter of the beauty of colours. Rather, Galilei advocated solo singing to the harmonic accompaniment of one or more instruments, and he mentions a piece he composed in that style and performed himself to the accompaniment of *viole*. Unfortunately, the piece does not survive, but another of his attempts in that style – a setting of a single verse from Dante's *Inferno* – has been preserved.[33] This example clearly demonstrates Galilei's conception of harmonically accompanied monody as written in four-part chordal polyphony.

Other evidence of polyphonic conception in monody can be found in Christofano Malvezzi's publication of the music to *La Pellegrina*, performed in Florence in 1589. The six intermezzi for Bargagli's play include four solo songs: Antonio Archilei's *Dalle più alte sfere,* Malvezzi's *Io che l'onde raffreno,* Emilio del Cavalieri's *Godi turba mortal* and Jacopo Peri's *Dunque fra torbid'onde*.[34] According to Malvezzi's description of the performance of these pieces, the first was accompanied by a *leuto grosso* and two chitarroni, the second by lute, chitarrone and *arciviolata lira,* and each of the last two by a single chitarrone.[35] While Malvezzi's own piece is an arrangement of a five-part madrigal for which he provides all five voice parts in the print, the others seem to have been conceived as solo songs. Yet instead of providing tablature, he notates the accompaniment in four-part polyphony. In the first three songs, all for solo soprano, the highest voice of the accompaniment duplicates the vocal line but in a simplified form. In Peri's song, the vocal part is an embellished version of the tenor line of the accompaniment. A similar style of accompaniment is also employed in Luzzasco Luzzaschi's *Madrigali per cantare et sonare a uno, e doi, e tre soprani,* which was published in Rome in 1601 but preserves a repertory dating from the 1570s and

---

[30] These songs are *Che faro o che diro?* (*Bottegari*, fol. 6v), which also appears in *Brussels 704*, p. 235, and *Fillide mia, mia Fillide bella* (*Bottegari*, fol. 14v), which is the second verse of Giulio Caccini's *Fere selvaggie* included in his *Nuove Musiche* (Florence, 1602).

[31] See Tim Carter, 'Giulio Caccini's *Amarilli, mia bella*: Some Questions (and a Few Answers)', *Journal of the Royal Musical Association* 113 (1988), pp. 250–73.

[32] The following discussion of Galilei is based on Tim Carter, *Jacopo Peri, 1561–1633: His Life and Works* (New York, 1989), pp. 110–21.

[33] *Così nel mio cantar,* included in Galilei's 'Discorso intorno' (1589), Florence, Biblioteca Nazionale, Ant. di Galileo 1, fols. 147v–148r. The piece is included as Example 1 in Carter, *Jacopo Peri,* p. 367.

[34] Modern edn in D. P. Walker, ed., *Musique des intermèdes de 'La Pellegrina'* (Paris, 1963). Malvezzi omitted a fifth song, *Io che dal ciel cader* by Giulio Caccini, from his edition. It survives as a continuo song in Florence, Biblioteca Nazionale Centrale, Magl. 66, Classe XIX, fols. 72r–74r, and in *Brussels 704*, pp. 15–16.

[35] The 'Nono' partbook includes the descriptions that are cited in Walker, *Musique des intermèdes,* pp. xxxvii–lviii.

1580s.[36] The three solo songs in Luzzaschi's collection also contain polyphonic accompaniments in four-part keyboard score that double the vocal part in a simplified form. Luzzaschi could easily and more economically have provided basso continuo parts for his songs, but chose not to do so. If basso continuo notation had been invented by 1591, Malvezzi could have done likewise. The most plausible explanation for these notational procedures is that this solo song repertory belonged to a tradition in which polyphonic accompaniment was an essential component of style; it was so essential that it could be notated only by means of a *partitura* or *intavolatura*.

This is not to say, however, that idiomatically composed Italian lute songs did not exist. It is simply that in the written tradition, as opposed to the improvised one, the normal style of accompaniment during the sixteenth-century was polyphonic, and because of this we possess no easily identifiable Italian examples.[37] This holds true even for sources from the first half of the century in which all accompaniments but one can be shown to have polyphonic models or whose style betrays such an origin. The one exception is *Se mai per maraveglia,* an anonymous setting of a *capitolo* (or *terza rima)* included in the second book of frottole arranged for voice and lute by Franciscus Bossinensis.[38] The lute accompaniment to this piece is written in an improvisatory style to match the recitational quality of the melody, and it even includes an instrumental ritornello. The writing is so idiomatic to the lute that a polyphonic model is hard to imagine, and the piece undoubtedly derives from the improvised tradition. Only one late sixteenth-century lute song, *Dura legge d'amor'* from *Bottegari,* has a similar idiomatic accompaniment.[39] This anonymous setting of a *terza rima* uses simple, chordal arpeggiation as its basic accompanimental style and, like the Bossinensis piece, begins with an introduction that also serves as a ritornello. Though the melody is more aria-like than recitational, this piece may also derive from the improvised tradition. *Bottegari* might contain other songs originally written for solo voice and lute, but the polyphonic style of the accompaniments makes an identification of such pieces speculative at best.

If the absence of idiomatically composed lute song in Italian sources seems odd to us, it is only because we know so little about improvised singing. In many ways, this was the purest form of humanist musical expression – one in which a solo singer would improvise the recitation of narrative poetry to a chordal, formulaic accompaniment on some appropriate instrument, usually a lute. The art of improvising poems in *terza rima, ottava rima,* and *sonetto* to music was common throughout the

---

[36] Facsimile rpt by Studio per Edizioni Scelte (Florence, 1980).

[37] A modest number of Spanish solo songs with idiomatic vihuela accompaniments can be found in the collections of Milan (1536), Narváez (1538), and Mudarra (1546).

[38] Bossinensis, *Libro secondo* (Venice, 1511; facsimile rpt Geneva, 1982), fols. 5v–6r.

[39] See the MacClintock edition, p. 109.

sixteenth century, but our knowledge of it has been limited primarily to composed, polyphonic settings that derive from and thus reflect some of the attributes of improvised song.[40] Other than the *capitolo* by Bossinensis, mentioned above, the most direct links to improvised song in the sixteenth century are harmonic formulas in Italian lute tablature that appear in printed and manuscript collections of Renaissance lute music.[41] Although many of the tablatures carry generic appellations like *aria per cantar stanze* or simply *aria da cantar*, many specify the poetic form for which they are designed, like *aria di terza rima* or *aria in ottava rima*. The largest single source for such harmonic formulas in tablature is *Bottegari*, which includes seven pieces of this type, all with melodies and three of them with texts. In addition, the same manuscript includes a number of pieces that exhibit formulaic and recitational qualities typical of improvised song. The Florentine manuscript *Cavalcanti*, another important source of *arie da cantar* in tablature, includes six examples, one of which carries a text.[42]

Lute song arrangements of polyphony normally present the uppermost voice of the vocal model as the sung part. However, in many sources of the late sixteenth century it is the bass line of vocal polyphony that was commonly sung solo with lute accompaniment. A letter to the Ferrarese court dated 1584, for instance, mentions a Roman singer named Vigio who 'possesses fanciful skills in singing *napolitane* and inventing words and tunes in good taste. He practices singing bass to lute accompaniment, and he has the sweetest voice.'[43] Giustiniani refers to what may be the first flowering of bass solo songs with instrumental accompaniment.[44] After briefly discussing the villanella in Rome (this passage is quoted above), and mentioning how it was commonly performed as a solo song accompanied by some instrument – most probably the lute – Giustiniani continues:

In the holy year of 1575 or a little after, a new mode of singing emerged [that was] very different from the first, and thus for a few years following, [it was] largely the mode of singing with a single voice to an instrument, following the practice of one Giovanni Andrea

---

[40] See William F. Prizer, 'The Frottola and the Unwritten Tradition', *Sm* 15 (1986), pp. 3–37, and James Haar, '*Improvvisatori* and their Relationship to Sixteenth-Century Music', in *Essays on Italian Poetry and Music in the Renaissance, 1350–1600* (Berkeley and Los Angeles, 1986), pp. 76–99.

[41] The sources dating from before 1600 include Antonio Becchi, *Libro primo d'intabulatura da leuto* (Venice, 1568); Giulio Cesare Barbetta, *Intavolatura di liuto* (Venice, 1585); *Cavalcanti*; *Florence 109*; Florence, Biblioteca Riccardiana, F.III.10431 (manuscript additions to the 1568 edition of Galilei's *Fronimo*); *Bottegari*, and *Vienna*. At least nine seventeenth-century lute sources also include such tablatures.

[42] These pieces are discussed in Coelho, 'Raffaello Cavalcanti's Lute Book (1590) and the Ideal of Singing and Playing'.

[43] Cited in Cardamone, *The 'canzone villanesca alla napolitana'*, p. 172.

[44] One isolated earlier example of a bass song survives as a manuscript addition to a printed copy of the play *Sacrifizio*, performed in Ferrara in 1554. The song, by Alfonso della Viola, survives as a single bass clef line with the instruction 'con la lira'. It is described and reprinted in Alfred Einstein, *The Italian Madrigal* , 3 vols. (Princeton, 1949), vol. I, pp. 301–2. We also know that the famous bass Giulio Cesare Brancaccio (see n. 45, below) was active as a singer in Italian *commedia* performances as early as 1545. See the discussion in Howard Mayer Brown, 'The Geography of Florentine Monody: Caccini at Home and Abroad', *EM* 9 (1981), p. 148.

the Neapolitan, and of Giulio Cesare Brancacci, and of Alessandro Merlo the Roman who sang bass with a range of 22 notes, [and] with a variety of diminutions new and agreeable to everyone's ears. They inspired composers to write pieces as much to be sung with a few voices as with a solo voice to an instrument in imitation of the above-mentioned and of a certain woman named Femia, but obtaining greater invention and artifice. And arising from [those pieces] there came a few villanellas mixed [in style] between florid madrigals and villanellas, which one sees today in many books of the above-mentioned authors and of Orazio Vecchi and others.[45]

A few ornamented Italian lute songs for solo bass survive in a manuscript copy of Giovanni Bassano's *Motetti, madrigali et canzoni francese . . . diminuiti per sonar con ogni sorte di stromenti, & anco per cantar con semplice voce* (Venice, 1591).[46] While we may suppose that Bassano's ornamental style was similar to Giustiniani's description, none of Bassano's examples cover as much as three octaves in range, and they are settings of madrigals rather than villanellas. Closer to the practice described by Giustiniani, though certainly much simpler, are the more than 130 arrangements of madrigals, villanellas, and canzonettas with either mensural parts for bass voice or texted intabulations in which the text corresponds to the bass voice of the tablature. They can be found in the printed collections by Galilei, Terzi, and Besard, as well as in the *Cavalcanti, Landau-Finaly, Haslemere, Lucca,* and *Montreal* manuscripts.[47]

Among the many illuminating parts of Giustiniani's discourse is the passage about how the solo songs for bass by Merlo, Brancaccio, and Giovanni Andrea inspired the creation of a new genre that mixed the styles of madrigals and villanellas. That new genre was the canzonetta and it was invented around 1580 by Orazio Vecchi, a fact alluded to by Giustiniani.[48] Given this connection, it might not be just a coincidence that Vecchi is the most frequently represented composer in the Italian lute song repertory at the end of the sixteenth century and the dominant figure in the bass solo song repertory with lute accompaniment.[49] Vecchi's works figure most prominently

---

[45]   *Discorso sopra la musica*, cited in *Discorsi,* ed. Banti, pp. 21–2. 'L'anno santo del 1575 o poco dopo si cominciò un modo di cantare molto diverso da quello di prima, e così per alcuni anni seguenti, massime nel modo di cantare con una voce sola sopra un istrumento, con l'esempio di un Gio. Andrea napoletano, e del sig. Giulio Cesare Brancacci e d'Alessandro Merlo romano, che cantavano un basso nella larghezza dello spazio di 22 voci, con varietà di passaggi nuovi e grati all'orecchio di tutti. I quali svegliarono i compositori a far operare tanto da cantare a più voci come ad una sola sopra un istrumento, ad imitazione delli soddetti e d'una tal femina chiamata Femia, ma con procurare maggiore invenzione et artificio, e ne vennero a risultare alcune Villanelle miste tra Madrigali di canto figurato e di Villanelle, delle quali se ne vedono oggi di molti libri de gl'autori suddetti e di Orazio Vecchi e altri.'

[46]   Though this print was lost during World War II, a manuscript copy survives in Hamburg, Staats- und Universitätsbibliothek, and is described in Ernst T. Ferand, 'Die Motetti, Madrigali, et Canzoni . . . des Giovanni Bassano (1591)', in *Festschrift Helmuth Osthoff zum 65. Geburtstag* (Tutzing, 1961), pp. 75–101.

[47]   One cittern source can be added to the list: Virchi's *Primo libro* (1574) which includes the lowest parts of seven *canzoni napolitane* in score with tablature accompaniments for 6-course cittern.

[48]   DeFord, 'Musical Relationships . . .', pp. 116–18.

[49]   At least 66 different lute songs in eight different sources can be attributed to Vecchi. See Ruth DeFord, *Orazio Vecchi: The Four-Voice Canzonettas with Original Texts and Contrafacta by Valentin Haussman and Others,* Recent Researches in the Music of the Renaissance 92–3 (Madison, WI, 1993), vol. I, pp. 8–10.

in *Cavalcanti,* which is the largest source of songs for bass voice with lute. Of the seventy-one texted intabulations in this manuscript, all with texts corresponding to the bass, thirty-two are arrangements taken from Vecchi's first three books of *Canzonette . . . a quattro voci* (Venice, 1580–5). One of Vecchi's canzonettas, *Quando mirai sa bella faccia,* appears in Terzi, whose text corresponds precisely to the vocal bass. Terzi leaves no doubt that the bass part is to be sung, with his directions that 'the words are for singing the bass' ('le parole sono per Cantar il Basso'), 'the words are beneath the bass part' ('le parole sono sotto à la parte del Basso') and 'the words for singing are beneath the bass' ('le parole per cantare sono sotto al Basso').[50] In addition, four of the twelve texted intabulations for bass voice in *Montreal* are by Vecchi.[51] In *Cavalcanti,* the tenor voice is texted only when it is the lowest sounding part and when the text would otherwise be incomplete, as in Vecchi's *Mentre io campai,* found both here and in the *Montreal* manuscript.[52] While the practice of texting the tenor when the bass rests seems to be the norm, there are exceptions. For instance, in the triple-metre section of Vecchi's *Hor ch'io son gionto quivi,* text is provided for the tenor even though it duplicates what the bass has just sung.[53] The same repetition of text can also be observed at the beginning of Giulio Renaldi's five-part canzonetta *Se di dolor io potessi,* found in Terzi.[54] It would seem, therefore, that part of the art of singing bass solo involved occasionally taking whatever part was lowest at the moment, like a vocal *basso seguente.* It is a procedure that can also be seen in Bassano's ornamented bass line version of Rore's *Anchor che col partire* where, for a brief moment towards the end of the piece, the tenor line is included in the divisions.[55]

Another important contributor to the bass song repertory with lute accompaniment was Vincenzo Galilei. Bound into a copy of his *Fronimo* of 1568 are Galilei's own manuscript additions consisting of nine madrigals and one *napolitana* arranged for bass voice in mensural notation with a lute tablature arrangement of the vocal model on the opposing page.[56] A similar format can be seen in *Lucca,* which includes seven canzonetta intabulations with block texts, three of which have bass parts in mensural notation on non-adjacent folios.[57] In the 1584 edition of *Fronimo,* Galilei included two songs, one each for bass and for treble voice, to be sung to the lute. The bass song is a four-part motet notated in open score with lute tablature, but

---

50   Terzi, pp. 8, 74 and 77.
51   *Montreal,* fols. 5r–6r, 59r. See the incipits given in Coelho, *The Manuscript Sources,* pp. 368–9, 383.
52   *Cavalcanti,* fol. 50v; *Montreal,* fol. 6r.
53   *Cavalcanti,* fol. 75v.
54   *Il secondo libro de intavolatura,* pp. 53–4.
55   *Motetti, madrigali* (Venice, 1591), p. 27.
56   *Landau–Finaly;* see Palisca, 'Vincenzo Galilei's Arrangements'.
57   *Occhi dell alma mia,* fols. 32r and 47r; *Donna mi fuggi ogn'hora,* fols. 42v & 45r; and *Sian fiumi e fonti,* both parts on fol. 44r. The manuscript includes other bass parts but without accompanying tablatures.

with text provided only for the bass voice.[58] The same format can be found in Besard's *Thesaurus harmonicus* of 1603. Here, the ten three-part villanellas by Luca Marenzio are printed in mensural notation but with French tablature accompaniments, and like the piece in *Fronimo,* only the bass voice part is texted.[59] While Galilei's madrigal and motet arrangements do not precisely match the type of bass song described by Giustiniani, they are, along with Bassano's ornamented versions of madrigal bass lines, a direct link to monodic settings of madrigal texts for bass voice and continuo that were to flourish in the early seventeenth century, some of which do exhibit a three-octave vocal range.[60]

As shown above, all of the sixteenth-century lute song sources suggest that polyphony demanded an accompaniment in which one duplicated as faithfully as possible the texture and voice leading of the vocal model. To achieve this goal, intabulators made use of a variety of nominal pitch levels for the lute. The usual procedure was to determine the range of the vocal model and then imagine a suitable pitch for the lute. Galilei explains that 'each note may be used on whatever string and fret you wish, provided that the position [on the fretboard] is capable of embracing comfortably the extremes [of the composition's range]' ('ciascuna Nota si possa usare in qual si voglia corda, & tasto, pur che la posta sia capace d'abbracciare comodamente gli estremi').[61] Although Galilei is speaking in reference to solo intabulations, the same must have applied to accompaniments. Galilei fails, however, to mention important factors that relate to the lute's playability and timbre. In general, one should make use of open string resonance when possible, avoiding a tuning that forces one to play only fretted notes, and one should also adopt a tuning that does not require the lutenist to play consistently on the highest frets, except for special effect. In order to use the 'best' part of the lute (loosely defined by the first five fret positions of the upper four or five courses), intabulators tended to associate pieces in high clef combinations with the higher nominal lute tunings (C and D), medium-range pieces with medium tunings (G and A) and low clef combinations with lower tunings (D and E). There are exceptions, however, such as *Io dicea l'altro* and *Et io vo' pianger* in Anerio (Rome, 1600), in which the former (with low clefs of c^4, c^4, and f^4) and the latter (with high clefs of c^1, c^1, and c^1) are intabulated for a

58 *In exitu Israel,* fol. 17r. The song for treble voice, *Qual miracolo Amore,* is in three parts.

59 Except for the missing text in the upper parts, the mensural parts in Besard are identical to versions found in Marenzio's first four collections of *Villanelle et arie alla napolitana a tre voci,* published in Venice in 1584, 1585, and 1587 (facsimile rpt Bologna, 1984). While Besard may have made his own lute arrangements based on these prints, it is possible that he simply plagiarized (presumably switching the Italian tablature into French) from the now lost 'Canzonette Marenzio per il liuto'. See n. 16 above.

60 See, for instance, *Sfogava con le stelle* by Ottavio Valera, included in Francesco Rognoni, *Selva de varii passaggi parte seconda* (Milan, 1620), pp. 72–3.

61 *Fronimo,* p. 12.

medium-sized lute tuned in A. It seems clear that in these two pieces the intabulator intended to exploit the same extremes of range that he avoids elsewhere.

The number of different pitch levels in any single source ranges from as few as two (G and A) in Gorzanis (Venice, 1570) to as many as all seven diatonic tones in *Bottegari*. Such a variety does not imply that one needs seven different lutes to perform this repertory. Rather, *Bottegari* makes it clear that singers should adjust their pitch to the lute at hand by his inclusion of instructions like 'the voice takes [its note] from the fourth fret of the top string' ('pigliasi la voce al 4° tasto del canto').[62] As one can see in MacClintock's modern edition, where all of the vocal parts have been transposed to fit with a lute in G, the use of many nominal lute tunings serves to equalize melodic ranges so that a single singer with a single lute can perform virtually every piece in the book. The only requirement is that the pitch level of the lute be suited to the voice range of the singer, which was a common practice during the Renaissance.[63]

While many solo lute song sources reveal a variety of nominal tunings, and largely will work with a single singer and a single lute, the sources of ensemble vocal music with lute present a more complicated situation. These sources show that sometimes a variety of lutes must be used to produce the best musical effect. In Fiorino (1571), for instance, all of the villanellas can be performed by the same singers because of a consistency of voice ranges: twenty-six pieces use a clef combination of c^1, c^2, and c^4 and the remaining six vary only slightly. The tablatures show nominal pitches of G (four pieces), A (nineteen pieces), C (six pieces), and D (three pieces). If all of the works are played on a single instrument, one tuned in A, for example, then the four pieces in G tuning will be transposed up a step, which poses no serious problem for the singers. The pieces in C and D, however, will transpose down a third and fourth respectively, and in some cases make for improbable if not impossible vocal transpositions. For these few pieces, one must choose between a higher-pitched lute and different singers. Since Fiorino's collection contains no textual thread that would make necessary a complete performance, the singers could be selective of the pieces they sang, depending on the availability of a variety of lutes. In fact, only one source of Italian vocal music with lute seems to require complete performance. In his *Dialogo pastorale* (Rome, 1600), Giovanni Francesco Anerio takes a single poem describing the birth of Christ and provides a different musical setting unified by key for each of the sixteen strophes. Six different clef combinations are found – the standard c^1, c^2, and c^4 for eleven of the sixteen canzonettas plus *voci pari*

[62] For more on pitch and the lute intabulation process, see Brown, 'Bossinensis, Willaert and Verdelot', and John Ward, 'Changing the Instrument for the Music', *JLSA* 15 (1982), pp. 27–39.

[63] See, for instance, early sixteenth-century documents relating to the purchase of an appropriately sized lute for Isabella d'Este, discussed in William Prizer, 'Lutenists at the Court of Mantua in the Late Fifteenth and Early Sixteenth Centuries', *JLSA* 8 (1980), pp. 18–20.

combinations for high as well as low voices. If tonal unity is to be maintained, a minimum of six singers is needed along with three different lutes – bass lute in D, mean lute in A, and treble lute in D. By contrast with collections designed for solo voice with lute, the different tunings do not equalize the vocal ranges. But regardless of whether a single lute is used for all sixteen pieces (which breaks the tonal unity) or three lutes, it is impossible to perform the entire collection with just three singers.

We can distinguish three overlapping phases of accompanimental style in sixteenth-century lute tablatures. The main style, evident throughout most of the century, can best be described as 'straight', in which the vocal model is arranged literally (see Ex. 4.1). Only minor alterations are noticeable, such as the occasional omission or addition of a single note, the simplification of a rhythm, or the inclusion of ornamentation. Only a few sources with 'straight' intabulation accompaniments, such as Antonelli (1570), are completely devoid of ornaments, while in all of the others at least some light cadential ornamentation can be found. A few sources such as Fiorino (1571) and Adriaensen (1584), however, do include heavily ornamented passages. 'Straight intabulation' accompaniments can either include or omit the canto part of the vocal model. In the early sixteenth century, all of the frottola arrangements present literal intabulations (with some decoration) of only the tenor and bass parts with the alto omitted completely and the soprano (the part to be sung) given in mensural notation.[64] A few decades later, Adrian Willaert arranged the lower three voices of Verdelot's four-part madrigals in tablature with the top line sung, and a similar procedure is followed in the Verona manuscript.[65] While these earlier sources seem to suggest that it was normal practice to omit the uppermost part in the arrangement, sources from the second half of the century indicate that it was just as common to include it. Most of the sources with 'straight intabulation' accompaniments, like Antonelli (1570), Gorzanis (1570), Fiorino (1571), Adriaensen (1584), Fallamero (1584), Galilei (1584), Bellasio (1592), and Terzi (1599), include the cantus in the arrangement. In *Bottegari,* on the other hand, one finds 'straight' intabulations, some with the cantus included, like Rore's *Anchor che col partire,* and some without, like Palestrina's equally popular five-part madrigal *Vestiva i colli.*[66]

[64]   Paris, Bibliothèque Nationale, Rés. Vmd. ms. 27 (facsimile rpt Geneva, 1981); Bossinensis, *Tenori e contrabassi . . . Libro primo* (Venice, 1509; facsimile rpt Geneva 1977); Bossinensis, *Tenori e contrabassi . . . Libro secondo* (Venice, 1511; facsimile rpt Geneva 1982); and *Frottole . . . per cantar et sonar col lauto* ([1520]). A complete facsimile and transcription of this last collection can be found in Francesco Luisi, *Frottole di B. Tromboncino e M. Cara 'Per Cantar et Sonar col Lauto'* (Rome, 1987).

[65]   Willaert, *Madrigali di Verdelotto* (Venice, 1536; facsimile rpt Florence, 1981); Verona, Ms. 223 (*ca.* 1548–60).

[66]   *Modena 311,* fols. 34v and 41r–v, and MacClintock edition, pp. 107–8 and 126–9. All the concordant versions of *Anchor che col partire* are for lute in either G or A and include all four voice parts. See Adriaensen (1584, 1592, and 1600) and *Cavalcanti.* Of the five concordant versions of *Vestiva i colli,* the two for lute in A (*Bottegari* and *Landau-Finaly 2*) omit the top part. The versions in Adriaensen (1584, 1592, and 1600) are for lute in D and include all five voice parts.

Ex. 4.1   *Ancor che col partir*, Gasparo Fiorino, *La Nobiltà di Roma* (Venice, 1571), pp. 52–3.

During the last three decades of the sixteenth century a second, less literal phase of vocal accompaniment can be discerned. The first indication of this trend can be seen in Gorzanis (1570) which includes two examples that might be termed 'free intabulation' accompaniments. One of these, *Se scior si vedra il laccio,* a three-part villanella by Pitio Santucci, survives in four other lute song sources.[67] The concordant versions of this work all have 'straight intabulation' accompaniments, except for the version in *San Gimignano* whose variants one might attribute to corruption. The version by Gorzanis, however, omits the vocal part, simplifies voice leading and rhythm, and frequently expands the rather thin two-part accompaniment to three parts. Except for Gorzanis, all other sources from the 1570s include only accompaniments in the 'straight intabulation' style.[68] By the 1580s, however, arrangers begin to take more liberties. In Verovio's *Diletto spirituale* (1586), for instance, the arrangements mostly follow their vocal models in a literal manner, but occasionally transpose the top line down an octave, thicken the texture on long-note chords, and simplify a few rhythms. With the publication of Verovio's *Ghirlanda di fioretti* just three years later, the scope of these liberties expands and the 'free' arrangement of vocal polyphony becomes a clearly identifiable style of accompaniment. The amount and type of modification allowed in the 'free' style varies from source to source and can include any or all of the following: transposition of either of the

---

[67]   Gorzanis (1570), p. 26. The concordances are in: Antonelli (1570), p. 33; *Bottegari*, fols. 1v and 45r; *Florence 109*, fol. 2r; and *San Gimignano*, fol. 29v.

[68]   The only other source of 'free intabulation' accompaniments that might date from the 1570s is *Bottegari*. It carries the date 1574 but much of its contents may date from the 1580s and some pieces possibly from the 1590s. The few pieces with identifiable vocal models show a mixture of pieces in both 'straight' and 'free' styles.

upper lines down an octave; omission of part or all of any line except the bass; transposition down the octave of individual bass notes or sections of the bass line; rhythmic simplification of rapid note values; and the addition of cadential suspensions, harmonic filler, and even new counterpoint. In almost every case, the alterations make the arrangement more idiomatic for the lute. The prime consideration seems to be that the accompaniment should fit into the framework formed by the vocal model. Except for the bass part, any line is expendable in part or in total as long as some semblance of the original polyphonic integrity is retained.

Almost all of these traits can be seen in Ruggiero Giovanelli's three-part canzonetta *Vermiglio e vago fiore* (Ex. 4.2). This lute accompaniment is arranged for a lute tuned nominally in D to facilitate the relatively high ranges of voice parts notated with a clef combination of g^1, c^1, and c^4. Less than half of the piece is intabulated literally (see bars 1, 5, 6, 7, and 11). But even in these 'straight' bars, a few notes are altered, such as the re-articulation of the suspended note in bars 7 and 11, and the transposition of a bass note up the octave in bar 5. Otherwise, the vocal model is treated freely with the addition of new counterpoint in bars 3 (beat 1) and 5 (beats 3–4), and from bar 14 (b. 4) to the beginning of bar 16 (not shown in example), where a new melody is created that lies above the upper voice parts. In the second half of bar 3 the bass line is ornamented and in the first half of bar 10 the ornamentation of the vocal bass is transposed up the octave. Rhythmic simplification can be found in bars 3 and 9, the cadential chord in bar 8 is filled out to five parts, and various notes of both of the upper parts are omitted throughout the piece.

A somewhat different procedure is seen in Bottegari's arrangement of Giovanelli's three-part villanella *Mi parto, ahi sorte ria!* (see Ex. 4.3). Omitting the top voice completely, this accompaniment uses the second line and the bass as a framework that is filled out mostly to a three-part texture. For the most part, the top notes of the accompaniment closely follow the middle voice, deleting only those fragments of melody that would take the player's left hand higher than the fifth fret (see bar 10). In the first two and a half bars, however, *Bottegari* ignores the middle voice completely, even though it lies conveniently on the fourth and fifth frets, and in spite of the fact that the suspension it creates is a salient feature of the polyphony. Instead, *Bottegari* uses block chords without thirds, placing a downbeat where there is none in the vocal model, and re-striking a chord where the suspension resolves.

An unusual example of 'free intabulation' style is the accompaniment provided for the three-part villanella *Fiamenga freda,* probably by Emanuel Adriaensen (see Ex. 4.4). Adriaensen provides two accompaniments for this piece – one a 'straight' intabulation, and the other a 'free' intabulation (with modest cadential ornamentation) in which almost every chord is enriched to four, five, and six voices. The

Ex. 4.2   Ruggiero Giovanelli: *Vermiglio e vago fiore, Ghirlanda di fioretti musicale* (Rome, 1589), pp. 13–14, and *Canzonette per cantar et sonar . . . Libro primo* (Venice, 1591), fol. 4v.

bass part is transposed down the octave whenever possible, and the melodic integrity is maintained intact in the *canto primo* only. In the 'free' version, the only place at which Adriaensen reverts to a more literal transcription of the vocal model is in an imitative section around bars 19–21 where he adds only a few notes to keep a constant quaver motion. Unlike other 'free intabulation' arrangements, this one goes to extremes to create a full texture – sacrificing, in the process, the

Ex. 4.3   Ruggiero Giovanelli: *Mi parto, ahi sorte ria* (a) *Bottegari*, fols. 2v–3r (b) *Il primo libro delle villanelle* (Venice, 1588), 'Tenore' and 'Basso'. 'Cantus' is the same in both sources.

original polyphonic texture in favour of one that allows the lute to exploit its capability for playing full resonant chords. Adriaensen employed a similar style in his arrangements for three and four lutes, where he assigns each lute the bass line (with little regard to appropriate octave) and a different upper voice part with chordal filler. This seems to suggest an ensemble function for the full-textured arrangement of *Fiamenga freda* – an ensemble of voices, in this case, rather than lutes.

Ex. 4.4   Emanuel Adriaensen: *Fiamenga freda, Pratum musicum* (1584), fols. 57v–58r

If one accepts this hypothesis, then perhaps Adriaensen's intent in including such a 'free' arrangement alongside a literal one was to distinguish between two accompanimental styles: (1) the 'straight' style for accompanying a solo voice, when the polyphony would be incomplete unless presented in the accompaniment, and (2) the 'free', full-textured style for accompanying the full complement of voices, in which case literal duplication of the voice-leading is unnecessary.

From here it is but one step to the third style, or phase: an accompaniment composed above the bass voice part without duplicating the voice-leading or texture of the vocal model. Unfortunately, such accompaniments are rare in the Italian lute song repertory. One of the earliest examples may be the anonymous *Vola vola pensier,* which is found as a texted intabulation in three manuscripts and in a version for soprano and bass voices with lute in Adriaensen's *Pratum musicum* (1584), where it is described as an 'aeria à la Italiana'.[69] As seen in Ex. 4.5, the bass line is doubled (with only a few minor differences) while the only recognizable doubling of the melody (down the octave) occurs in bars 10–12. In general, there is no attempt to keep the texture consistent. It is mostly in three or four parts, but some bass passages are played *tasto solo* (cf. bar 5) and a few individual bass notes are left unharmonized.

The full range of accompanimental styles can be seen in Verovio's *Ghirlanda* (1589), which includes arrangements mostly in the 'free' style, but also two 'straight' intabulations and two examples of chordal accompaniments, both by Felice Anerio.[70] In *Al suon non posa il core* (see Ex. 4.6), the counterpoint of the three-part vocal model is largely obscured by a chordal accompaniment in four parts constructed above the bass. The top line of the accompaniment frequently coincides with one of the upper lines of the vocal model, but no effort is made to continue the contrapuntal thread of any line other than the bass. In the imitative passage (bars 13–15), for instance, there is no attempt at doubling either of the upper parts, and the syncopated exchange of those parts in bars 5–6 (not shown here) is reduced to simple chords following the bass line. Anerio's other piece in this style, *Mentre il mio miser core,* exhibits similar traits but goes slightly further in disregarding the voice-leading of the upper parts by ignoring a sustained 6–5 suspension in favour of a block root-position chord and by placing chords above the bass line even when the upper voices are silent. The effect is similar to what one might obtain by playing from the bass part and following the rules for unfigured basso continuo as outlined by Agostino Agazzari almost twenty years later.[71]

Like Verovio's *Ghirlanda,* *Cavalcanti* contains a wide variety of accompanimental styles ranging from 'straight' through a variety of 'free intabulation' arrangements. In addition, it includes one example of a free chordal accompaniment: the texted tablature arrangement for bass voice of Vecchi's four-part canzonetta *Quando mirai sa bella faccia d'oro* (see Ex. 4.7). Here, the upper three parts are ignored completely in favour of a chordal accompaniment above the bass line. The texture varies from

---

[69] *Pratum,* fol. 58v. The manuscript sources are *Cavalcanti,* fol. 51r; *Florence 168,* fol. 10v; and *San Gimignano,* fol. 13v. None of these sources specify as to whether the vocal model was originally in two parts, as given in Adriaensen, or more.

[70] *Al suon non posa il core,* pp. 29–30, and *Mentre il mio miser core,* pp. 49–50. See also the Vincenti reprint (1591), vol. II, fol. 2v, and vol. III, fol. 6v, respectively.

[71] *Del sonare sopra'l basso* (Siena, 1607; facsimile rpt Milan, 1933).

Ex. 4.5   *Vola vola pensier*, Adriaensen, *Pratum musicum* (1584), fol. 58v

single bass notes on the fastest note values (quavers) to five-note chords. As one can see in bars 6 and 7, not only is the texture of the vocal model disregarded, but there is no attempt at preserving a consistent texture within the accompaniment. In the first bar, for example, a full chord is placed on the solo bass entry and again when the tenor voice enters. Like Anerio's *Mentre il mio miser core,* the accompaniment seems to have been 'realized' with only the bass partbook as a guide, a conjecture supported by a significant number of pitch discrepancies between the tablature and the upper voices of the vocal model (see bars 7, 11, and 12).

Italian lute song accompaniments from the late sixteenth century illustrate a conscious transition from the literal polyphonic transcription to a style freely composed

Ex. 4.6   Felice Anerio: *Al suon non posa il core, Ghirlanda* (1589), pp. 29–30, and Vincenti, *Canzonette* (1591), II, fol. 2v

above the bass line of the vocal model. The last step in the process provides a direct link with improvised accompaniment above a basso continuo. Although continuo parts do not appear until the 1590s in the earliest manuscript sources of Italian monody,[72] we know that musicians improvised above bass lines earlier than this.

---

[72] See William V. Porter, 'The Origins of the Baroque Solo Song: A Study of Italian Manuscripts and Prints from 1590–1610', Ph.D. diss., Yale University, 1962.

Ex. 4.7   [Orazio Vecchi]: *Quando mirai sa bella faccia d'oro* (a) four-part version, *Canzonette
. . . libro primo* (1580) (b) *Cavalcanti*, fol. 60r (bottom system).

Alessandro Striggio, for instance, writes in 1584 that 'I had written out the
intabulation [of the piece] for the lute, but I left it behind in Mantua. But it will not
matter, for Signor Giulio [Caccini] can easily improvise above the bass on the lute or
the harpsichord.'[73] With the creation of monody and the invention of basso continuo
notation, there was less of a need for intabulated accompaniments. Nevertheless,

[73] Cited in Carter, *Jacopo Peri*, p. 257.

continuo realizations in tablature for lute and theorbo persisted into the early seventeenth century, mostly as pedagogical examples that reflect only the most rudimentary steps in learning to improvise from a bass line.

It seems clear that coming from the context of Renaissance lute song, the seventeenth-century Italian tablature accompaniments for lute and theorbo look backward to the sixteenth century – the last vestiges of an earlier practice – rather than forward to Baroque accompanimental styles. The doubling of the voice part in the theorbo accompaniments of Kapsberger, Corradi, and Castaldi points backwards to earlier 'straight' and 'free' intabulation styles, and while we may find such doublings unacceptable in modern performance, the practice at least has historical roots. Similarly, Rossi's madrigal accompaniments for theorbo belong to Renaissance intabulation practice. The problems with these tablatures are caused by Rossi's inability to reconcile a style of accompaniment with an instrument whose re-entrant tuning makes it unsuitable for intabulating equal-voiced polyphony. While some of the stylistic problems with the lute accompaniments in *Brussels 704* can be explained as an amateur's marginally successful attempts at learning to play from a basso continuo, one can see the correlation between the style of these accompaniments and those found in Verovio's *Ghirlanda,* which are likewise in four parts and built above each note of the bass voice. In the end, armed with a forward-looking perspective, one is able to make more useful assessments of the early seventeenth-century tablature accompaniments for lute and theorbo, as well as recognizing 'old-fashioned' and 'progressive' styles, or what is common and what is uncommon practice.

5

AUTHORITY, AUTONOMY, AND
INTERPRETATION IN SEVENTEENTH-
CENTURY ITALIAN LUTE MUSIC

VICTOR ANAND COELHO

Italian players, whether accompanying or playing [solo] pieces, have no merit other than being able to produce a lot of sound from their instruments. Regardless of the player, they produce a sound with such an unpleasant harshness, that it offends the ears rather than flatters them. One would think that they might break the instrument at each stroke of the hand.

Jacques Bourdelot[1]

in France, where there is no self-esteem, no one plays cleanly or delicately.

Alessandro Piccinini[2]

Bourdelot's criticism of noisy Italian lutenists and Piccinini's swipe at the disrespectful French underlie the distinct national (and nationalistic!) styles of performance that had emerged in lute music at the beginning of the seventeenth century. The French *luthistes* of this period are unified in their compositional style, consistent in their choice of instrument (eleven-course lute), and, as a result, more cohesive in their approach to performance than the Italians. Moreover, their music was stylistically and historically connected to its own time. It is rare that a French manuscript of this period would contain music from the middle of the sixteenth century, for example. Through their replacement of the old tuning with new ones, the French had re-invented their tradition and established a new history for the instrument.

Lute music in seventeenth-century Italy, on the other hand, reveals a plurality of styles, instruments, and performance traditions. Contemporary music written in a modern idiom by composers like Kapsberger and Piccinini co-existed with a 'classical' repertory of the sixteenth century that was still cultivated by amateurs and

---

[1] *Histoire de la musique* (The Hague, 1743), cited in Edmond Vander Straeten, *La musique aux Pays-Bas avant le XIXᵉ siècle*, 8 vols. (Brussels, 1867–88; rpt New York, 1969), ii, p. 376. The *Histoire* was first published in 1715, but largely written in the final decades of the seventeenth century; see Philippe Vendrix, *Aux origines d'une discipline historique: La musique et son histoire en France aux XVIIᵉ et XVIIIᵉ siècles* (Liège, 1993), pp. 52–3.

[2] 'in Francia, dove non si stima alcuno, il quale non suoni netto, e delicato', *Intavolatura di liuto, et di chitarrone* (Bologna, 1623), Ch. II, p. 1.

students. Not one but at least four sizes of lute were used by Italian lutenists during this time: seven- and eight-course short-neck lutes for the earlier repertory, along with fourteen-course archlutes and theorboes for the most contemporary styles, not to mention 'giraffes' like the nineteen-course theorbo of *Kapsberger 1640*.[3] It is safe to say that neither the newly invented techniques described in the prints of Kapsberger and Piccinini nor the music contained therein should be considered as the performance standard by which seventeenth-century Italian lute music should be judged. Rather, it would be more accurate to think of three very distinct performance traditions that were cultivated by seventeenth-century Italian lutenists. These are:

(1) a *modern professional* tradition, largely for theorbo or archlute, written in a contemporary style incorporating effects and techniques such as slurs, arpeggios, tremolos, and a variety of trills; its main exponents were Kapsberger, Giuseppe Baglioni, Andrea Falconieri, and the *fratelli* Piccinini, which constituted the Roman school, as well as the anonymous composers of *Modena B* and *Paris 30*;

(2) a *courtly professional* tradition, written in a more conservative idiom by court lutenists such as Santino Garsi da Parma and Lorenzo Allegri, and intended for courtly events, such as banquets, wedding festivities, or *balletti;* usually this music comes down to us for archlute (*Kraków 40153, Nuremberg 2,* and *Nuremberg 3),* and occasionally for lute ensemble;

(3) a *domestic* tradition made up of amateur and student players who, for the most part, played smaller instruments. Their books often contain works by 'classical' composers like Francesco da Milano, conservative contemporaries such as Santino Garsi da Parma, settings of famous dances like the *Barriera,* the *Spagnoletta,* and the *Pavana d'Espana,* and arrangements of popular *arie* and canzonettas.

This musical and stylistic patchwork makes the *seicento* a particularly appropriate historical model for examining issues of lute performance practice that are relevant to our own time. Like us, Italian lutenists of this period understood the concept of 'early music' and the need to confront it on its own terms. At the same time, they also recognized the existence (and the trappings) of 'authenticity' – a concept that was already discussed by Vincenzo Galilei in his *Fronimo* of 1568/1584[4] – forcing lutenists to adjust their techniques and instruments in order to meet the demands of new and old music, short of inventing different modes of playing altogether. Like us,

---

[3]   For a summary of lutes in seventeenth-century Italy and their distribution among the manuscripts, see Victor Coelho, *The Manuscript Sources of Seventeenth-Century Italian Lute Music* (New York, 1995), pp. 27–38. For an explanation of all sigla used in this chapter see pp. 140–1.

[4]   For an English translation, see Vincenzo Galilei, *Il Fronimo* (1584), trans. by Carol MacClintock (Stuttgart, 1985). The most detailed study of the *Fronimo* is in Philippe Canguilhem, 'Les deux éditions de *Fronimo* (1568 et 1584) et la place du luth dans la pensée musicale de Vincenzo Galilei', doctoral thesis, 2 vols., Université François Rabelais, Tours, 1994.

seventeenth-century Italian lutenists were caught in a historical 'swirl' of tradition and modernity, to which players adapted through their autonomous strategies of invention, revision, and, most of all, interpretation.

For a period in such stylistic and historical flux as the *seicento*, then, we must resist making aprioristic assumptions about the existence of a 'normative' performance practice, and recognize instead a diversity of approaches. To this end, documents such as treatises and prefaces to printed books are too few in number, too limited by their coverage of technique rather than performance, too poorly written, and too restricted in overall circulation to be of much use. A more promising approach to understanding the diversity of lute performance during the *seicento* is through a consideration of the concepts of *authority* and *autonomy*, which, in my opinion, define the fundamental parameters of historical practice and modern interpretation within which all performance is created. *Authority* refers primarily to the performer's use of an established text – an *Urtext* as far as is possible – and secondarily to the choice of an appropriate instrument (as revealed by the music or by contemporary visual sources), and deference to an established tradition in matters regarding style. The printed source, particularly if published during the composer's lifetime, is the usual index of *authority* in performance, and we have generally accepted its role in revealing what the composer ostensibly intended us to see (though it is not clear whether the composer performed it that way). Not surprisingly, the Italian repertory played by modern lutenists on recordings and in concert has come from prints and, with few exceptions, their performances have digressed little from these scores; by and large, they have approached printed sources as if they were prescriptive and authoritative.

Autonomy, on the other hand, deals with the options that are (and were) available in varying the authoritative score. It is what the player can do with the music within acceptable stylistic and historical boundaries.[5] *Autonomy* is the province of manuscript sources, which, when they contain concordances to prints, show how different players imposed their personality, interpretive preferences, and technical abilities upon the music. They display the artistic licence of a performer, his autonomy in modifying and personalizing the authority of the text. The extent of variation between the authoritative text of a piece and an autonomous reading of it depends on many factors: region (Milan or Naples, for example), skill of performer, purpose (private academy or banquet), context of the manuscript (professional, pedagogical, or retrospective anthology),[6] distance in time from the original, and experience or musical acculturation of the audience to the repertory (fashionable courtiers, erudite

---

5   Those familiar with the incisive work on performance by Richard Taruskin should equate his use of the term 'authority' (that is, interpretation) with my definition of 'autonomy'. See his chapter 'Tradition and Authority' in *Text & Act: Essays on Music and Performance* (New York and Oxford, 1995), pp. 173–97.

6   On these distinctions, see Coelho, *The Manuscript Sources*, pp. 19–26.

academicians, or foreign visitors, for example).[7] Sometimes a lutenist will alter a text for technical reasons, in order to facilitate passages or even to render them more complex; or they can be based on an aesthetic preference. Other revisions can be to the musical vocabulary itself, such as chromatic alterations or the rewriting of cadences, which are often necessary when modernizing a piece that is several decades old. Occasionally manuscripts call for a larger or smaller instrument than that prescribed by the print, which almost invariably results in a thickening or a thinning of chordal textures and the addition or deletion of bass notes.

Manuscripts, then, are the product of players, their local traditions, and of their autonomy as musicians. They show what changes can occur to an 'authoritative' musical text when it is exported to the various sectors – near and far, professional and amateur – of actual performance, sub-regionalized through the dialects of written and oral transmission, varied according to personal taste, and eventually, if a composer is lucky, revived by a younger generation. In the case of the latter, manuscripts reveal how lutenists re-contextualized and modernized the past through elaboration and revision. Along these lines it is important to reflect upon how performance traditions of all musical cultures are inextricably linked to context. A print, for example, is context-neutral: it is created not for a single person or specific performance, but for a market. A lute *manuscript*, on the other hand, is the written evidence of music as it is disseminated into the hands of individual players, and is usually context-specific. Pieces in manuscripts thus qualify as the closest thing we have to 'recordings' by lutenists of past eras, since they 'capture' a specific performance in time.

Let us consider an example drawn from one of the most important Italian lute manuscripts of the sixteenth century, *Siena*, in order to understand the way in which authority and autonomy operate within performance.[8] In addition to being the largest anthology of Italian lute fantasias of the Renaissance, *Siena* is also one of the central manuscript sources for the music of Francesco da Milano (1497–1543). The manuscript was copied between *ca.* 1580 and the late 1590s by a virtuoso, professional lutenist who must have had an immense knowledge of the repertory. The manuscript thus shows how Francesco's music was transmitted, interpreted, and revived a half-century after his death by a skilled player.[9] Not surprisingly, *Siena*

---

[7] As Kate Brown states in her article 'Representations', in *Performing Practice in Monteverdi's Music*, ed. Raffaello Monterosso (Cremona, 1995), p. 267: 'listening to various solutions as illustrated by recordings of Monteverdi from the last thirty years, it becomes obvious that there is no right solution: from Leppard to Rooley (regardless of personal preferences), it is clear that they are using the same source material to produce music that sounds radically different – and the major cause of the differences is not so much the state of academic knowledge but the estimated capability of the audience to understand it, not to mention changing tastes'.

[8] The Hague, Gemeentemuseum Ms. 28 B 39. A facsimile has been published as *Tablature de luth Italienne dit Siena Manuscrit (ca. 1560–1570)*, ed. Arthur J. Ness (Geneva, 1988).

[9] On Francesco's revival in the late sixteenth century and the making of his posthumous reputation, see Victor Coelho, 'The Reputation of Francesco da Milano (1497–1543) and the Ricercars in the Cavalcanti Lute Book', *Revue Belge de Musicologie* 50 (1996), pp. 49–72.

offers different readings of Francesco's music when compared to earlier printed versions of the same pieces. *Ricercar 5* (fol. 23r–v) is one such example.[10] One of Francesco's most popular ricercars, given its appearance in several Italian, German, Lowlands, and English sources through the early seventeenth century,[11] the work was printed in each of the three surviving prints devoted to Francesco's music that appeared during the composer's lifetime, Sultzbach's *Intavolatura di viola o vero lauto . . . Libro Primo* and *Libro secondo* published in Naples in 1536,[12] and the *Intabolatura de liuto . . .* brought out by Marcolini of Venice in the same year. These three versions are identical with each other, and all subsequent concordances, with the important exception of *Siena*, are based on this 'authoritative' text. The *Siena* reading of fifty years later, on the other hand, adds numerous embellishments, motivic extensions and repetitions, and a rewriting of cadences. These changes fall into the categories I have described above as examples of manuscript 'autonomy', and they can be summarized as follows (see Examples 5.1a to 5.1j):

5.1a: *Siena* adds a 4–3 suspension (over an implied C) to the cadence in bar 14 and displaces the piece rhythmically by augmenting the rhythmic values. In bar 17, *Siena* provides more closure by ornamenting the cadence on F with a turn, like a *cadenza finale*, as compared to the more conventional internal formula used in *Sultzbach*.

5.1b: In bar 23, *Siena* changes the appoggiatura E♭ that appears in Sultzbach (bar 22, alto voice) to the chord-tone B♭, and 'de-ornaments' the cadence on C in bars 24–5.

5.1c: *Siena* eliminates the diminution in bar 30 (*Sultzbach*).

5.1d: *Siena* diminishes the rhythm in bar 39.

5.1e: In bars 47 and 52, *Siena* suspends the dissonance rather than restriking it, which is common in *Sultzbach*.[13]

5.1f: In bar 54, *Siena*'s raising of the E♭s in *Sultzbach* to E♮ pushes the phrase more tonally towards the final F through its 'modern' dominant C, whereas the E♭s in *Sultzbach* mirror bar 22 (see 5.1b, above) in its movement towards the more

---

[10] I use the standard numbering as established in Arthur J. Ness, ed., *The Lute Music of Francesco Canova da Milano (1497–1543)*, vols. I and II, Harvard Publications in Music 3–4 (Cambridge, MA, 1970).

[11] See *ibid.*, p. 18 for a list of concordances.

[12] A facsimile of this print has been published as Francesco da Milano, *Intavolatura de viola o vero lauto I–II* (Geneva, 1988); the *Libro secondo* is in Neapolitan tablature.

[13] *Sultzbach* is a Neapolitan print, so perhaps Piccinini's suggestion of 'restriking the dissonance as they do in Naples' (*Piccinini 1623*, Ch. III) is based on a tradition whose roots extend back to the early sixteenth century.

[14] In other places, too, *Siena* raises the lowered second of a scale to *mi*, even in descending passages, e.g. bars 64 (*fa–mi*), 71, and 111. From bar 86, however, the opposite is the case, in which *Siena* consistently uses *fa* where *mi* is given in *Sultzbach*, e.g. bars 86, 95, and 99

Ex. 5.1a–j   Francesco da Milano, *Ricercar 5* (Ness edition): versions from *Siena*, fol. 23r–v (top system) and *Sultzbach*, fols. 8v–11r (lower system).

5.1a

5.1b

5.1c

5.1d

5.1e

5.1f

5.1g

5.1h

5.1i

5.1j

'archaic' (seen from the eyes of *Siena*) plagal relationship with B♭.[14] Confirming this tonal orientation, *Siena* extends the phrase through a parenthesis consisting of two new repetitions (adding five bars to the work), bars 57–61, resulting in a postponement of the B♭ cadence in bar 62.

5.1g: Consistent with previous passages in which *Siena* reduces the *Sultzbach* ornamentation, the ornamental turns cadencing on C and on F in bars 73–6 are eliminated, probably as a way to extend the continuity of this canonic passage without the cadential punctuation that is so typically evoked by this type of turn.

5.1h: bars 77–82. *Siena* animates the canonic section by fragmenting the voices in quick hocket-like alternation. This is achieved by simply repeating bars 77–9 as 80–2. *Siena* syncopates bar 77 and eliminates the augmented sixth (!), which does not appear in the Marcolini print.

5.1i: bar 112. *Siena* simplifies the fingering of the suspension at the expense of the voice leading.

5.1j: bars 114–21. *Siena* alters the tenor voice in bar 115, then truncates the drive to the cadence by eliminating the repetition of bars 106–8/109–11, as read in *Sultzbach*. The motivation for this change is probably to weaken the sense of final closure since *Siena* also rewrites the final cadence to end on the dominant, as if the ricercar is simply a *prima pars* to another work, similar to the two-part madrigals common during the 1580s and beyond.

The *Siena* revisions are clearly the work of the skilled lutenist/scribe of the manuscript, and they represent not only his autonomous reading of the piece but a contemporization of it, according to the stylistic conventions of his own time. Certain portions of the work are revisions, but other sections introduce totally new passages to the existing score. Consequently, it is no longer simply 'Francesco's work'. Nevertheless, it is this version, made some fifty years after the 1536 prints, that was included in Arthur Ness's complete edition of Francesco's music (a parallel might be if Mozart's version of *Messiah* had been used for the Handel complete edition), and it is also the version chosen by Paul O'Dette in his 1986 recording of Francesco.[15] In other words, both the *Urtext* edition and a recording made by one of the foremost lutenists of our time promote a version of this piece that is not only many layers removed from the original text printed in Francesco's time, but one that is significantly the work of an anonymous lutenist from the hills of Tuscany[16] for whom Francesco was already, in the 1580s, a 'classical' composer.

Now, if original sources, which ostensibly preserve the composer's intentions, are the precondition for any serious performance or scholarship, as we are all taught, why is the *Siena* version of Francesco's ricercar *not* a problem from a performance practice standpoint (though it certainly is from a text-critical one[17])? What validates this version as appropriate, and what can it tell us about the autonomous reading of a 'fixed' musical text? Finally, what implications does this comparative study impress upon the issue of performance practice in the seventeenth century? The many changes revealed by *Siena* underlie the importance of the performer's autonomy in effecting changes to a musical text within general stylistic confines. They show how a piece is open to interpolation and interpretation through extension, repetition, suppression, elaboration, and alteration. These techniques have been generally regarded as elements of compositional style – that is, the *composer's* 'authority' – but they are actually inseparable from the *performer's* natural 'autonomy'.

Unfortunately, all but a few modern lutenists who play this repertory have virtually ignored the manuscript sources of this music and remained religiously close to the texts found in printed sources. There is still apprehension about the 'authenticity' of manuscripts vis-à-vis printed sources. Is the *Siena* version 'authentic', and would Francesco have 'approved' of it? For the former, we can answer that it is 'authentic' in so far as it is transmitted by an original source and represents the flexibility in performance employed by Renaissance lutenists in adapting pre-existing works for their own use. As for whether Francesco would have 'approved' of it, what we do know is that the intabulations of vocal works by Francesco and his contemporaries clearly demonstrate the significant degree of latitude taken by performers in transforming the original text of a model and subjecting them to much the same treatment of personalization and modernization as we have seen above with *Ricercar 5*.

---

[15]   *Intabolatura da Leuto*, Astrée CD E7705. Chiesa's edition (transcribed a minor third lower for guitar) reproduces the 1536 Marcolini version. See Francesco da Milano, *Opere complete per liuto*, ed. Ruggero Chiesa (Milan, 1971), vol. I, pp. 9–12; for a detailed list of all the variants of this ricercar that exist between the sources, see pp. lv–lxiii.

[16]   For possible identifications of the *Siena* copyist, see Dinko Fabris's review of the Minkoff facsimile of the manuscript (cf. n.8, above) in *JLSA* 20–21 (1987–8), pp. 165–70.

[17]   It should be pointed out that the Sultzbach prints were discovered only after Ness's edition was in production, though the nearly identical Marcolini version was certainly available.

Since the idea of 'seventeenth-century performance practice' is, of course, a concept of musical style and procedure rather than a mere chronological distinction, I have gone to some length in order to forge a link between trends in Italian lute practice of the late sixteenth century and the deepening of these tendencies in the years after 1600. To summarize the themes we have touched upon so far:

(1) *Performance practice issues are most safely approached from a fixed musical text* and the relationship between that *point de départ* and the performer's art – not initially from theoretical descriptions or 'rules' contained in prefaces.

(2) *Manuscript sources are more revealing about performance than prints* since they are performance- and context-specific, and hence 'freeze' aspects of performance in time, as a study of variant readings can show.

(3) *Composition and performance are allied activities*, in that performance practice relies on an acceptable amount of compositional imposition, like troping, on a fixed text by a performer.

(4) *Performance, like speech, is closely linked to generational or historical relevance*, in which performance practice can be seen as an evolving mode of communication that reflects the stylistic characteristics, regional conventions, and musical aesthetics of a certain period and its audience.

In the remainder of this chapter, I shall approach seventeenth-century performance practice within the context of these issues. My goal is not to provide a set of rules, but to illuminate what I believe were the conceptual procedures of performance as understood by lutenists of various strata and backgrounds during the seventeenth century, and integrate these ideas into a concept of modern interpretation. Using manuscripts as the main sources, I will attempt to 'thaw' those performances 'frozen' in lute and theorbo tablatures, and show how they can inform our knowledge of the area between textual authority and performance autonomy.

INSTRUMENTS AND THEIR PLAYERS

We can now return to some of the rudimentary issues of performance practice of the *seicento*, and examine them first in the light of our discussion above. Some seventy sources of Italian lute music are known to us from between 1600 and 1691. Fifty of these are manuscripts, of which twenty-three are for lute (seven to ten courses), fourteen are for archlute (eleven to fourteen courses), and thirteen are intended for theorbo (eleven to eighteen courses).[18] All of the lute manuscripts employ 'Renaissance tuning' with occasional variants for the bass courses, and the odd experiment with the new French tunings; the theorbo manuscripts use the standard

---

[18] See Coelho, *The Manuscript Sources*, pp. 34–5 for a complete breakdown of instruments represented in the manuscript sources. On the distinctions between lute, archlute and theorbo as well as a list of tunings, see *ibid.*, pp. 33–8, or the relevant articles in *The New Grove Dictionary of Musical Instruments*, ed. Stanley Sadie (London, 1984).

Italian re-entrant tuning in which the highest two courses are tuned one octave lower. Treatises and surviving instruments confirm that a fourteen-course theorbo was standard, though the earliest theorbo sources all call for an instrument of eleven or twelve courses only *(Kapsberger 1604, Berkeley 757* [fascicle 2], *Kraków 40591, Frankfurt)*, and by 1619, *Modena B* calls for an eighteenth course (see Plate 6), which is similar to the nineteen-course theorbo required for *Kapsberger 1640.*

Manuscript sources containing vocal pieces with lute accompaniments reveal that the normal pitch of the lute was g^1 (i.e. highest string tuned to g^1) and the theorbo was tuned a step higher, which is also confirmed by Praetorius and Kircher. A few sources call for a lute in a^1, which suggests an instrument of dimensions such as the seven-course Vendelio Venere in the Accademia Filarmonica in Bologna, whose vibrating string length is 58.4 cm. Certain ensemble pieces in the manuscripts *Nuremberg 2* and *Nuremberg 3* call for bass lutes in D to play thick, intabulated accompaniments.[19] The tiorbino, a small fourteen-course theorbo tuned an octave higher, is specified only in *Castaldi*, but it could have been used in some of the thirteen theorbo manuscripts as well as a 'character' instrument in certain types of performances.[20] There is no reason why it should not be used more today in the same contexts. Its high-pitched tuning (open third course to b^1) is ill suited for accompanying high voices, to be sure, but the instrument's bright sound compensates for its narrow playing range, which is one of the limitations of the theorbo as a solo instrument.[21] The lute shown in *A Concert*, painted by the Roman Antiveduto Grammatica, is probably a tiorbino: it may have been much more popular than is generally assumed, particularly in Rome where the theorbo tradition was strong, given this associate of Caravaggio's well-known penchant for depicting people and objects from everyday surroundings.[22]

Not a single Italian source calls for an instrument in *nouveaux accords*, which were becoming standard in France, though at least two progressively minded Italian lutenists flirted with their possibilities. A manuscript lute treatise by Pier Francesco Valentini explains the most common of the new French tunings (in D minor) and gives examples of realizing bass lines, ornamenting final cadences, and intabulation using this tuning;[23] and *Florence 45*, written by the Florentine Court lute teacher

---

[19]   See Coelho, *The Manuscript Sources*, pp. 110–15.

[20]   Mason, after Wessely-Kropik, cites an archival source from 1661 that mentions the use of the tiorbino during an oratorio 'to play to the angel above the altar'. See Kevin Mason, *The Chitarrone and its Repertoire in Seventeenth-Century Italy* (Aberystwyth, 1989), p. 9, n. 15.

[21]   Although the theorbo has an acceptably wide range, from an open fourteenth course at F to an open third course at a, its normal playing compass is somewhat constricted to within the high tenor range.

[22]   The work has been reproduced widely; see, for example, Keith Christiansen, *A Caravaggio Rediscovered: The Lute Player* (New York, 1990), p. 27.

[23]   *Rome 4433*, fols. 28r–29v: 'Di una certa accordatura di Leuto alla Francese.' A facsimile of the manuscript is in *Pier Francesco Valentini: Il Leuto Anatomizzato / Ordine . . .* (Florence, 1989) with an extensive introduction by Orlando Cristoforetti. The treatise is summarized in Coelho, *The Manuscript Sources*, pp. 150–4.

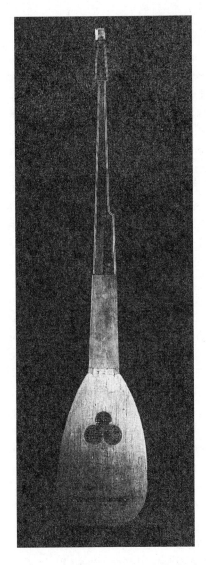

Plate 6   Eighteen-course theorbo by Matteo Sellas (Venice, *ca.* 1630). Paris, Musée de la Musique, Cité de la Musique. Inv. E 547 (photograph by Joël Dugot)

Giacinto Marmi, contains a chart showing this tuning (fols. 11v–12v), followed by a few fragments as examples.[24]

The continued presence of seven- and eight-course lutes in almost half of the manuscripts may be surprising, given that the majority of surviving instruments from this period are lutes with extended necks. Furthermore, only one of the nineteen

---

[24]   Pierre Gaultier's lutebook of works in various new tunings for ten-course lute was published in Rome in 1638, but it cannot be considered as an Italian source musically.

printed sources is not for either archlute or theorbo.[25] Nevertheless, short-necked lutes did indeed remain popular in Italy well after 1600, and they define a particular area of performance practice that is best understood by considering the relationships among instrument, repertory, context, and player. As in vocal music of the same period, there emerged in seventeenth-century lute music a historical and stylistic distinction between old and new, or *prima* and *seconda* practices. A clear stratification developed within lutenists by class (professional or amateur) and the instruments they played. In the previous century a professional musician like Francesco and an amateur novice learning the lute played the same instrument; the stylistic stability of sixteenth-century lute music and the well-defined needs of players required little more than a six-course lute, occasionally in different sizes.[26] All of Vincenzo Galilei's music, except at the very end of his enormous manuscript of 1584, calls for a six-course instrument, which was for him, an avowed purist, the 'classic' lute. Molinaro's lute book of 1599 is written for an eight-course instrument, but most of the pieces can be played on seven courses.[27]

With the stylistic changes that took place after 1600, however, professional lutenists were required to learn new roles, such as playing continuo and participating in larger bands containing diverse rather than like instruments, and newer styles of music, all of which necessitated the use of different instruments. A single player like Kapsberger, for example, wrote for four instruments: lute (1611), eleven-course theorbo (1604), nineteen-course theorbo (1640), and guitar (lost). All evidence shows that by the 1620s, the theorbo had surpassed the lute as the instrument favoured by professionals, and with the meteoric rise in popularity of the guitar, guitarists also played theorbo and vice versa. (By removing the first course of the theorbo, courses 2–6 will be identical to guitar tuning, e, b, g, d, A; a guitarist can thus play continuo on either instrument without changing left-hand fingering.) Seven of the nine prints published from 1620 to 1669 are either exclusively or partially for theorbo, and the bulk of theorbo manuscripts are concentrated within this period as well. In 1628, Giustiniani reported that 'in the past the lute was also much in use, but this instrument is almost completely abandoned since the theorbo has been introduced'.[28] Bouchard wrote to Mersenne six years later from Rome that because of the theorbo 'the lute and the viol are almost out of use in Rome'.[29]

[25] The *Balletti Moderni facili per sonar sopra il liuto* (Venice, 1611; rpt Geneva, 1980), calling for a seven-course lute.

[26] An excellent survey of lutes and lute construction at the end of the sixteenth century is in Robert Lundberg, 'In Tune with the Universe: The Physics and Metaphysics of Galileo's Lute', in *Music and Science in the Age of Galileo*, ed. Victor Coelho (Dordrecht and Boston, 1992), pp. 211–39.

[27] *Intavolatura di liuto di Simone Molinaro Genovese* (Venice, 1599; facsimile rpt Florence, 1978).

[28] Vincenzo Giustiniani, *Discorso sopra la musica* (1628), trans. Carol MacClintock (American Institute of Musicology, 1962), p. 79.

[29] For the entire passage, see Victor Coelho, 'G. G. Kapsberger in Rome, 1604–1645: New Biographical Data', *JLSA* 16 (1983), p. 129.

Nevertheless, manuscripts show that all players, even aspiring theorbists, began their studies on the lute. The thirteen existing theorbo manuscripts are either professional books, such as *Modena B*, or else student books that already assume an intermediate level of competence on the instrument, like *Rome 4145* and *Bologna*, which contain works by Kapsberger and Piccinini, respectively. Nowhere among the theorbo manuscripts is there a source intended for the true beginner, which is a source-type that is encountered frequently within the manuscript lute tablatures, e.g. *Berkeley 759* and *Brussels 16.662*.

Documentary evidence confirms this method of pedagogy. In 1612, a young Belgian lutenist named Philippe Vermeulen was sent to Rome to learn to play the theorbo, so that he might bring back to the north the latest Italian styles and make them better known at his own court.[30] But when he began studying the lute in Rome, the Archbishop of the Lowlands wrote sternly to his ambassador Philippe Maes, that 'instead of working at bettering himself on the lute, [Vermeulen] should take pains to become a master of the theorbo, and that, moreover, he work towards that goal by studying with some capable man in that profession . . .';[31] a month later, the Belgian ambassador responded that

following your instructions, I have spoken on behalf of Philippe Vermeulen with some teachers of lute and theorbo about what you said, who tell me that ordinarily one instrument goes with the other, and that moreover if he plays the lute well, he will subsequently learn to play the theorbo without difficulty. As for salary, they ask two escuz a month for each instrument, which makes ten florins in all. Nevertheless, I will make inquiries of others. . .[32]

Maes's original information was correct, and at the beginning of August he confirmed that 'practically everybody tells me it is better that [Vermeulen] continue to learn first to play the lute, and that afterwards, in one month, two, or three, he will easily learn to play the theorbo . . .'[33]

Well, not quite so easily. Maes's letter of a few months later confirms that even with the best teachers – Vermeulen was taught by no less than Kapsberger, after he failed in his attempts to contract Filippo Piccinini – mastery of the theorbo does not come without sacrifice:

In response to your letters of before 22 September [1612], I have looked for the Sr Piccenini, brother of the musician or lutenist now dead in the service of the nuncio;[34] but some five or

---

30   Some items of this correspondence appear in Vander Straeten, *La musique aux Pays-Bas*, vol. II, pp. 376–88, which I have corrected and supplemented with other letters from this exchange following my 1990 examination of these documents in Brussels, Archives Générales du Royaume (AGR), Papiers d'Etat et de l'Audience': *Negociations de Rome de 1582–1636*. All of the shelf numbers cited by Vander Straeten have since been changed.

31   Vander Straeten, p. 378.

32   *ibid.*

33   *ibid.*

34   Maes is therefore searching for Filippo Piccinini (1575–1648), who from all accounts equalled if not surpassed his brother Alessandro in fame during the early seventeenth century. The dead brother mentioned by Maes was

six months have passed since he left here from the employ of the illustrious Cardinal Aldobrandini to join the [service of the] Duke of Savoy, where he can still be found, having taken with him all of his furniture and clothing, so that if Your Highness wishes to have the music books left by his brother, you must therefore write to him . . .

I have since received your last letter of 29 [September], but am disturbed that you have not written me better news regarding Philipe Vermeulen, who in this state cannot continue much longer to live here; seeing that his parents are not sending him sufficient allowance so that he is practically naked, I am forced to extend him credit of some twenty or thirty escuz just so he can clothe himself. I leave to you his needs for food, which are at least 100 escuz annually. I suppose I could hire [him as] another member of my staff or a valet, but he could do nothing for me in this respect since he is from the morning to the evening locked in his room practising the theorbo, on which he hopes now to play well after some time, as his teacher confirmed to me a few days ago . . .[35]

As solo virtuosos and the professional players in the continuo pits graduated from lutes to theorboes and archlutes, the larger group of amateurs, students, and nobles continued to own seven- and eight-course instruments on which they played a 'classical' repertory rather than a modern one. They valued this music as they did the venerable classics of Plutarch, Livy, Petrarch, and Tasso upon which their education was formed. Amateur anthologies like *Como, Montreal, Paris 29*, or the Berkeley lutebooks show that the lute music equivalents of these 'great books' were Francesco (particularly his monothematic fantasias nos. 33 and 34[36]), stylish court dances drawn from Caroso's *Il Ballerino* (1580/1600) such as the *Barriera* (easily the most widely disseminated piece in the seventeenth-century Italian manuscript repertory), settings of popular tunes such as the *Spagnoletta* and *La Monica* (= *Une jeune fillette*), the patriotic *Aria di Fiorenza*, short formulas to accompany the recitation of poetry in *terza* and *ottava rima*, arrangements of popular canzonettas and, just to be contemporary, non-obtrusive, conservative modern music by Santino Garsi da Parma and the Cavaliero del liuto.[37] The most progressive lute music of the day by the likes of Kapsberger and Piccinini did not enter into the amateur musical diet; consequently, neither did the need for 'professional'-size instruments.

The large number of retrospective manuscript anthologies of lute music show that the cultivation of the lute by learned and noble society continued long after the lute itself declined as a solo instrument in Italy. Consequently, as long as Renaissance

Girolamo Piccinini (b. 1573), who obviously died sometime around the time of this letter. This document contradicts Cristoforetti's dating of Girolamo's death to 1615. See Cristoforetti's introduction to *Alessandro Piccinini: Intavolatura di liuto, et di chitarrone...*(Florence, 1983), p. [ii].

[35]   Vander Straeten, *La musique aux Pays-Bas*, vol. II, p. 381.

[36]   For an examination of the Francesco repertory known to lutenists after his death, see Coelho, 'The Reputation of Francesco da Milano . . .'

[37]   On the manner in which lutenists used these formulas, and for a study of a typical Italian lutebook compiled by a noble amateur, see Victor Coelho, 'Raffaello Cavalcanti's Lutebook (1590) and the Ideal of Singing and Playing', in *Le concert des voix et des instruments à la Renaissance*, ed. J.-M. Vaccaro (Paris, 1995), pp. 423–42.

lute music was still being played by a large amateur and student public – a parallel can be drawn here to the continued popularity of Arcadelt's madrigals in seventeenth-century Italy – lute makers of the early seventeenth century enjoyed a still-vigorous market for short-necked models.

The presence of so many short-necked lutes in the seventeenth-century manuscripts suggests some interesting possibilities for modern players, particularly those who tour and like to play eclectic programmes. We have already mentioned that pieces by Kapsberger and Piccinini rarely found their way into amateur sources. This is not because amateurs played instruments that were too small – even amateur manuscripts for archlute and theorbo (*Kraków 40591, San Francisco*) exclude music by Kapsberger and Piccinini. Quite simply, amateurs just did not care much for 'modern' music. On the other hand, more benign contemporary music by Santino Garsi da Parma, Caroso, and a small 'top ten' of popular dances[38] fill amateur anthologies and manuscript tutors, and these works show how lutenists freely adapted the music to fit the size of the instrument. Garsi's famous *Gagliarda della Marchesa di Sala*, for example, is one of the many pieces that comes down to us in versions for different-sized instruments. In the Florentine manuscript *Brussels 16.663* (*ca.* 1600–10), the piece is written for 6 courses. In *Kraków 40032* (1590–1611), a reliable source of Santino's music,[39] *Paris 941* (1609–16), *Paris 29* (*ca.* 1610–20), and *Pesaro b.14* (*ca.* 1610–25), a seventh course is present, and in *Rome 570* (*ca.* 1608–15) and *Kraków 40153* (1620–1), the last-named source copied in the hand of Santino Garsi's son, Donino, ten courses are required. Many other examples of adapting the music to the instrument can be found in these sources, and they reveal the autonomous decisions made by lutenists in the context of their own needs.

Unfortunately, doctrinaire notions about 'authenticity' have convinced most modern players that similar compromises or adaptations are inappropriate. To invoke such orthodoxy as playing Francesco *only* on a six-course lute or Piccinini *only* on a fourteen-course archlute contradicts the practices of lutenists in Italy during the seventeenth century. While the 'correct' instrument as designated in a print is always preferable and often unequivocal, the use of a different lute and the occasional transposition of a few bass notes are in no way violations of seventeenth-century performance practice; rather, these adaptations are well within the tradition of the time. Moreover, it is not always clear, even in professional prints, what

---

[38] Such as *La Adoloratta, La Passionata, La Barriera*, the *Gagliarda dele cinque mentite*, and *La Tamburina*, to name just a few. For the dispersion of these, see Coelho, *The Manuscript Sources*.

[39] *Kraków 40032* is the earliest source of Garsi's music and contains more pieces by him than any other manuscript. An edition of this important manuscript, edited by John Griffiths and Dinko Fabris, is forthcoming. In the meantime, see Coelho, *The Manuscript Sources*, p. 14 for a general description. A tablature incipit inventory of the manuscript is in *Berliner Lautentabulaturen in Krakau: Beschreibender Katalog der handschriftlichen Tabulaturen für Laute und verwandte Instrumente in der Bibliotheka Jagiellońska Kraków aus dem Besitz der ehemaligen Preußischen Staatsbibliothek Berlin*, ed. Dieter Kirsch and Lenz Meierott (Mainz, 1992), pp. 1–53. For a list of concordant versions of the work, see Coelho, *The Manuscript Sources*, p. 584, no. 25.

instrument was intended by the composer. While there is little doubt about what is meant when specifying the *arciliuto* or *tiorba*, the word 'lauto' could mean many things at the beginning of the seventeenth century. In his *Libro primo di lauto* (Rome, 1611), Kapsberger calls for an eleventh course, which, given his professional status, might suggest an archlute strung in the disposition of 6 ('petit jeu') + 5 ('grand jeu'). But the eleventh course (B♭) is used only once in the entire print, and both O'Dette and Smith use ten-course lutes in their recordings.[40] Moreover, with a few small adaptations, almost all of the pieces in the book can be accommodated easily and convincingly to an eight-course lute with the seventh and eighth courses tuned to F and C, respectively (rather than F and D), which is one of the eight-course configurations used by Pietro Raimondi in the amateur anthology *Como*. Twenty of the thirty-two pieces in *Kapsberger 1611* can be played on such an instrument, requiring no change at all to the music: toccatas 1 and 8; gagliarde 1–11; and correnti 1, 2, 5, 6, 8, 10, 11. Toccatas 2, 3, 4, and 6, gagliarda 12, and correnti 7 and 9 require the transposition of only one or two bass notes which have no impact whatsoever on the voice-leading. In sum, all but five pieces from Kapsberger's *Libro primo* can be played on the same eight-course Renaissance instrument one uses for Molinaro, Dowland, or Laurencini.

Similarly, Piccinini's 1623 book for lute and theorbo specifies for the former an *arciliuto*, but Piccinini was already fifty-four years old at the time of this book's publication and many of the works were probably written for a smaller instrument during the composer's years in Ferrara during the 1590s. (Piccinini writes in his preface that he 'invented' the *arciliuto* around 1594.[41]) Whereas Kapsberger normally reserves his use of octave bass courses for cadential emphasis or harmonic support, Piccinini's dances contain many ill-advised passages on the bass courses that sound much better an octave higher (e.g. *Corrente prima*, bars 47–51; *Corrente XIII*, bars 27–31), a criticism that can also be made about many of the disappointing archlute works by Pietro Paulo Melii. Perhaps these are earlier works by Piccinini that he later revised for a larger instrument, similar to the Garsi example cited above. Some pieces, like *Corrente terza, Corrente quinta,* and *Corrente XII* are distinctly earlier works requiring a maximum of seven courses, and even the famous *Passacaglia* from his posthumous 1639 tablature calls for no larger than a seven-course lute.

One of the most interesting examples of adapting the music to fit the instrument is the occasional interchangeability seventeenth-century players allowed between lute and theorbo. Both of the central theorbo sources, *Modena B* and *Paris 30*, contain concordances with Kapsberger's 1611 lute book, which predates both manuscripts.

---

[40]   Paul O'Dette, *'Il Tedesco della Tiorba': Kapsberger, Pieces for Lute*, Harmonia Mundi HMU 907020; Hopkinson Smith, *Giovanni Girolamo Kapsperger, Intavolatura di Lauto*, Astrée E 8553.

[41]   *Piccinini 1623*, p. 8, Ch. XXXIIII: *Dell'Arciliuto, e dell Inventore d'esso*. For a translation, see Mason, *The Chitarrone and its Repertoire*, p. 26.

Both concordances are dances: the *Gagliarda 3ᵃ* (*Kapsberger 1611*, p. 17; *Modena B*, fol 15r), and the *Corrente 3ᵃ* (*Kapsberger 1611*, pp. 25–6; *Paris 30*, fol 26v). Since Kapsberger's dances are rarely contrapuntal – the correnti are particularly transparent in texture – only a few changes to the tablature are required to adapt the dances for theorbo. Indeed, the same can be done to many of the other dances in Kapsberger's lute collection. It is entirely possible that either or both of the two unique dances by Kapsberger that appear in these manuscripts were adapted from his lost lute book of 1619, which was in circulation before either of the two manuscripts were completed. These adaptations are the work not of amateur or student lutenists, but of courtly professionals, and they show the flexible and autonomous practices that existed at the highest and most respected level.

Turning to the issue of right-hand position and technique, we can gain remarkably consistent information from seventeenth-century paintings and surviving instruments. They show that from *ca.* 1590, Italian lutenists used the right-hand technique known as 'thumb out', and they are unequivocal in their depiction of the lutenist's right hand closer to the bridge than during the sixteenth century. Piccinini mentions that the best sound on both lute and theorbo is produced by plucking the strings halfway between the rose and the bridge,[42] though paintings often show the lutenist's hand much farther to the right (depending on the size of the instrument) of the rose. The right hand continued to be anchored by the small finger resting on the soundboard – this is confirmed once again by both Piccinini (Ch. V) and by paintings – just below or behind the bridge. Many surviving instruments even reveal a small indentation on the belly of the lute from where the finger was planted, confirming the accuracy of the paintings. But almost no lutenist today plays so close to the bridge as did our seventeenth-century counterparts, nor has any modern theorbist (to my knowledge) adopted the position described in *Kapsberger 1640*, in which the right hand was anchored by the *ring* finger at the bottom of the bridge, rather than by the fifth: Kapsberger's reasons for this position were to be contained in his book entitled *Il Kapsperger della Musica*, which never appeared. Generally, scale passages continued to be played by alternating downstrokes of the thumb with upward strokes of the index finger. The standard symbol of using dots in the tablature to show the notes played by the index finger was maintained in many manuscripts as well as in *Piccinini 1623*. However, archlute sources like *Kraków 40153, Perugia*, and *Venice* call for the index and *middle* fingers to play scale passages, similar to modern classical guitar technique. Piccinini permits this fingering when during scale passages the thumb must play another part, and he encourages its use for the evenness in sound that is produced. Clarity of prose not being one of Piccinini's strengths, he refers to this technique as 'arpeggiation' (Ch. XI); arpeggiation as we

---

[42] *Piccinini 1623*, Ch. IIII, p. 1. See Fabris, in this volume, p. 38.

know it and as played on the theorbo, he calls 'pizzicate' (Ch. XXIX). As for the use of nails, seventeenth-century paintings of lutenists are inconclusive on this subject, but Piccinini mentions their use on the thumb, index, middle, and ring fingers and describes their optimal shape without apology or justification, suggesting that they were not at all uncommon. While the great Julian Bream was roundly criticized for his use of nails (and a footstool) by the first generation of modern flesh players, in recent years the tide has turned somewhat, and many professional lutenists have shown the advantages of nails for some repertories after around 1550.

PEDAGOGY, PREFACES, AND VARIATION

The notions of autonomy, flexibility, adaptation, and the 'open score' were emphasized early on in the training of a seventeenth-century lutenist. Once again, the manuscripts are a rich source of information on this subject since almost half of them are pedagogical books. From these we can reconstruct fairly accurately the education of lutenists and trace some of the musical procedures they used to their source.

The root of this training lies with the lutenist's familiarity with genres, and the relationship between genre and performance. With the decline of contrapuntal and derivative forms like the fantasia and intabulation, combined with the need for lutenists to play more than one instrument, lute technique underwent a definite and perceivable change at the beginning of the seventeenth century, equal in scope to the transformations in vocal and keyboard technique at the same time. The parallel rise of more sectional and discursive genres, like the toccata, led to a subjectivity in overall approach. These newer genres demanded a flexible and explosive technique that could be used to dramatize individual moments of a piece – rather than overall symmetry, as in the Renaissance fantasia – through timbral and dynamic contrast, while at the same time exploiting the new dimensions in sound that were being opened up by larger instruments. The newest inventions in technique are found in theorbo sources, since the instrument, which was invented specifically for accompaniment, had to be adapted for a solo repertoire. These included slurs, strums, different varieties of arpeggios and trills, tremolos, highly syncopated rhythmic groupings, triplets, and cross-stringing for scales. Many of these 'new' techniques were used as effects within the new dramatic style of seventeenth-century toccatas. They are described in an unusually detailed passage from Giambattista Marino's epic poem *L'Adone*, which should be considered as an important source of seventeenth-century performance practice. In a recent article I have shown how Marino's intricate knowledge and specialist terminology about the lute seem derived from *Piccinini 1623*, whose author was one of Marino's close colleagues in Rome.[43] Archlute

---

[43]   Victor Coelho, 'Marino's *Toccata* between the Lutenist and the Nightingale', in *The Sense of Marino: Literature, Fine Arts and Music of the Italian Baroque*, ed. Francesco Guardiani (New York and Toronto, 1994), pp. 395–427.

manuscripts (*Florence 45, Perugia, Venice*) reveal that some specific theorbo techniques were eventually borrowed by lutenists. In the Roman pedagogical book *Perugia*,[44] both the sign ·//· and the actual pattern of theorbo arpeggiation, first described in *Kapsberger 1604*, are employed for some pieces.[45] Their use is restricted to (1) toccatas, (2) chords that last a full bar, and (3) pieces at the end of the manuscript, beginning with the concordance of *Toccata 5ª* from *Kapsberger 1611* on pp. 90–2, which suggests some specificity in the use of this technique.

If there is one lesson that is emphasized more than any other in pedagogical books, it is that of variation technique. In the conventional sense, variation is the principal procedure used in multi-sectional pieces based on recurring harmonic or bass schemes, such as passamezzos, passacagli, ciaccone, and settings of the *Ruggiero*, *Romanesca*, *Folia*, *Bergamasca*, and *Aria di Fiorenza*. Variation principle is a fundamental strategy in theorbo composition: since the instrument cannot easily sustain contrapuntal textures because of its re-entrant tuning and its restricted range, the theorbo composer must rely on melodic and rhythmic variation as the main source of textural and sectional contrast. The majority as well as the most elaborate of the works in *Kapsberger 1604* are variation pieces: the *Ruggiero* (nine *partite* [= theme plus eight variations]), *Aria di Fiorenza* (nine *partite*), *Folia* (nineteen *partite*), *Romanesca* (five *partite*), and *Passamezzo* (three *partite*). Beyond this, the technique of variation underlies most other genres as well.

The archlute manuscript *Perugia* and the theorbo source *Rome 4145* provide particularly good insights into this type of pedagogical training, for these sources appear to have been supervised and at least partially copied by the professional lutenists Andrea Falconieri and Kapsberger, respectively. *Perugia* contains, in addition to a diverse repertory of dances and an important collection of toccatas, actual taught lessons that were copied into the book. Sprinkled throughout the manuscript in a subsidiary (and inexperienced) hand are short pieces with titles such as *Ceccona per A, Ceccona per B*, followed by the description 'Mutanza' and instructions 'to copy this' ('Copiare questa'). A reconstruction of these lessons shows that they revolve primarily around asking the student to invent a ciaccona bass, transpose it to different scale degrees (e.g. pp. 12–15: *Ceccona per A, Ceccona per B*, etc.[46]), and then vary it ('Mutanza') using diminutions, ornamented cadential formulas, and arpeggios. These 'mutanze' are based on standard scale and arpeggio patterns, which the lutenist learns in order to create various rudimentary harmonic formulas that can

[44]   A facsimile of *Perugia* has been published as *Libro di Leuto di Gioseppe Antonio Doni, MS. Perugia, sec. XVII*, ed. Dinko Fabris (Florence, 1988).

[45]   Kapsberger's 1611 lute book mentions nothing about arpeggiation. On theorbo arpeggiation, see Victor Coelho, 'Frescobaldi and the Lute and Chitarrone Toccatas of "Il Tedesco della Tiorba"', in *Frescobaldi Studies*, ed. Alexander Silbiger (Durham, 1987), pp. 137–56.

[46]   For an explanation of these titles, see Coelho, *The Manuscript Sources*, pp. 134–5.

be expanded and elaborated in different contexts. They can also serve to embellish other ciaccone in the manuscript. Plate 7 and Ex. 5.2 show how one of these lessons is illustrated in *Perugia*.

Variation technique is also the main lesson in *Rome 4145*. The manuscript opens with the *Ruggiero* and six of the nine *partite* from *Kapsberger 1604*, followed by *Toccata 1* from the same print, all in Kapsberger's hand. A new hand copied the next seven works, which consist of two dances, both followed by their *doubles*, and three short *arie*, possibly accompaniments to vocal works. Almost half of the remaining pieces are passacaglia or ciaccona settings, which are usually followed by blank pages intended for the student to complete the settings, compose a variation, or transpose them.[47] As in *Perugia*, some of these passacagli are based on the same theme but transposed to different pitches. Completing these exercises allows the player to build up a repertory of possibilities in realizing a repeated bass line or chordal scheme in different transpositions. This principle of variation also underlies the ornamenting of final cadences, or *cadenze finali*. Continuo players were expected to have many ornamented cadence formulas committed to memory for realizing the long held notes that often appear at the end of monodies and *arie* of the early seventeenth century, among other types of final cadences. Some manuscript books contain intabulated exercises of this nature (*Kraków 40591*, fol. 62v; *Paris 31*, fol. 45r). In the manuscript treatise *Il Leuto Anatomizzato* (*Rome 4433*), Pier Francesco Valentini devotes sections to ornamenting interior and final cadences (fols. 16r–18r) even providing examples using D minor tuning (fols. 28r–29v). The theorbo section of *Modena 239* contains ninety-eight examples of *cadenze finali*, offering ornamented solutions to bass lines descending or ascending by thirds, fourths, with 7–$\sharp$6 and 4–3 suspensions, and other types of movement.[48]

Variation technique is thus a licence for autonomy and improvisation – or improvised composition – and this is why many of the seventeenth-century manuscripts are compiled in the manner of a 'fakebook'. Most of the pieces in *Paris 29, Pesaro b.10*, and *Paris 941*, for example, provide the player with just one strain of a bass scheme or tune, from which lutenists were to create longer settings through elaboration and variation. Taken as a whole, these manuscripts show how variation technique is used in (1) pieces based on repeating patterns, (2) ornamented repeats for the binary or ternary sections of dances, (3) *Nachtänze* for dance pairs based on the same thematic material, (4) settings of *La Monica* (sometimes just called *Alemana*), which is one of the most popular variation pieces in the entire repertory and especially liked by theorbists, (5) popular tunes like the *Pavaniglia* (Spanish Pavan) and the *Spagnoletta*, and (6) programmatic works like the *Battaglia* and *Barriera*.

---

[47] A list of directions on fols. 13v–14r includes the direction to 'complete a passacaglia'.

[48] See Coelho, *The Manuscript Sources*, pp. 101–4; for a larger study including facsimiles, see Mirko Caffagni, 'The Modena Tiorba Continuo Manuscript', *JLSA* 12 (1979), pp. 25–42.

Plate 7   *Perugia*, p. 114, *Ceccona per A* (courtesy of the Archivio di Stato, Perugia)

Variation is also an integral strategy used in the composition of toccatas. Most of the toccatas by Kapsberger and Piccinini, for example, are constructed around the presentation of two or three subjects and their subsequent elaboration, though the procedure of such elaboration is anything but conventional.[49] The quintessential

<hr />

[49]   For a discussion of the relationships between the common strategies used in toccatas and seventeenth-century poetry, with particular emphasis on Piccinini, see Coelho, 'Marino's *Toccata*'.

Ex. 5.2   transcription of Plate 7

unpredictability of these works is due to the possibilities that can be achieved through variation, since it is a technique that is adaptable to many different kinds of polyphonic or homophonic textures, unlike the stricter procedures of counterpoint, canon, fugue, or even canzona. It is not irrelevant here to cite a similar rise in variation-type pieces during the nineteenth century, when composers increasingly employed strict theme-and-variation, as well as variation derivatives such as cyclic form and developing variation, in order to free themselves from the formal restrictions and harmonic requirements of sonata principle and classical symphonic form. In the seventeenth century, variation technique can similarly be seen as a liberating device that can be found in a variety of genres. Example 5.3 shows how the seemingly unlimited invention of *Toccata 1ª* from *Kapsberger 1611* is, in fact, based on a simple variation principle of three motives and their mutations.

VARIANTS AND AUTONOMY

As we have noted above, printed books provide an 'authoritative' text that was, in most cases, approved by the composer,[50] but they do not succeed in telling us how this music is actually performed. Even when 'instructions' are provided in introductory prefaces, as in *Kapsberger 1604/1640* and *Piccinini 1623*, only the purely technical information – how to arpeggiate, how to interpret rhythms in triplets, how to play trills, tremolos, *accenti*, and slurs – is relatively unambiguous. *When* to trill, *when* to use the tremolo, and *when* to ornament, on the other hand, are never specified to the precision that modern players would like. If a lute teacher at a master class today was asked by a young player about where to ornament in a particular piece and he replied vaguely with, 'Here you should do one sort of ornament, there another, according to what is suitable', students would demand an immediate refund; it would be of little solace to the student that the teacher was simply quoting from *Piccinini 1623*. Rather, what is implicit behind the various techniques and effects that are described, but not *prescribed*, by Kapsberger and Piccinini, is the granting of autonomy in using ornaments 'in every place it is possible',[51] 'in an unlimited number of places',[52] 'in all places where there are long or short pauses',[53]

---

[50] Of the main prints, *Piccinini 1623* was obviously approved by the composer and contains a list of errata; Castaldi was the engraver of his own print, and *Kapsberger 1604* and *Kapsberger 1611* were brought out by members of the composer's close patronage circle; only *Kapsberger 1640* seems to have a chequered history, and might not have represented the composer's original intentions. Leone Allacci (*Apes Urbanae* (Rome, 1633), pp. 159–60) listed *Kapsberger 1640* as being ready for publication by 1633, but seven years elapsed before it was finally published. Furthermore, only a single copy of this print survives (British Library), no concordances exist between this print and the manuscript sources, and one can notice the appearance of a second engraver's hand from p. 47.

[51] *Piccinini 1623*, Ch. XI, p. 3, on arpeggiation.

[52] *ibid.*, Ch. XVII, p. 3, on the second type of tremolo [trill].

[53] *ibid.*, Ch. XIX, p. 4, on where to ornament.

Ex. 5.3   G. G. Kapsberger, *Toccata 1ᵃ*, from *Kapsberger 1611*: motives a, b, and c, and their 'variations'

and on 'every chord as much as possible'.[54] Such 'codified flexibility' invites comparisons with Girolamo Frescobaldi's preface to his 1627 book of toccatas, which suggests variable tempos, allows the player to make 'cuts' in the overall form of the piece, and permits arpeggiation and some ornaments at the player's discretion.[55] What these authors seem to be saying is, 'here are the techniques and a few rudimentary guidelines since all of this may be new to you, but ultimately you are the player, and you make the decisions'. By encouraging this autonomy, the role of the composer has been placed in the hands of the performer. Consequently, significant interpretive differences can, did, and should exist in the performance of a single piece by different performers. Concordances contained in manuscripts reveal these variants, and they help define some of the autonomous strategies used by lutenists of the *seicento*.

The theorbo manuscripts *Modena B* (dated 1619) and *Paris 30* (dated 1626) are ideal for a comparison along these lines. Both are professional books copied less than a decade apart, and they are identical both in their selection of genres and in their arrangement. Unique works by Kapsberger and possibly Piccinini are found in both

54 *Kapsberger 1640*, p. 2, regarding trills and *accenti*.

55 A study of the parallels between Frescobaldi's and Kapsberger's toccatas is in Coelho, 'Frescobaldi and the Lute and Chitarrone Toccatas of "Il Tedesco della Tiorba"'. An expanded and more copiously illustrated version of this study is in Victor Coelho, 'G. G. Kapsberger "della tiorba" e l'influenza liutistica sulle *Toccate* di Frescobaldi', in *Girolamo Frescobaldi nel IV centenario della nascita*, ed. Sergio Durante (Florence, 1986), pp. 341–57. Another study that is highly relevant to this discussion is Etienne Darbellay, 'Liberté, variété, et "affetti cantabili" chez Girolamo Frescobaldi', *RdM* 61 (1975), pp. 197–243. Frescobaldi's rules have been reprinted many times; a readable, accessible version is in Lorenzo Bianconi, *Music in the Seventeenth Century* (Cambridge, 1987), pp. 95–6.

manuscripts, as well as pieces culled from *Kapsberger 1604* and the lute source *Kapsberger 1611*, arranged for theorbo. Although the tablatures seem to have been copied in different cities, the stylistic origins of the repertory are unmistakably Roman. Despite their common ancestry, however, the three concordances between the two manuscripts offer some interesting variant readings. They show how two contemporary theorbists thought about the same pieces and how the styles of both are the result of their autonomous decisions on a fixed text.

Neither the Modena nor the Paris theorbists were apprehensive about imposing new formal divisions onto the models they chose to copy, or about extracting sections from larger pieces to suit their own needs. In the *Folia* copied from *Kapsberger 1604* that appears in *Paris 30* (fols. 17r–18v), only three of the eighteen variations were selected (nos. 1, 10, and 12), an editorial practice that sets a liberating precedent for the modern theorbist performing for modern audiences, given the length of most printed variation sets from this time. A different strategy was planned for the *Partita* (*Paris 30*, fol. 14v), which was extracted from the *Passamezzo*, also from *Kapsberger 1604*, but divorced from its theme and the other two variations. In addition to the possibility that it was played autonomously – it is the most impressive variation of the set – it was more probably combined with the untitled passamezzo moderno and its *partita* on fol. 29r–v. The *Gagliarda* on fol. 20r, also based on the passamezzo moderno, provides a natural *Nachtanz*.

A more intrusive example of revising the printed text can be seen in the *Gagliarda HK* (*Paris 30*, fol. 24r–v), concordant to *[Gagliarda] 11ª* from *Kapsberger 1604* (see Exs. 5.4a–b). The six-bar phrase (2 + 4) of Kapsberger's original – unusual when compared to most other galliards of the time but typical of the mannerisms that Kapsberger injects into his dances – has been extended in *Paris 30* by two extra bars to create a more conventional eight-bar unit of 2 + 2 + 4. As we will see in the next example, the variants encountered in the Paris manuscript are consistent by their clarification of unusual or imbalanced passages. The ornamented repeat composed by the *Paris 30* theorbist (Ex. 5.4c), is an actual example of how a player varied a binary repeat, and it is of particular value here since written-out repeats are rarely found in Kapsberger's work.

A more detailed approach to editing works is present in Ex. 5.5, in which *Paris 30* compresses the version in *Modena B* for the same reasons of attaining rhythmic clarity that guided the revision of Ex. 5.4. In the *Modena B* reading of this anonymous *Corrente* (Ex. 5.5a), the 'A' section contains twenty bars while the 'B' section is thirty-one bars long, compared to sixteen bars and twenty-eight bars, respectively, in *Paris 30* (5.5b). Instead of adding bars to achieve more orthodox phrase-lengths, as in Ex. 5.4, the Paris copyist suppresses the cadential deflection of bars 15–18 in favour of a clearer and more direct arrival at the tonic, G major. The rearrangement of material is more ingeniously accomplished in the 'B' section, in which the Paris

Ex. 5.4 (a) *Gagliarda 11ᵃ*, from *Kapsberger 1604*, p. 58
         (b) *Gagliarda* from *Paris 30*, fol. 24r–v
         (c) Ornamented repeat of 5.4b, bars 9–16

copyist avoids the rhythmic difficulties present in *Modena B*, bars 36–9, by telescoping bars 34–7 into two bars, as shown by the arrows.

Perhaps the most common variant that exists between concordant versions of a single piece involves the density of chord voicing. It is rare to find a concordance in the seventeenth century that does not contain at least a few chords that are more thickly or thinly voiced than the analogous chords in the model. When a concordance exists for a larger or smaller instrument than that intended by the model, it is, of course, natural to expect the addition, elimination, or transposition of bass notes. But when concordant versions are written for the same size of instrument, as in Ex. 5.5, chord voicing is a flexible decision that is guided by personal taste, sonority, technical ability, and context – i.e. using thicker chords in order to produce more

Ex. 5.5
(a) *Modena B, Corrente AP* [Alessandro Piccinini?], fol. 9r
(b) *Paris 30, Cor[rente]*, fol. 9v

sound when playing in a crowded or large room. In another study, for example, I have shown that the unusually thick chordal textures in *Nuremberg 2* and *Nuremberg 3* were written specifically for lutenists participating in a large ensemble that performed for various grandiose events related to the 1608 wedding celebrations for Cosimo II Medici and Maria Maddalena of Austria.[56]

As lutenists of the early seventeenth century became experienced at playing continuo, they learned how to voice chords according to the musical context. Moreover, with the introduction of new arpeggiation patterns and the appropriation of certain techniques from the guitar, like strumming, the player could draw spontaneously on a variety of possibilities for playing chords. In Ex. 5.5b, the Paris theorbist uses thinner chords on most occasions (see bars 2, 6, and 24), sometimes suppresses bass notes (bars 4, 19), or adds them (bars 9, 25, and 43), occasionally changes the chord voicing (bars 8, 22), that alters the timbral quality of the chord when using a left-hand fingering in a lower position (bar 8), which has particularly interesting implications for all sorts of passages. Ex. 5.4 shows a contrary approach, in which the Paris theorbist significantly thickens Kapsberger's original textures at almost every chordal event in various ways including the addition of bass notes. Many of Kapsberger's dances, especially for lute, are in fact so thinly scored that a convincing 'realization' along the lines of Ex. 5.4b is not only possible, as Hopkinson Smith has recently demonstrated, but justified by historical practice.[57]

The performance practices of seventeenth-century Italian lutenists are founded not on a common aesthetic goal, but on highly individual traditions that reveal the subjective, autonomous, and interpretive abilities of players. The elements and foundations of these practices are commensurate with the diversity of source-types, which are divided between pedagogical lute books for the student, lute and archlute anthologies containing a 'classical' repertory for the amateur, and professional books, usually for theorbo, that transmit the most progressive genres and styles of the early seventeenth century. In all of these books, the invention and autonomy of the player takes precedence over the musical text: performance practice is inextricably linked to interpretation and the choices made by the performer. Pedagogical sources show that this notion of the 'open score' was part of a lutenist's training from the beginning, in which the principle of variation was taught as a basis of musical composition.

Although the period continues to defy any strict codification of 'rules', the sources we have just studied show how performance varies according to context, and between the practices of élite professionals and those of amateurs or students. Just as our knowledge of art history is based not only on the Giottos, Leonardos, and Titians, but also on the thousands of anonymous frescoes and oils that grace the chapels of small Italian towns, I believe that we must base our understanding of this

---

[56] See Coelho, *The Manuscript Sources*, pp. 110–15.

[57] See n. 40, above.

repertory not just on professional books, but also on the information-rich corpus of amateur and domestic manuscript sources. Embedded in these tablatures are the pedagogical principles that underlie both amateur and professional training. Since these manuscripts reveal procedures rather than just pieces, they provide an entrée into the practical solutions lutenists used to adapt to the changing techniques, styles, and musical aesthetics of the early Baroque, and they can provide a link between the historical practices of seventeenth-century lutenists and the goals of the modern interpreter of this music.

EXPLANATION OF SIGLA

Berkeley 757	Berkeley, University of California Music Library, Ms. 757
Berkeley 759	Berkeley, University of California Music Library, Ms. 759
Bologna	Bologna, Archivio di Stato, Fondo Malvezzi-Campeggi, Ms. IV–86/746
Brussels 16.662	Brussels, Bibliothèque du Conservatoire Royale de Musique, Ms. Littera S. No. 16.662 (rpt Brussels, 1980)
Brussels 16.663	Brussels, Bibliothèque du Conservatoire Royale de Musique, Ms. Littera S. No. 16.663 (rpt Brussels, 1980)
Castaldi	*Capricci a due strumenti cioé tiorba e tiorbino* (Modena, 1622; rpt Geneva, 1981)
Como	Como, Biblioteca comunale, Ms. 1.1.20 (rpt Como, 1980)
Florence 45	Florence, Biblioteca Nazionale Centrale, Ms. Fondo Magl. XIX 45
Frankfurt	Frankfurt-am-Main, Private library of Matthias Schneider, Ms. without shelfmark
Kapsberger 1604	*Libro primo d'intavolatura di chitar[r]one* (Venice, 1604; rpt Florence, 1982)
Kapsberger 1611	*Libro primo d'intavolatura di lauto* (Rome, 1611; rpt Florence, 1982)
Kapsberger 1640	*Libro quarto d'intavolatura di chitarrone* (Rome, 1604; rpt Florence, 1982)
Kraków 40032	Kraków, Biblioteca Jagiellonska, Mus. Ms. 40032
Kraków 40153	Kraków, Biblioteca Jagiellonska, Mus. Ms. 40153
Kraków 40591	Kraków, Biblioteca Jagiellonska, Mus. Ms. 40591
Modena B	Modena, Archivio di Stato, Ms. Archivio Ducale Segreto per materie, musica, e musicisti, Busta IV [Fascicle B]
Modena 239	Modena, Biblioteca Estense, Ms. G.239
Nuremberg 2	Nuremberg, Bibliothek des Germanischen National-Museums, Ms. 33748/M.271 [2]

Nuremberg 3	Nuremberg, Bibliothek des Germanischen National-Museums, Ms. 33748/M.271 [3]
Paris 29	Paris, Bibliothèque Nationale, Mus. Rés. Vmd. Ms. 29
Paris 30	Paris, Bibliothèque Nationale, Mus. Rés. Vmd. Ms. 30
Paris 31	Paris, Bibliothèque Nationale, Mus. Rés. Vmd. Ms. 31
Paris 941	Paris, Bibliothèque Nationale, Ms. Fonds Conservatoire National Rés. 941
Perugia	Perugia, Archivio di Stato, Archivio Fiumi-Sermattei della Genga, Ms. VII–H–2 (rpt Florence, 1988)
Pesaro b.10	Pesaro, Biblioteca musicale statale del Conservatorio di Musica 'G. Rossini', Rari Ms. b.10
Pesaro b.14	Pesaro, Biblioteca musicale statale del Conservatorio di Musica 'G. Rossini', Rari Ms. b.14 (mod. edn by I. Cavallini [Bologna, 1979])
Piccinini 1623	Alessandro Piccinini, *Intavolatura di liuto, et di chitarrone, Libro primo* (Bologna, 1623; rpt Florence, 1982)
Piccinini 1639	*Intavolatura di liuto* (Bologna, 1639; rpt Florence, 1982)
Rome 570	Rome, Biblioteca Apostolica Vaticana, Ms. Mus. 570 (*olim* Casimiri 36)
Rome 4145	Rome, Biblioteca Apostolica Vaticana, Ms. Barb. Lat. 4145
Rome 4433	Rome, Biblioteca Apostolica Vaticana, Ms. Barb. Lat. 4433
San Francisco	San Francisco, Frank V. De Bellis Collection of the California State University and Colleges, Ms. M2.1.M3
Venice	Venice, Biblioteca Nazionale Marciana, Ms. Italiano classe IV, no. 1793

6

PERFORMANCE INSTRUCTIONS FOR THE SEVENTEENTH-CENTURY FRENCH LUTE REPERTORY

WALLACE RAVE

Past descriptions of performance traits applicable to the extensive repertory of French lute music composed between *ca.* 1630 and the end of the seventeenth century were based largely on the published tablatures of Denis Gautier (or Gaultier), Jacques Gallot, and Charles Mouton. While these provide explanations of the performance symbols and *agrément* (ornament) signs employed, there exist other significant documents as well. The discussion that follows provides summaries of and commentaries on three other performance guides, one early, one from the middle of the period, and one from the 1680s. Further, I will examine representative lute compositions taken from two manuscript tablatures that are exceptionally rich in performance information, and compare them to published versions of the same works.

JEHAN BASSET'S TREATISE

As a prominent and respected lute teacher in Paris, Jehan Basset was asked by Marin Mersenne to contribute his lute treatise to the priest's *Harmonie Universelle*, published in 1636.[1] In his instructions Basset provides a discussion of what he calls *tremblements*. He observes that the comma is usually understood to mean a *tremblement* proper, that is, an 'inverted mordent' or an appoggiatura from above. He then presents signs for *accent plaintif* (an appoggiatura from below, later to be called *port-de-voix)*, *martelement* (mordent? see below), *battement* (trill), and *verre cassé* (vibrato; this was too much used in the past, which may be why it is now neglected, he thinks). On p. 79 he claims he has invented some of the *caractères* himself, although he adds that he has employed the more common symbols, 'since they are used by the more understanding in this profession' (p. 83).

---

[1] Marin Mersenne, *Harmonie Universelle, contenant la théorie et la pratique de la musique* (Paris, 1636). A facsimile edition was published in 1963 by the Centre National de la Recherche Scientifique. The lute performance instructions are in Propositions ix and x of the 'Livre Second des Instruments'.

Some of the Basset's descriptions are not only quite detailed but occasionally surprising. He describes the *martelement* not simply as a mordent but as a trill in which the lower note is the neighbouring pitch. If the lower pitch is an open course he employs an 'x'; if not, then an inverted 'v' is used (pp. 80–1). He distinguishes between an inverted mordent and a trill, using a different symbol for each (comma and 'z', respectively).[2] In another distinctive instruction he says that a trill should begin on the upper neighbour but the stop should then be pulled off forcefully, the trill continuing by 'beating' the course with the same finger (p. 81). This implies a strongly accented beginning that may have been rhythmically distinct from the continuation of the trill. A compound ornament is created by combining *accent plaintif* and *battement,* and another consists of an *accent* with a *verre cassé*. Basset further specifies that an appoggiatura from below must take half the duration of its note of resolution (p. 80), that the right-hand thumb should be extended towards the rose, that the little finger on the right hand should be close to the bridge but not behind it, and that the lute should be supported by and held against a table.

Basset then moves on to matters of right-hand technique, stressing the importance of sustaining pitches, and illustrating the signs used in tablature for striking the courses: *p* for thumb, onc to three dots for fingers, oblique and curved lines for sustains (*tenues*), and the use of numbers to indicate right-hand fingering (p. 85). All of these are symbols that are commonly encountered in seventeenth-century French lute music. But the extensive detail with which embellishment procedures are described far outweighs in significance other facets of Basset's instructions. Even what little information he supplies about left-hand fingering is in conjunction with the performance of *agréments*, and he notes that never had they been so frequent, nor so diverse, as in the present (p. 79).

The compositions by Basset, Mesangeau, and Chancy printed by Mersenne on pp. 87–9 of the *Harmonie Universelle* share many traits with other French lute works from the 1630s and slightly before, such as the employment of the *nouveaux accords*.[3] But it comes as a surprise that these works include only the comma for (probably) the appoggiatura from above, an occasional 'x' for the mordent, and markings for *tenues* and strokes with the right-hand index finger, all regularly employed in contemporaneous tablature sources. Mersenne remarks that the reader can apply to Basset or himself to discover how the former's method is to be applied to these

---

[2] The distinction between a trill and appoggiatura from above, the latter indicated by a comma, is often made in performance descriptions; for instance, in his late-century publications, Mouton distinguishes between an X" denoting a trill and a comma. In the *Pieces de luth de Denis Gaultier* the comma signifies only an appoggiatura if on a short duration, which is repeated if on a longer note.

[3] On p. 87 Mersenne lists two tunings: 'old' tuning and tuning no. 8, but not no. 10; the numbering is based on Table II in Wallace Rave, 'Some Manuscripts of French Lute Music 1630–1700: An Introductory Study', Ph.D. diss., University of Illinois, Urbana, 1972. A corrected and updated list of tunings can be found as Appendix B in David Ledbetter, *Harpsichord and Lute Music in 17th-Century France* (Bloomington, 1987).

compositions (p. 90). On the other hand, Basset notes in reference to the comma that 'most people use no other character to express all the different species [of ornaments]' (p. 79) – an offhand comment, perhaps, but when noted in conjunction with a wry remark he makes near the outset of Proposition X, takes on added significance:

Although many clever men have cultivated this art with much skill and dexterity, among which there are some who succeed so happily today in France, nevertheless there is [among them] only Adrian le Roy who has committed to writing some precepts of his instruction. They [the others] perhaps hope to acquire more glory in keeping this art hidden rather than divulging it . . .[4]

While some lutenists may have been reluctant teachers, it is likely that many were not, but were nevertheless inclined to 'hold back' information in their training of students, resulting in a condition of dependence among students with regard to their acquisition of pieces. The plausibility of this suspicion is supported, I believe, by the prevalence of manuscript collections made for student players. Teachers prepared anthologies of music for students, or entered works over time in the blank and lined pages of books then available for that purpose. Consideration of the music thus preserved, what its notation tells us about its performance, and how this relates to printed music and verbal descriptions of playing techniques, should thus prove informative, and help penetrate some of the reticence of lute players in revealing the secrets of their art.

Two volumes for lute were published by Pierre Ballard in 1631 and 1638, both entitled *Tablature du luth de différent autheurs sur les accords nouveaux*.[5] Chronologically flanking Mersenne's mighty tome, they contain music by Mesangeau, Dubut, Dufaut, and Chancy, among others.[6] In fact, among prominent composers in the new style only Ennemond Gautier (the 'vieux' Gautier) is not represented. The Ballard prints reveal *agrément* signs (comma, and much less frequently, 'x'), oblique

---

[4]   'Encore que plusieurs habiles hommes ayent cultivé cet art avec tant d'adresse & de dexterité, dans lequel il y en a qui reüssissent aujourd'huy si heureusement en nostre France, il n'y a neantmoins qu'Adrian le Roy que ayt donné par escrit quelques preceptes de son instruction, ils ont peut-estre creu acquerir plus de gloire à tenir cet Art caché, qu'à le divulguer . . .' (pp. 82–3). The reference to le Roy concerned his *Instruction de partir toute musique facilement en tabulature de luth* (Paris, 1557).

[5]   An earlier Pierre Ballard collection was published in 1623; only the title page is now extant. It is likely, though, that it contained a repertory older in style than the contents of the later volumes. Rather than *accords nouveaux*, the volume's title specifies 'l'accord ordinare et extraordinaire'. The tunings in question probably were the common 'Renaissance' and a number of *scordature* based on it, as found in other publications and manuscripts stemming from near the beginning of the seventeenth century.

[6]   Nearly the complete contents of these publications can be found in tablature and modern transcription in *Œuvres de Chancy, Bouvier, Belleville, Dubuisson, Chevalier* (Paris, 1967), *Œuvres de Dufaut* (Paris, 1965, 2nd edn, 1988), *Œuvres de Mesangeau* (Paris, 1971), all three edited by A. Souris and M. Rollin, and in *Œuvres des Dubut* (Paris, 1979) edited by M. Rollin and J.-M. Vaccaro.

and horizontal lines for *tenues*, and the dot customarily used to indicate a stroke with the index finger of the right hand. All of these signs are identical to the ones Mersenne employed in his tablature selections. The same symbols occur in greater or lesser measure in contemporaneous manuscripts. Although it cannot be declared unequivocally that the printed sources were not subjected to editing, they do transmit widely distributed versions of the compositions included.[7] As such, their contents can be taken as an index to *brisé* style in its early stages.[8]

Among the few manuscript sources sheltering works concordant with the Ballard prints, one is labelled herein *CNRS,* and another will be called *Dal 5.*[9] In the *Œuvres de Mesangeau*, it was persuasively argued that entries in both sources were made by the hand of René Mesangeau himself, that the manuscripts were essentially contemporaneous with the Ballard anthologies, have considerable repertory in common though mostly without composer specifications, and were compiled for students, at least one of whom was not far advanced.[10] As a result, both manuscripts display an impressive amount of performance information.[11] Because no work from it has yet been the basis for a modern edition, the following discussion will centre on the contents of *Dal 5.*

The study of *Dal 5* is complicated somewhat by the existence of entries made by at least three individuals.[12] Most of its pieces were entered by Mesangeau, but music was also copied into these pages by two other lutenists within the same time period, since works entered by all three are intermingled. Mesangeau rather brusquely overstruck and altered entries made by another hand of his own compositions on fols. 36v–37r. One hand, with entries intermittently from fol. 5r on, consistently employs an 'x' instead of a comma.

In its early folios *Dal 5* includes both right- and left-hand fingerings, providing in conjunction with careful placement of *tenue* lines an unusually detailed guide to performance. While left-hand fingering disappears by fol. 9r, the entries by

---

[7]   The most spectacular instances of 'editing' known to me occurs in the published anthologies of Jean-Baptiste Besard, *Thesaurus harmonicus* (Cologne, 1603) and the *Novus Partus* (Augsburg, 1617). Besard went to extremes in transforming the compositions of others into stylistic equivalents of his own, to the point that some have little in common with their appearances elsewhere.

[8]   Courantes by Mesangeau appear in a manuscript of the 1620s, Prague Univ. knihovna, Ms. IV G 18; they are presented in *Œuvres de Mesangeau*. However, there is little about them to suggest the new lute style, and they bear no performance markings or *agréments*.

[9]   *CNRS* is in reference to its present owner, the Centre National de la Recherche Scientifique, sometimes called 'Pa. Reymes'. *Dal 5* (or 'Panmure 5') is Edinburgh, Nat. Library of Scotland, Panmure mss., acq. 2763 no. 5 (from the collection of Lord Dalhousie).

[10]   *Œuvres de Mesangeau*, pp. xvii–xx; for a list of compositions shared by the two sources, see Rave, 'Some Manuscripts', p. 114.

[11]   Samples of both manuscripts can be inspected conveniently by recourse to facsimiles of a page from each included in the Mesangeau edition.

[12]   This does not include a work on fol. 57v which may have been entered by yet another person, nor pencilled-in additions on fol. 27v of ten- and eleven-course alternatives to pitches originally notated an octave higher.

Mesangeau continue to be very specific. There are few uncertainties about *agréments*, and sustained pitches are identified not only in the accompaniment (in the bass, mostly) but in the melody as well. Nothing is redundant; symbols are employed only where extended durations would not occur via open courses. It is important to note stylistic implications in this regard: while there is little question, I believe, that *style brisé* was eminently suited to the amateur player partly because of frequent employment of unstopped courses, the desire for treble/bass continuity encouraged their use as well.

The few instructions for left-hand fingering reinforces our observation about durations: Ex. 6.1 shows the third bar of a courante on fol. 7v. All chord members on the first beat could have been stopped with just the index finger, but Mesangeau requires the top pitch to be stopped with the second finger (the pertinent dots are always to the left of letters). This allows it to be sustained as specified while the first finger executes an appoggiatura on the passing note in the bass.

That the notational symbols do not leave much to chance can be seen in the Mesangeau *Allemande* in Ex. 6.2. A comparison with a concordance of this work contained in the 1638 Ballard print (no. 21 in the *Œuvres de Mesangeau*) reveals several discrepancies. Most of them involve rhythmic redistribution (e.g. bars 14–15), the addition or deletion of chord pitches (bars 12, 14), the placement of signs for *agréments*, and rhythmic details (at several points the two versions are at variance as to whether or not a dotted-quaver-and-semiquaver pattern is appropriate). Even without direct comparison the reader can observe the care taken in marking sustained pitches (a few included in the Ballard print are omitted, but new ones appear), slurs (not used in the Ballard collections), and right-hand use. The dot and vertical line below the initial chord at the opening of the second couplet specify that the index finger strikes the top course while the others are sounded by the thumb. In some other works Mesangeau indicated a sweep across the courses by means of a plus sign, placed either above a chord (a downstroke with the index finger) or below (probably a thumb sweep).

There are several observations to be made from this evidence. I have already referred to the extraordinary care with which Mesangeau has tried to ensure, by sign, fingering, and frequent dependence on open courses, that longer durations are maintained. As noted above, the prominence of unstopped bass courses (*bourdons*) in the new style may have stemmed more from the desire to maintain continuity of sound in the part-writing, even at the expense of clarity, than from any other factor. The presence of so many ornaments strengthens the perception of sonorous continuity; to some extent the actual placement and manner of execution may have been less significant than their mere presence, as Basset's comment about their increased significance in the new style can be taken to imply. Even the looser, more *brisé* texture itself, where present, may have evolved from a need to maintain musical

Ex. 6.1   *Dal. 5:* Anonymous courante

Ex. 6.2   René Mesangeau: *Allemande* from *Dal. 5*, fol. 44v

continuity without recourse to advanced technique. Complemented by a lower tessitura, the new style involved a more intimate, less assertive approach to performance, marked by traits designed to create sustained musical flow. Few manuscript tablatures, not even *CNRS*, can approach the wealth of detailed performance markings found in *Dal 5*. While all tablatures of French lute music published later include verbal descriptions of the symbols employed, rarely if ever is this true of manuscripts prepared by teachers.

THE BURWELL LUTE TUTOR

The music of Ennemond Gautier was far more extensively distributed in manuscripts than was Mesangeau's. While the informant responsible for the Burwell lute tutor (henceforth *Burwell*), thought to have been a Gautier student himself, cites Mesangeau as having given the lute 'his first perfection', he considered Gautier *le vieux* 'as the sun among the stars'.[13]

Although he lived in England, the *Burwell* informant/teacher claimed extensive knowledge about French lutenists and their performance. A fount of good advice, he nevertheless addresses the performance of *agréments* in rather perfunctory fashion. The essential comments about trills or 'shakes' are that many perform them too vigorously, some even striking each pitch individually, and that the Gautiers had condemned this excess. He overstates matters, though, in his claim that Gautier of Paris (Denis) 'would have no shake at all' (p. 34). A 'fall' (an appoggiatura rising in pitch) and roulades (the opposite) can have two or three pitches, he says, though it may be that he is merely describing slurred notes. A 'sigh or a pull' seems to be distinguished from two-note roulades only in concluding on an open course, while his 'stopped pull' concerns a mordent-like gesture using two stops, but again it is unclear with regard to employment. Like Basset, *Burwell* also claims the 'sting' (vibrato) is no longer used (p. 36; the usual symbol for it, an asterisk, appears occasionally in manuscripts, however) and that care should be taken to observe the 'tenues' (p. 30). Unfortunately, many of the tablature illustrations in *Burwell* are neither extensive nor complete enough to really be helpful.[14] Furthermore, one might have wished for an illustration clarifying the description of 'hammering' (p. 36), said to involve beating the strings several times without removing the finger very much, and explaining how this differs, if at all, from the trill.

Included towards the end of *Burwell* are complete compositions that show discrepancies among themselves regarding *agrément* symbols, a subject never actually

---

[13] *The Burwell Lute Tutor*, facsimile edition ed. Robert Spencer (Leeds, 1974); a modern edition with commentary appeared in: Thurston Dart, 'Miss Mary Burwell's Instruction Book for the Lute MS c1670', *GSJ* 11 (1958), pp. 3–69. References in the text are to the modern edition.

[14] An allemande by 'Mr Gaultier' intended to illustrate a stop on the eighth course was omitted; perhaps this was to have been the allemande by Vieux Gautier that his nephew later printed on pp. 54–5 of his *Livre de Tablature*.

discussed in the source. A *Courante Mr Pinel*[15] uses the comma for an appoggiatura from above, but writes as two different letters an appoggiatura from below, to be fitted within the duration of a crotchet. Immediately following is an allemande by the elder Gautier[16] which employs an inverted 'v' as the (inferred) sign for the same embellishment. It thus appears that each composition was obtained from a different source – one indication among several which suggest that the manuscript is a composite.[17]

Nevertheless, *Burwell* contains important passages on the questions of fingering and rhythm. As in Basset, note is made (p. 29) of the preference for striking adjacent courses in a chord with the first finger, over the use of one finger for each course, as formerly; the informant claims that the old way resulted in striking only the uppermost string of a course.[18] This technique is indicated by vertical lines following the letters. Additionally, sometimes the highest pitch of the chord is repeated by striking it with the middle finger following (notation is not given for this event). Aside from the implied concern for sonority – such as the emphasis on striking both strings of a course – these techniques ensure that chord members will not be sounded exactly together, especially if the top pitch is restruck. Once again, as in Basset's instructions, there is concern for proper right-hand technique: 'If a master give you a lesson, desire him to give you the fingering.' In another comment the author notes that it is good to strike the lowest string of a bass course a little before the other strings and courses: 'it is a rule that the thumb must always march first' (p. 32). In a chord made up of notes on adjacent courses, the thumb strikes all but the topmost (this may or may not contradict the comment above about the use of the index finger). Sarabandes must be played 'loosely' after the manner of the guitar, i.e. strummed sometimes with the thumb, sometimes with the forefinger only (p. 39). He does say – perhaps inconsistently, given his comment on p. 32 mentioned just above – that the notes of a chord are to be struck 'altogether at once'. When a chord made up of adjacent courses is repeated, it is sounded the first time with the thumb, then with the index finger.

---

15 *Œuvres de Pinel*, no. 44; although a *unicum*, this piece illustrates modes of *agrément* notation seen in other sources of Pinel's music. This entails the use of symbols similar to those found in *Les œuvres de Pierre Gaultier* (Rome, 1638; facsimile edn Geneva, 1974). They include an 'x' for trill, an asterisk meaning vibrato, a comma for *accent* (appoggiatura from above), a half circle below a letter probably signifying an inverted mordent, while a full circle seems to mean an appoggiatura from below. A *marteler* (quickly played mordent) is marked by this sign: ⌐ He also employs the usual curved lines for slurs and a few instances of *tenues*. Some however, are less often used in manuscripts, where the works of this composer are seldom encountered.

16 *Œuvres de vieux Gautier*, no. 8 (*unicum*).

17 The Vieux Gautier composition just mentioned is said to be in the 'goat's tuning' (*ton de chèvre*), by which is meant here a standard D minor tuning but with the sixth course raised to B♭ (tuning no. 13); however the same term is elsewhere explained (p. 21 of Dart's edition) as one in which 'all the little play [top six courses] is like the ordinary tuning', but with some *bourdon* courses sharpened.

18 The 'older' technique is specified in the Gautier prints, however.

Other revealing observations appear at the end of the treatise: a warning not to sing to the lute; that it is used commonly during the 'going to bed of the Kings of France'; that you should not play too many pieces or use too many tunings if you are to play well; and that 'you are but a bungler' if you play too fast, do not use the proper fingering, and do not keep the time. Regarding tempo, though (about which there is little explicit information from the time), he asserts that

When one plays alone you may take some liberty [with tempo] because you follow no other's playing. You may choose a slow time or a quick time, and besides allow something to the graces [rubato? less tempo rigidity?]; as when you walk alone, you walk as you please . . .

This might indicate that tempo need not be maintained rigidly; on the other hand, in conjunction with the remarks about 'hammering' cited above, it is related that 'all these things must be done without losing the measure . . .'

The 'soul' of the lute is best acquired by listening to violins, singing, and especially someone playing well; he adds,

you may get that art by breaking the strokes; that is, dividing of them by stealing half a note [i.e. duration] from one note and bestowing of it upon the next note. That will make the playing . . . more airy and skipping.

There follows a tablature illustration showing a scalar passage notated in quavers but to be played, for the 'humouring of a lesson', as dotted quavers and semiquavers, and not the reverse as could be inferred in the preceding quoted passage. The passage conforms to some of the common *dicta* for *notes inégales* – that they are based on the regular occurrence of a durational value shorter than a beat's length, and on pitch content dominated by stepwise melodic movement. Then there appears a brief passage illustrating *séparé* of a two-pitch chord with a crotchet's duration into two quavers. Furthermore, by extension from the recommendation above, the bass can steal half again of the time, thus producing a dotted quaver and semiquaver in performance from what was notated as two simultaneous pitches of a crotchet's duration, but with a short diagonal line placed between them; this is followed by another crotchet:

There is [notated] but two strokes here and two crotchets. You must make two quavers [of the first stroke] and a crotchet in breaking; that is, dividing the (chord) playing first the (bass pitch) and then the (pitch) of the second [i.e., the treble]. Besides that, you may make a quaver and half of the [bass note], and a semiquaver of the second.[19]

---

[19] *Burwell*, p. 47. Contributing to the ambiguity of the description is a (presumed) error in the tablature illustration in specifying the fret used for the bass pitch, plus the absence – one of many in the manuscript – of rhythmic indications. Further, the tablature places the diagonal line as if it were a *tenue* and not a *séparé*. However, a different hand made all the tablature entries in *Burwell*, perhaps including an error here. I can discover no other plausible interpretation of the passage.

These passages thus provide (1) an early mention of the technique of separating in time two (or more) pitches notated as a chord, (2) an early specification of *notes inégales*,[20] and (3) a description suggesting that both can be employed simultaneously!

In sum, the Burwell lute tutor was believed to have been compiled by John Rogers around 1670, but the character of its advice, the inclusion of music in four different tunings, the lute works included, and the composers named suggest that it reflects French practices from about mid-century.[21] It stresses many traits already advocated by Basset. Particularly notable in this respect is the extended instruction concerning right-hand technique. However, *Burwell*'s most distinctive contributions to our understanding of performance practice are, in my judgement, the descriptions of rhythmic nuances implying rubato-like flexibility. These include insistence on brevity of the notes concluding a cadential trill (to be as short as possible – most probably shorter than written), separation (*séparé*) into two shorter values of pitches notated as a simultaneity, a *notes inégales* process of lengthening a note on a beat at the expense of the offbeat pitch following, and the descriptions of strumming and the like, especially in the usual domain for such activity, the sarabande.

THE INSTRUCTIONS GIVEN BY PERRINE

A distinctive feature of solo lute manuscripts compiled around mid century is the appearance of short diagonal lines placed between pitches notated as chords; earlier tablatures seldom, if ever, include them. *Burwell* is the first document to describe their meaning. Later discussions of playing technique, the Gautier, Gallot, and Mouton prints included, mention them as a matter of course, and the symbol is employed regularly in their music. But none of them specifies the exact degree of deviation from the notated rhythmic value. To be sure, there would be no reason to expect unanimity on such a matter, and rhythmic flexibility in the performance of *séparés* may have been common. But the existence of a symbol for the technique implies it was more than a mere arpeggio, especially since certain right-hand techniques already assured arpeggiation (e.g. the sweeps with thumb or forefinger). The usual explanation given the symbol in most of the CNRS editions of seventeenth-century lute music has been *arpegé*. But this is not what was described by the *Burwell* informant, nor by the only writer to discuss the matter extensively, one Perrine (given name unknown).

---

[20] The description in the initial but not the latter passage is quoted in Stephen E. Hefling, *Rhythmic Alteration in Seventeenth- and Eighteenth-Century Music* (New York, 1993), pp. 51–2.

[21] Another English document of the 1670s, Thomas Mace's *Musick's Monument* (London 1676; facsimile edn Paris, 1966) confirms some of the observations found in *Burwell*, but its idiosyncrasies, insularity, and antique views place it far distant from contemporary practices in France, despite its good sense, sound advice, and humour.

Perrine's first publication, *Livre de musique pour le luth* (*privilège* granted in 1679), contains instructions for lute performance and an explanation of and justification for the author's method of staff notation for lute music, needed, he says, because reading tablature had caused most players to abandon 'ce Royal instrument'. In most respects his comments are conventional; however, a statement that *tenues* and 'Lettres séparés' in tablature are expressed by the note values in staff notation deserves some amplification. Unfortunately, Perrine appended only one piece, a well-known courante by Gautier *le vieux*, to illustrate his argument. Besides being far too brief to serve as an example, its notation was somewhat carelessly executed, which could not have helped the author's cause.

Perhaps it was awareness of this that led Perrine to issue his *Pieces de luth en musique* (hereinafter, *Perrine*), published in 1680 or slightly later.[22] It comprises an anthology in staff notation of compositions by Ennemond and Denis Gautier that begins with a revised version of the very courante appended to the earlier publication. Its contents have been frequently mistaken to be for keyboard performance, probably because the 'clavecin' is mentioned on the title page. This was most likely a ploy to increase sales; in fact, keyboard performance is mentioned within the text only once in passing, and the detailed notation is unequivocally designed for lute. The music proper is preceded by a description of lute technique and notational symbols, including, perhaps most importantly, staff-notated illustrations of *séparés*. Apparently Perrine now thought it advisable to give up the idea of exact notation of *séparés* implied in his earlier publication, reverting instead to the simple tablature symbol of the diagonal line, by now a commonplace.

The *séparé* illustrations Perrine provides are for three durations, each on both two- and three-note chords, followed by an explanation of how to proceed with four-note *séparé* chords. The order of pitches is always given as ascending; the lowest pitch generally receives half or more of the notated duration. For a quaver's duration, a two-note chord is split evenly; for both a dotted quaver and a crotchet, the top note receives only a semiquaver's duration. For three-note chords there is an even succession if on a dotted quaver, but on a crotchet the last two pitches evenly divide the final quaver duration; in a dotted crotchet the second pitch is sounded only after a delay of a dotted quaver, while the top pitch occupies the final quaver. The author then explains that the pitches of a four-note chord (found only, he says, in 'signe majeur' and 'la mesure binaire') of a crotchet's duration are either evenly distributed (an exception to the generality above about bass pitches), or the bass receives three-fourths of the duration, the other pitches to be separated during the remaining semiquaver value. He does not reveal why these options exist; perhaps he

[22]   Perrine, *Pieces de Luth en Musique avec des Regles pour les toucher parfaitement sur le Luth, et sur le Clavessin* (Paris, *privilege du Roy*, 1680; facsimile edn Geneva, 1983). 'En musique' means in staff notation.

was simply reflecting alternative customs of performance. Nor does he attempt to explain the inconsistency among the various examples in the durations assigned to the last-sounded pitch.[23]

Taken by itself, Perrine's discussion of *séparés* might seem excessively rigid and even misleading, the practical limits of notation acting rather as a Procrustean bed to which the actuality of rhythmic flexibility was made to conform. And this may well have been the case, remembering that he, too, advocated what can only be described as *notes inégales*:

Finally, it must be observed, in order to find the true movement of all sorts of pieces for lute, that the first parts, or first parts of parts of beats [*temps de la mesure*; i.e. first part of a crotchet or of a quaver] must be longer than the others.[24]

But such an inference must be tempered by realizing how conscientiously Perrine approached the challenge of providing staff notation for this music, specifying ornaments, right-hand strokes, and especially durations to a degree of precision not feasible in tablature notation.[25] Moreover, it will be recalled that *Burwell* had already broached the topic of *inégales*, albeit in sketchy fashion.

Most works in *Perrine* also appear in the published Gautier tablatures of more than a decade earlier. Not surprisingly, Perrine's readings are distinct in several respects from the tablature versions, not least in their greater frequency of *séparés*. In part this may be due to the generally restrained employment of *agréments* in the Gautier prints. But the *Livre de Tablature*[26] contains some music by Vieux Gautier in versions startlingly austere, nearly devoid of performance indications other than commas and the rare appearance of a sign for slur or *tenue*.[27] Perhaps Denis preferred not to 'interpret' his uncle's compositions, for they lack even right-hand fingering, although it is abundant in his own compositions. There is, however, an alternative explanation: 'final' versions of his late uncle's works might not have been achieved before Denis himself died, leaving actual publication to his widow. And there are other signs that he had not completed preparation: the *Avertisement* lacks an illustration for one of the ornaments (*l'etoufement* = smothering or damping the pitch, an effect not present or even mentioned in the earlier *Pieces de Luth*); and it ends with a notice of a forthcoming volume by M. de Montarcis which is claimed to be based on Gautier's method but which does not seem to have ever appeared.

---

23   *Perrine*, pp. 6–9. I have not seen in manuscripts any four-note chords bearing *séparé* signs. In the course of his review of the performance instructions given by Denis Gautier in his prints, David Buch reproduces Perrine's *séparé* examples; see his edition of Denis Gaultier, *La Rhétorique des Dieux*, Recent Researches in the Music of the Baroque Era 62 (Madison, WI, 1990), p. xiii.

24   Perrine, *Pieces de luth*, p. 9.

25   A few pieces in Perrine's notation can be seen in *Œuvres de Vieux Gautier*, nos. 68–73.

26   The *Livre de tablature des pieces de luth* (Paris, *ca.* 1672) has been reprinted in facsimile together with *Pieces de Luth de Denis Gaultier . . . (ca.* 1669) by Minkoff (Geneva, 1975).

27   *Burwell* (p. 33) reported that a 'cadence' (or 'trillo') had formerly only appeared at the end of a piece, but that 'old Gaultier' had 'intermixed' them 'in all parts'.

In this scenario, Denis would have had compositions by his uncle in 'core' versions lacking most of the accoutrements required for performance. This circumstance is reminiscent of the condition in which the music of Denis (plus at least one piece by his uncle) was presented in the manuscript known as *La Rhétorique des Dieux*, assembled about twenty years earlier. In that collection only a handful of *agréments* appear, and no other symbols are found except for indications for vertical alignment between pitches widely separated on the tablature staff.[28] Were these versions merely supplied in this format by Denis to the compiler of the manuscript, thus to be copied *verbatim*? There is no evidence that Gautier had a direct role in the manuscript's conception or preparation; most of the fanciful titles given the compositions in this source, for instance, appear nowhere else. Although the informant in *Burwell* had commented on the restraint of the Gautiers regarding *agréments*, the earlier Gautier print, unquestionably prepared by Denis, does exhibit performance guides of many sorts, as do his own compositions in the posthumous volume.

THE ROBARTS LUTE BOOK

Some notion of the discrepancies between the Vieux Gautier music in the *Livre de Tablature* and that in other sources can be illustrated in the first couplet of one of his courantes (Ex. 6.3). In this instance, the printed tablature version reveals no performance indications whatsoever. In comparison, *Perrine* shows considerable 'interpretation', particularly evident in its looser, more *brisé* approach.[29] The *Robarts* version, from a manuscript antedating both prints, was prepared explicitly for a student/amateur by a professional.[30] Its contents are laden with guides for the player, including indications for right-hand fingering and the usual *agrément*, *séparé*, and *tenue* signs (including an especially intriguing instance in bar 6). As is usual in manuscripts, no explanations are provided for the interpretation of performance symbols. It can be seen that in no single bar do the three sources agree completely among themselves. *Perrine* more often corresponds to *Robarts*, especially in the rhythmic separation of chordal pitches, although in this instance the former employs explicit notation instead of the *séparé* symbols used in the manuscript and commonly

---

[28] See the facsimile in the supplement to Buch's edition of *La Rhétorique*. The 'bare bones' of the pieces in *La Rhétorique* so distressed an earlier transcriber/editor that he substituted versions of works found also in the Gautier prints whenever possible, even in the facsimile volume. See *La Rhétorique des Dieux et autres pièces de luth de Denis Gautier*, ed. A. Tessier, Publications de la société française de musicologie, vols. 6–7 (Paris, 1932).

[29] (In his notation *p* = thumb; *a* = forefinger; an 'x' signifies an appoggiatura from above; the numbers refer to courses on which, exceptionally, the so-indicated pitches are to be played.

[30] *The Robarts Lute Book c. 1654–68*, introduction by Robert Spencer (Kilkenny, 1978). Among its symbols is one that looks like two adjacent commas; contexts suggest that it signifies a mordent.

⊕ eighth rest w/half note in original

Ex. 6.3   *Courante* by Vieux Gautier, opening couplet (three versions)

by Perrine himself. The suspicion that the *Livre* contains a 'core' version of this work is strengthened by the absence of even a *port-de-voix* on the downbeat, a nearly obligatory event found in both *Perrine* (notated) and *Robarts* (conventional symbol) that would perhaps be executed by any knowledgeable lutenist encountering the *Livre* version, anyway.

Robarts displays an abundance of *séparés*, and throughout the manuscript the musical contexts in which they appear suggest a performance according to the directions given in *Perrine*. This is true of some other manuscripts of this period, such

as *Pa. Viée*, dated 1653 by Johanes Viée, its original owner.[31] Performance infor-
mation in the latter source is copious and consistent and the usual symbols are found,
although an inverted 'v' placed before the letter here seems to denote *martelement*.
An asterisk (e.g. fol. 13r), perhaps a sign for vibrato, appears on rare occasions.
Again, the *séparé* signs of Perrine can be applied with confidence. It is unlikely that
Perrine's prescriptions represented some sort of doctrine; in the prints of Denis
Gautier, Gallot, and Mouton the symbol is described merely as separation. Clearly,
however, it indicated much more than casual arpeggiation. Its impact on the music
is considerable, even aside from obviously greater rhythmic activity. For instance, the
séparé technique ensures rhythmic delay in the melody, thus elevating the preceding
melodic pitch, if it is sustained, to the status of a suspension.

In an earlier article I discussed the effects a manuscript 'editor' or teacher could
have on the texts of compositions within manuscripts compiled at the end of the
seventeenth century or later.[32] The same applies for earlier sources as well; both
Robarts and *Pa. Viée* have tablature corrections, alterations, and additions, perhaps
made in the process of teaching. Note was made earlier of Mesangeau works that
underwent changes from one source to another even if the composer himself
provided the different 'versions'. Reminiscent of Jehan Basset, the informant in
Burwell goes so far as to say of one section in the tutor (p. 25):

[Chapter VII] is the golden key . . . the want of the knowledge whereof made the scholars
necessitated to continue their masters without profit or pleasure, they [their masters] never
writing the lessons as they must be played, that they may by word of mouth tell them one
thing this day and tomorrow another, that which they might write upon the book and
whereof they might perfect rules and sure precepts. For if they should give this secret, or
mark all upon the book so that the scholar of himself could learn any lesson . . . [Then] the
master should lose all his scholars but one.

The Mesangeau allemande discussed above exists in two other manuscripts; one is
CNRS, where it is substantially divergent from *Dal 5*, even though both were
notated by the composer himself, and from the Ballard printed version. Another
source, *Vm7 6211*,[33] the relevant portion of which dates from before 1650, contains
a notational style and repertory similar to *CNRS* and *Dal 5*, but without their
extensive performance information. Its reading of a Mesangeau work deviates
substantially from Ballard's printed version, yet some of the non-Mesangeau pieces
it contains were copied *verbatim* from the 1638 Ballard tablature, including a notational

---

[31] Paris, Bibliothèque Nationale, Rés. Vmf ms. 51.
[32] Wallace Rave, 'Remarks on Gallot Sources: How Tablatures Differ', *JLSA* 20–21 (1987–8 [©1992]),
      pp. 87–107.
[33] Paris, Bibliothèque Nationale, Ms. Vm7 6211.

error.[34] Was all this material obtained from Mesangeau, who would have altered his own piece yet again?

Perhaps a piece in *style brisé* was less an unalterable, finished composition than a core idea to be enhanced anew in performance or instruction by nuances and *agréments* applied *ad hoc*. What would have counted, then, was an extemporaneous performance manner, rather than a fixed compositional entity.[35] It is difficult otherwise to account for the infinitude of variables existing among versions of the same works within the repertory as a whole – that is, the extraordinarily high degree of inconsistency they exhibit. By mid century the style had become even more 'broken', if the appearance of *séparé* symbols is any guide, but there was little change otherwise; for instance, the same few dance genres continue to dominate, within them the same musical gestures appeared regularly, and composers continued to avoid the intricacies of motivic development and other techniques of expansion such as melodic sequence.[36] While compositions themselves were clearly valued for their quality, they seem not to have encompassed all of the performance nuances. Even in modern performances, music in the *style brisé* continues to fascinate, less for its logic, variety, or originality, than for the subtlety and freshness it requires in performance.

[34] Works by Bouvier and Dubut are on fols. 40r–42r; the latter (*Œuvres de Dubut*, no.1) contains the error mentioned in the text.

[35] For a parallel in the seventeenth-century Italian lute repertory, see Victor Coelho, *The Manuscript Sources of Seventeenth-Century Italian Lute Music* (New York, 1995), pp. 39–44, as well as Coelho's central thesis about 'autonomy' in his chapter in this volume.

[36] Attempts to demonstrate otherwise, as by Buch in the commentary for his edition of *La Rhétorique*, serve to underscore how subtle these techniques are, if present.

THE VIHUELA: PERFORMANCE PRACTICE, STYLE, AND CONTEXT

JOHN GRIFFITHS

This diversity of modes, melodies, consonances and duly proportioned rhythms, together with many other beauties are found by musicians on the vihuela, united in one, and more perfectly than on any other instrument. For from the vihuela comes the most perfect and deepest music, the gentlest and sweetest concord, that which most pleases the ear and enlivens the mind; moreover, that of greatest efficacy, which most moves and ignites the soul of those who hear it.[1]

For an instrument played as extensively as the *vihuela de mano* was in sixteenth-century Spain, it has left an astonishingly small inheritance of music, instruments, and other information related to its performance. We are nevertheless fortunate that limited resources should yield such a richness of perspectives. The present study begins by examining several of the cultural issues regarding the vihuela prior to considering questions of style, taste, and instrumental technique. The reasons for this approach are simple: an understanding of context develops an image of the cultural and intellectual world of the original practitioners, while more detailed questions of musical style and instrumental technique, respectively, delineate the artistic objectives of performance practice and strategies for its implementation. It is always my hope that informed, historically based practice should not be restricted by the limitations of source materials, but should produce artistic performances in which the final product is greater than the sum of all the parts.

The core of what we know about the vihuela consists of seven well-known books of printed music, a handful of pieces in manuscript, a small number of theoretical sources and illustrations, two surviving instruments, and a patchwork of documents that offer fleeting glimpses of the instrument and its world. The discovery

---

[1] Enríquez de Valderrábano, *Silva de sirenas*, fol. [5r]: 'Esta diversidad de tonos, sones, consonancias, y rhrthmos [*sic*] de devida proporción, con otros muchos primores músicos se hallan en una vihuela, todo iunto, y más perfectamente que en otro instrumento alguno. Ca en la vihuela es la más perfecta y profunda música, la más suave y dulce consonantia, la que más applaze al oydo y alegra el entendimiento, y otrosí la de mayor efficacia, que más mueve y enciende los ánimos de los que oyen.'

of new materials continues to augment and refine our knowledge of the instrument, its music, and its players, while John Ward's 1953 account of the vihuela and its performance practice remains the most authoritative, central point of reference.[2] More recent studies have examined the early development of the instrument prior to the emergence of notated vihuela music, the Italian variant of the vihuela known as the *viola da mano*, and a number of newly identified manuscript sources of music.[3] More significantly, it is now understood that the vihuela was not exclusively a court instrument, but that it was popular among the middle class and as important a means in its own day as the modern compact disc in increasing access to polyphonic art music.[4]

The life of the *vihuela de mano* stretches from the last quarter of the fifteenth century until the early 1600s. The emergence of the Renaissance vihuela has been traced from the mid fifteenth century, largely on the basis of iconographical evidence.[5] Ian Woodfield places the origins of the vihuela in Aragon around the middle of the fifteenth century as a single instrument that was both plucked and bowed; independent, differently constructed plucked and bowed models began to emerge from the 1480s. The Spanish origins of the instrument are attested to by Tinctoris in *De inventione et usu musicae* (*ca.* 1487), who describes it as 'hispanorum invento'. Most of the iconographical representations before 1500 show the plucked vihuela being played with a plectrum. Woodfield's claim that the bowing technique of the *vihuela de arco* resulted from the adoption of the Moorish underhand bowgrip of the *rabel* might also have parallels in plucked performance. Civic records offer complementary written evidence about players from this period. While most of the early iconography shows vihuelas being played in allegorical liturgical configurations, there are several references to blind players of the bowed *vihuela de arco* and *rabel* who were *oracioneros*, presumably professional ballad singers. Apprenticeship contracts show these musicians to have spent periods of between three and six years learning their repertory from memory and to play the bowed instruments mentioned.[6] While these documents are not specifically related to the plucked vihuela, they come from the period when no distinction is made between plucked and

[2] John Ward, 'The "Vihuela de mano" and its Music, 1536–1576', Ph.D. diss., New York University, 1953.

[3] The early history of the vihuela is documented in Ian Woodfield, *The Early History of the Viol* (Cambridge, 1984); the *viola da mano* is discussed in Ward, 'The Vihuela de mano', pp. 59–63, and James Tyler, *The Early Guitar* (Oxford, 1980). For details of recovered manuscripts, see Juan José Rey, *Ramillete de flores: Colección inédita de piezas para vihuela (1593)* (Madrid, 1975); Antonio Corona-Alcalde, 'A Vihuela Manuscript in the Archivo de Simancas', *The Lute* 26 (1986), pp. 3–20; John Griffiths, 'Berlin Mus. MS 40032 y otros nuevos hallazgos en el repertorio para vihuela', in *España en la Música del Occidente*, ed. Emilio Casares et al., 2 vols. (Madrid, 1987), vol. I, pp. 323–4; and Antonio Corona-Alcalde, 'The Earliest Vihuela Tablature: A Recent Discovery', *EM* 20 (1992), pp. 594–600.

[4] See John Griffiths, 'At Court and at Home with the *Vihuela de mano*', *JLSA* 22 (1989), 1–27.

[5] Literary reference to the vihuela has been traced back to the anonymous *Libro de Apolonio* (*ca.* 1250).

[6] Among the players in the documents reported by Pallarés Jiménez are Juan de Vitoria and Juan Pérez de Guernica (1462), Ramón Recalde and Iñigo García Landa (1466), and García Jiménez and Juan Sánchez de Córdoba (1469), in each case master and apprentice.

bowed models, and further research might be able to connect the practices of these *oracioneros* directly to the accompanied singing of secular *romances* like those found in the sixteenth-century vihuela books. Although referring to the *vihuela de arco,* the report by Tinctoris to having heard it used 'ad historium recitationem' similarly waits to be connected directly to this tradition.[7]

Numerous early references to the vihuela link it to Moorish culture, and they locate its use within an urban, rather than courtly, context – one that points to a direct link with oral tradition. The Moorish connection is confirmed by documents recently brought to light in Zaragoza that refer from 1463 to Moorish instrument makers such as Juce and Lope de Albariel, 'maestros de hacer vihuelas y laudes', that is, master builders of vihuelas and lutes.[8] While most of the iconography presented by Woodfield of late fifteenth-century vihuelas is of Valencian provenance, parallel documentary evidence from Zaragoza confirms the continuing practice there of vihuela playing by Christian, Jewish, and Moorish musicians.[9] In line with the assumption that the decline of the lute in Spain was a consequence of the expulsion or conversions of non-Christians, we find instances of musicians described in the 1480s as lutenists who are cited by 1500 as vihuelists.[10] It is precisely at this time that the presence of the vihuela is noted at court.[11]

During the period in which Spanish tablatures were printed (1536–76), vihuela performance practice is more attentively documented, after which our knowledge again becomes hazier. Although manuscript sources exist after 1580 that document a continued practice, it is nevertheless the period in which taste and musical styles began to change radically in Spain and vihuela playing declined in favour of the guitar. In the early seventeenth century its waning fortunes are aptly portrayed in Sebastián de Covarrubias's *Tesoro de la lengua Castellana o Española* (1611), in a definition more heavy-hearted than customary in lexicography:

This instrument has been highly esteemed in our time, and there have been most excellent players, but since the invention of the guitar, there are only few who devote themselves to the

---

[7] *De inventione et usu musicae* (*ca.* 1487). Tinctoris had visited Catalonia during his employment at the court of Naples. See Woodfield, *The Early History of the Viol,* p. 79.

[8] Miguel Angel Pallarés Jiménez, 'Aportación documental para la historia de la música en Aragón en el último tercio del siglo XV', 5 parts, *Nassarre* 7/1 (1991), pp. 175–212; 7/2 (1991), pp. 171–212; 8/1 (1992), pp. 213–74; 8/2 (1992), pp. 171–244; 9/1 (1993), pp. 227–310.

[9] For example, Rodrigo Castillo, lutenist and vihuelist active between 1488 and 1500; Mossé Patí *'judío, tañedor de vihuela'* active 1485–8; and Alí Aucert, a Moor who entered the service of don Pedro de Mendoza in 1489 on the condition that he teach him to play the vihuela, are reported in Pallarés Jiménez, 'Aportación documental' Pt. III, Documents 69 and 139; Pt. IV, Documents 75 and 110.

[10] The page Rodrigo Castillo (in the documents mentioned in n. 9) is described in 1488 as a 'tañedor de laúd', and in 1500 as a 'tañedor de vihuela'.

[11] Between 1489 and 1500 Rodrigo Donaire was a salaried member of the House of Castile as a player of the vihuela and a singer, although the references fail to clarify if he played the vihuela *de arco* or *de mano.* See Tess Knighton, 'The *a cappella* Heresy in Spain: An Inquisition into the Performance of the Cancionero Repertory', *EM* 20 (1992), pp. 574–6.

study of the vihuela. It has been a great loss, because on it could be played all kinds of notated music, and now the guitar is no more than a cowbell, so easy to play, especially in the strummed way, that there isn't a stable boy who isn't a guitarist.[12]

Not surprisingly, the most informative sources for information on vihuela technique and musical style are the seven known printed vihuela tablatures, by Luis Milán (*El Maestro*, 1536), Luis de Narváez (*Los seys libros del Delphín*, 1538), Alonso Mudarra (*Tres Libros de Música*, 1546), Enríquez de Valderrábano (*Silva de sirenas*, 1547), Diego Pisador (*Libro de música de Vihuela*, 1552), Miguel de Fuenllana (*Orphénica Lyra*, 1554), and Esteban Daza (*El Parnasso*, 1576).[13] Additional practical information is contained in a few paragraphs found in the *Libro de Cifra Nueva* (Alcalá de Henares, 1557) of Venegas de Henestrosa, the earliest of the Spanish publications whose titles advertise their appropriateness for any polyphonic instrument – keyboard, harp, or vihuela.[14] The *Declaración de instrumentos musicales* by Juan Bermudo also offers considerable insight; Santa María's *Arte de tañer fantasía* is less central.[15] These sources have all been examined with reference to performance practice by Ward and in Joan Myers's survey of vihuela technique.[16] In addition, Charles Jacobs has investigated questions of tempo and metre,[17] and both Annoni and Freis have made detailed studies of the information given by Bermudo relating to the vihuela.[18]

The ambitions of sixteenth-century vihuelists may have been quite different from the goals of performers today. The players were largely members of the professional classes for whom the courtly model of society was dominant, and their spiritual and intellectual lives were influenced by the currents of humanism and religious piety

---

[12] 'Este instrumento ha sido hasta nuestros tiempos muy estimado, y ha habido excelentísimos músicos; pero después que se inventaron las guitarras, son muy pocos los que se dan al estudio de la vihuela. Ha sido una gran pérdida, porque en ella se ponía todo género de música puntada, y ahora la guitarra no es más que un cencerro, tan fácil de tañer, especialmente en lo rasgueado, que no hay mozo de caballos que no sea músico de guitarra.'

[13] Full titles and detailed inventories are given in Howard Mayer Brown, *Instrumental Music Printed Before 1600* (Cambridge, MA, 1965).

[14] Luis Venegas de Henestrosa, *Libro de Cifra Nueva para Tecla, Harpa, y Vihuela* (Alcalá de Henares, 1557), ed. Higinio Anglés in *La música en la corte de Carlos V. Con la transcripción del 'Libro de Cifra Nueva para Tecla, Harpa y Vihuela' de Luys Venegas de Henestrosa (Alcalá de Henares, 1557)*, Monumentos de la Música Española 2–3 (Barcelona, 1944; rpt 1965). This interchangeability is repeated in the titles of two other important sources: Tomás de Santa María, *Libro llamado Arte de tañer fantasia, assi para Tecla como para Vihuela, y todo instrumento, en que se pudiere tañer a tres, y a quatro vozes, y a mas* (Valladolid, 1565), and Hernando de Cabezón, *Obras de Musica para tecla, arpa y vihuela* (Madrid, 1578).

[15] Juan Bermudo, *Comiença el libro llamado declaración de instrumentos musicales . . .* (Osuna, 1555); rpt ed. Macario Santiago Kastner, Documenta Musicologica 11 (Kassel, 1957); Tomás de Santa María, *Libro llamado arte de tañer fantasía* (Valladolid, 1565), translated as *The Art of Playing Fantasia*, ed. Almonte C. Howell and Warren E. Hultberg (Pittsburgh, 1991).

[16] Joan Myers, 'Vihuela Technique', *JLSA* 1 (1968), pp. 15–18.

[17] Charles Jacobs, *Tempo Notation in Renaissance Spain*, Musicological Studies 8 (Brooklyn, 1964).

[18] Maria Therese Annoni, 'Tuning, Temperament, and Pedagogy for the Vihuela in Juan Bermudo's *Declaración de instrumentos musicales* (1555)', Ph.D. diss., Ohio State University, 1989; Wolfgang Freis, 'Perfecting the Perfect Instrument: Fray Juan Bermudo on the Tuning and Temperament of the *vihuela de mano*', *EM* 23 (1995), pp. 421–36.

that were present in many aspects of Spanish life. Many of the players were amateurs with professions in law, public administration, and the church. Some were professional soldiers, such as the poet Garcilaso de la Vega (1503–36) and the vihuelist Luis de Guzmán (d. 1528) whose music was known to both Bermudo and Narváez.[19] Of the published vihuela composers, Narváez, Fuenllana, and Valderrábano were professionals, Luis Milán was a gentleman courtier, Alonso Mudarra a cleric, and both Diego Pisador and Esteban Daza remained middle-class amateurs. Both professionals and non-professionals such as Luis Milán would have performed habitually at court, and it was probably in these surroundings that the young page Luis Zapata heard Narváez and remembered him as an extraordinarily gifted improviser.[20]

Court performances most closely resemble the modern concert in both their acoustic conditions and the dynamics between performer and audience, but they were also isolated events within a society whose social rituals did not include public concerts. Most of the surviving references to vihuela playing do not describe court settings. In the main, they are abstract representations of the prowess of individual players that are silent about both the music they played and the settings in which they were heard. Some accounts appear to derive from small gatherings, however, or circumstances where the commentator is perhaps the only witness of the performance. One such description is of the small informal gathering celebrated in the Madrid home of the organist Bernardo Clavijo, as given by Vicente Espinel in *La vida del escudero Marcos Obregón*. He writes that 'hearing maestro Clavijo on the keyboard, his daughter Bernardina on the harp and Lucas de Matos on the seven-course vihuela, imitating each other with serious and uncommon turns, is the best thing that I have heard in my life'.[21]

The real purpose of many sixteenth-century literary references to the vihuela, it would seem, is the enumeration of the personal qualities and talents of virtuous or exemplary individuals. Such references reveal the musical capacity of a good vihuelist to be equated with moral virtue and spiritual enlightenment along the lines advocated by Castiglione, who lived the last year of his life in Spain and whose influential *Cortegiano* was first published in Spanish translation in 1534. An important aspect of vihuela playing was the individualistic pursuit of enlightenment and edification through study and self-improvement. Social performance at intimate domestic

---

[19]   See Juan José Rey, 'El vihuelista Luis de Guzmán', *RM* 4 (1981), pp. 129–32, and Garcilaso de la Vega, *Obras con anotaciones de Hernando de Herrera* (Seville, 1580).

[20]   Luis Zapata, *Miscelánea* (*ca.* 1592), ed Pascual de Gayangos, Memorial Histórico Español 9 (Madrid, 1859), p. 95; translated in Ward, 'The Vihuela de mano', p. 381. Descriptions of Milán's own performance practices are recorded in his *El Cortesano* (1560) and discussed in Luis Gasser, *Luis Milán on Sixteenth-Century Performance Practice* (Bloomington, 1996), Ch. 2.

[21]   'Pero llegado a oir al mismo maestro Clavijo en la tecla, a su hija doña Bernardina en el arpa y a Lucas de Matos en la vihuela de siete órdenes, imitándolos los unos a los otros con gravísimos y no usados movimientos, es lo mejor que he oído en mi vida.' *La vida del escudero Marcos Obregón* (*ca.* 1616), Colección Austral Nº 1486 (Madrid, 1972), *relación* III, *descanso* 5.

gatherings of family and friends extends from this base. As tablature notation enabled any person to play sophisticated and complex music by numbers, without any knowledge of music theory or compositional style, study had multiple rewards. In their domestic role, the printed vihuela manuals may be transmitting a code that relates only partially to public performance, but includes advice on practices relevant to private activity. Thus, suggestions such as those of Daza and Pisador that commend the vihuelist to sing one voice of the fantasias in their books as they play may relate less to public performance convention than as guidance to the domestic performer on how to gain maximum understanding and benefit from private music making.

IMPROVISATION AND EMBELLISHMENT

Vihuela practice shared with the lute a heritage in improvisation, although the development of the sixteenth-century instrumental style is also much indebted to the dominant tradition of vocal polyphony. Just over two-thirds of the extant vihuela repertory is made up of intabulated vocal music. Applied to music emanating from both the vocal and the inherently instrumental traditions, improvisation and embellishment were important ingredients of instrumental practice. Although cantus firmus compositions do not abound in the repertory – Narváez's book includes some variations on hymn melodies and a basse danse – both Venegas de Henestrosa and Fuenllana make specific reference to such playing in their discussion of right-hand technique, and a small number of pieces in the manuscript sources suggest that cantus firmus improvisation may have been more widespread than the printed sources would have us believe. A closely related practice was to improvise or invent variations on repeated harmonic grounds, a technique apparently derived from improvising accompaniments in the performance of strophic *romances*. The numerous variations on *Conde Claros*, *Guárdame las vacas* (or *Romanesca*), and the *Pavana* show how vihuelists created independent instrumental pieces by developing each variation from idiomatic devices such as chords, arpeggios, scale movement, motivic imitation, or other sophisticated forms of counterpoint. Cantus firmus melodies appear to have been treated similarly.

Though melodic embellishment of vocal pieces was a distinct practice, intabulations contain little embellishment other than at cadences. In agreement with Bermudo and Pisador, Fuenllana expressed his opinion that unembellished intabulations allow the player to preserve both the polyphonic integrity and tempo of the original model; accordingly, in most of his arrangements, he restricted himself to cadential ornamentation.[22] He does, however, provide embellished versions of a few pieces, such as Claudin de Sermisy's *Tant que vivray*. Valderrábano was of a similar

---

[22] *Orphénica lyra*, introductory fol. v r.

mind, stating that unadorned works were less difficult to play, particularly given the current vogue for complex counterpoint. His stated preference was to leave embellishment to the taste and technical ability of the player, although he advertises that he adds embellishments in a few works as a model for those who wish to play in this way. Bermudo goes so far as to admonish those players who 'destroy good music with importune glosses', and considers it an audacity for any instrumentalist to attempt to 'improve' compositions by eminent masters.[23] It must be remembered that in all these cases writers are expressing their taste and personal preference, and in so doing all are also tacitly acknowledging a practice of embellishing intabulated vocal pieces.

PLACING MUSIC ON THE VIHUELA

Composing or arranging for the vihuela meant fitting music to an instrument for which the intervallic relationship between strings was more important than a concept of fixed pitch. Pisador, for example, indicates that the vihuela has no fixed mode because it is arranged with semitone frets, and explains that players should be aware of melodic motion, cadences, and finals.[24] His views are shared by the majority of other vihuelists. Most vihuela pieces – intabulations and original compositions – locate the root note of the final chord on the open sixth, fifth, or fourth course, or at the second fret of those courses, depending mainly on the range of the piece, with mode being a secondary consideration. This formula ensures the advantageous use of open strings and a vocabulary of idiomatic chord configurations that reappear in piece after piece. Much of Bermudo's discussion of intabulation is directed towards this outcome, and the seven vihuelas for which he provides templates offer the intabulator a practical tool for making intabulations accordingly. As has been clarified frequently in modern literature, these are not references to vihuelas of different size and pitch; they are conceptualizations of the fingerboard to facilitate intabulation and performance.[25] To this end Bermudo describes vihuelas in *Gamaut, Are, Bmi, Cfaut, Dsolre, Elami,* and *Ffaut.* According to this practice, the intabulation of a piece of music in mode 1 with a final D on V/2 gives a vihuela in *Gamaut* or G; the same piece arranged so that the D final is on V/0 supposes a vihuela in *Are* or A; and, should it fall on VI/0, a tuning in *Dsolre* or D is imagined.[26] An intabulator who has difficulty conceiving the relationship of notes to the fingerboard can construct a template of the fingerboard or make use of those illustrated in Bermudo's treatise.

[23]   *Declaración*, fol. 84v. An almost identical admonition is made on fol. 29v.
[24]   *Libro de música*, introductory fol. Aiii v.
[25]   Ward, 'The Vihuela de mano', pp. 37ff.; Antonio Corona-Alcalde, 'Fray Juan Bermudo and his Seven Vihuelas', *The Lute* 24 (1984), 77–86; Annoni, 'Tuning, Temperament, and Pedagogy', pp. 89ff.
[26]   Roman numerals indicate the course, arabic numerals specify the fret.

IMPROVISING AND COMPOSING FANTASIAS

The composition of original fantasias was the pinnacle of the vihuelist's art. Most of the fantasias in Milán's *El Maestro* are fundamentally distinguished from those by all subsequent composers in that they are less dependent upon techniques derived from vocal composition and more closely connected to instrumental improvisation.[27] Milán's recourse to a reservoir of melodic cells, motives, textural complexes, cadential formulas, and even entire passages is evident from the recurrence of these devices in many pieces. He was a musician who composed directly onto the instrument by means of improvisation using partially pre-composed materials. The extent to which this represents a more widespread practice is a question to which no other evidence can be brought to bear.

Later vihuela fantasias rely more extensively on vocally derived practices. Bermudo offers vihuelists a graded pathway to acquire mastery on the instrument through the intabulation of duos from Mass movements, and simple three-part polyphony, before tackling works in four or more voices by Morales, Gombert, and others. All of this he regards as prerequisite to inventing one's own fantasias, specifically so that they should be 'in good taste'.[28] One could not find a more explicit expression of aesthetic goals. Whether there were many vihuelists able to improvise fantasias of the kind that is included in the printed repertory is not revealed by surviving documents. It seems clear, however, that in a number of cases fantasias were composed on paper and transferred to the vihuela by exactly the same process used in intabulating vocal works. The fantasias of Daza and Pisador are the most likely to have been conceived in this fashion.[29]

SINGING AND PLAYING

The vihuela repertory includes works that were intended primarily to be sung to accompaniment, as well as pieces in which singing was an option. Obligatory or optional, the evidence points to the vihuelist being also the singer. The books of Mudarra, Valderrábano, Pisador, and Fuenllana include accompanied songs as well as intabulated vocal works with the vocal part notated on a separate mensural staff, which are incomplete unless both voice and vihuela participate together. In the

---

[27] John Griffiths, 'The Vihuela Fantasia: A Comparative Study of Forms and Styles', Ph.D. diss., Monash University, 1983, Ch. 2.

[28] Bermudo, *Declaración*, fol. 99v.

[29] Although there is no direct documentation of this practice, the music of both composers suggests the likelihood of score composition and subsequent intabulation. In Daza's case, the dogged adherence to detailed aspects of vocal compositional practice leads to this conclusion, while in Pisador's music it is the density of his thematic imitation – often totally obscured and inaudible on the vihuela – that suggests a similar working method. Regarding Pisador, see John Griffiths, 'The Vihuela Fantasia', pp. 315–64 and Esteban Daza, *The Fantasias for Vihuela*, ed. John Griffiths, Recent Researches in Music of the Renaissance 54 (Madison, 1982), pp. xi–xiv.

tablatures of Milán, Valderrábano, Pisador, and Fuenllana, the figures corresponding to the vocal parts are printed in red, while the books of Mudarra and Daza signify sung parts with apostrophes (*puntillos*) at the upper right-hand corner of the tablature figures, with the text printed beneath. In numerous instances, the vihuelists indicate that these parts are shown so that the works can be sung if desired. Pisador and Daza extend this practice to their fantasias as well.

Vihuelists evidently performed intabulations in flexible configurations: as solo pieces; with one or more of the voices sung; or possibly together with other instruments. On this last point information is indeed scarce. One of the few references is given by Bermudo, who recommends placing a handkerchief under the strings to form a new nut in order to conform to the pitch of others when playing *en concierto*.[30] Considerable discussion has also centred on the issue of whether or not sung vocal lines should be doubled by the vihuela.[31] Apart from specific cases where separate mensural notation and tablature precisely declare the composer's intentions, the absence of reference to the problem in sixteenth-century sources suggests that it was not a crucial issue for players and there is no suggestion that a particular practice existed. Pisador's choice of notational format has more to do with legibility and notational clarity than performance practice. In the second and seventh books of his *Libro de música,* the three-part villancicos and villanescas are notated with red ciphers 'so that the voice they indicate may be sung by the player', while four-part pieces are notated with the vocal part on a separate staff.[32] Several of his transcriptions of cantus firmus Masses indicate the cantus firmus in red figures, perhaps more for didactic reasons than as a performance direction, and the majority of the motets show one voice in red, although Pisador designates other motets 'to play without singing'. With regard to his thirteen fantasias based on pre-existing themes 'sobre pasos remedados', statements of the theme are also printed in red and indicated to be sung as 'this will be a most pleasurable thing for him who plays and sings them, for the theme is found in all the voices'.

No preference is shown in the repertory for any particular voice range, and intabulations can be found showing any one of the voices – soprano, alto, tenor, or bass – in red ciphers or by *puntillos*. In the *libro segundo* of *Silva de sirenas,* Valderrábano presents a collection of motets and Mass sections in which either tenor or bass parts are shown in red 'para cantar y tañer' while the *libro tercero* comprises songs, intabulations of motets, villancicos, and other songs printed with an upper voice on a separate mensural staff and a specific indication for the vihuelist to sing them in falsetto ('para cantar en falsete').

[30]   Bermudo, *Declaración*, fol. 30r.
[31]   For example, Jesús Bal y Gay, 'Fuenllana and the Transcription of Spanish Lute Music', *AcM* 2 (1939), pp. 16–27.
[32]   'para que la voz que por ellas va señalada, la cante el que tañe', quoted here and following from the prologue of Pisador's *Libro de música*.

TEMPO AND METRE

The earliest four printed vihuela books include explicit indications of the desired tempo, which constitute the earliest known tempo markings in European music. Milán provides verbal instructions to guide the performer, using phrases such as 'algo apriessa' ('somewhat fast'), 'con el compás batido' ('with a beating pulse'), 'compás a espacio' ('a slow beat'), or 'ni muy apriessa ni muy a espacio sino con un compás bien mesurado' ('neither very fast nor very slow but with a well-measured beat'). While most of his music is to be played with a regular pulse, he also includes fantasias in a style that require internal tempo changes. Grouped together in each of the two *libros of El Maestro* are pieces that show 'más respeto a tañer de gala que de mucha música ni compás' ('more respect for "gallant playing" than much other music, nor for the beat'). His so-called *de gala* or 'gallant' style consists of chords mixed with passage work that is commonly called playing *dedillo* ('consonancias mescladas con redobles que vulgarmente dizen para hazer dedillo') in which the intention of the author is that 'all that is in chords should be played slowly and all that is in running notes fast, and pause on each fermata' ('todo lo que será consonancias tañerlas con el compás a espacio y todo lo que será redobles tañerlos con el compás apriessa, y parar de tañer en cada coronado un poco').[33]

In subsequent publications, Narváez, Mudarra and Valderrábano adapted traditional mensural signs to indicate two or three performance speeds. Narváez uses the symbols Ⓓ for pieces to be played quickly or 'apriessa', and ₵ for those to be played slowly or 'muy de espacio'. Mudarra uses three mensural signs Ⓓ, C, and ₵ to show tempos of fast, moderate and slow – 'apriessa', 'ni muy apriessa ni muy a espacio', and 'despacio', respectively. The signs employed by Valderrábano show a similar range of tempos with the signs ₵ for 'a espacio' (slow), ₵· 'más apriesa' ('faster') and ₵·· 'muy más apriesa' ('very much faster'). While in the vast majority of instances the tempo indicated by signs provides relatively useful guidance to the performer, it does appear that the vihuelists were not entirely consistent in their application. In comparing, for example, two consecutive fantasias in Mudarra's first book, we find works identical in most respects – mode, length, textural density, difficulty, compositional style – yet one is marked to be played at a faster speed than the other.[34] In some instances where markings appear to be anomalous, such as the *Romanesca* and *Pavana de Alexandre* in Mudarra's first book, slow tempo markings do not result in slow tempos when the given sign is taken to indicate the duration of the written tablature bar instead of the musical pulse. In both cases, slow tempos are given because the pieces are respectively notated in 3/2 and 4/2, so that the bars are of longer real-time duration than the more common 2/2 ones.

---

[33] *El Maestro*, fol. Diii r.

[34] *Tres libros*, fols. v r and vi r; Fantasias 5 and 6 in the Pujol edition, Monumentos de la Música Española 7 (Barcelona, 1949; rpt 1984).

The vihuelists who published after 1550 chose to break with the new tradition established in the 1530s and 1540s. It was certainly not due to their lack of familiarity with the earlier books. Pisador instructs his readers that tactus (*compás*) 'can be of greater or lesser interval as the player may desire' ('puede ser de mayor espacio o menor como quisiere el que tañe'). Towards the end of his preface (fols. viii v–ix), Fuenllana stresses the need to play evenly as one of the necessities of good performance, but concerning tempo his pronouncement is so intertwined with references to the ability of the player and the difficulty of the works, that it appears more to do with establishing a tempo relevant to the player's competence than to any ideal performance tempo. Fuenllana was more concerned to define an aesthetic objective for the performer, advocating a goal of unhurried forward movement rather than giving prescriptive tempo indications. Good taste, it seems, was more the manner of the performance than its speed:

Concerning the tempo with which these works should be played, I only wish to say that each should conform to the technical ability of his hands and the difficulty of the work, for he who has ability has licence to play any work with more liberty and dexterity, even if it be a difficult one. And he who does not have such ability should play with a slower beat, especially at the beginning, until knowing how to play the work accurately, and to maintain the integrity of the composition. And finally, both those who have skill and those who lack it, it seems to me that in any work they might play whether easy or difficult, they should choose the average, so that the beat is neither fast nor very slow.[35]

INSTRUMENTS AND PLAYING TECHNIQUE

From the variety of sizes shown in pictorial representations of the vihuela and by customary reference in the sources to its intervals rather than its pitch, it is unlikely that vihuelas were built to a standard size. Bermudo used the term *vihuela común* (common vihuela) to describe the instrument that he thought of as usually tuned in G, or sometimes A, irrespective of how those pitches translated into modern equivalents. In practice, pitch, according to Milán, was established empirically by the size of the instrument and the thickness of its strings. The variety of sizes is confirmed by Valderrábano's music for two vihuelas which calls for instruments tuned up to a fifth apart. Empirically, it is evident that much music in the surviving

---

[35] *Orphénica lyra*, introductory fol. v r: 'En lo que toca al compás con que estas obras se han de tañer, solo quiero dezir, que cada vno se deue conformar con la dispusición de sus manos, y difficultad de la obra, pues él que las tuuiere con ellas se tiene la licencia para tañer con más libertad y destreza, qualquiera obra, aunque tenga difficultad. Y él que no tuuiere tanta soltura de manos deue tañer con el compás reposado, en especial a los principios, hasta tener conocimiento de la obra que tañe por vsar de limpieza en lo que tañere, y guardar la verdad de la compostura. Y al fin assí los que tienen manos, como los que carecen dellas, me parece que en toda obra que tañeren, ora sea fácil o difficultosa, deuen de elegir el medio: quiero dezir, que ni el compás vaya apressurado, ni muy de espacio.'

tablatures is difficult if not impossible to play on instruments with a string length of over 72 cm, as found on the only surviving vihuelas in Paris and Quito.[36] The music is much easier to negotiate on instruments with a string length of 60 cm or less. It could even be the case that string lengths became shorter during the course of the century: the music of the later tablature books is much more manageable on an instrument with a vibrating length of 55 cm or less. Small instruments like this might have been known from quite early on if the proportions of the vihuela depicted in the frontispiece of Narváez's book are reliable.

The common vihuela was an instrument of six courses tuned to the same intervals as the lute – fourth, fourth, major third, fourth, fourth – although variants with four, five, and seven courses were also played. All these variant forms of vihuela are discussed by Bermudo in his *Declaración*. Fuenllana includes a group of pieces for the five-course vihuela, and pieces for four-course instruments are included in both *Orphénica lyra* and Mudarra's *Tres libros*. These instruments are all vihuelas in the generic sense of the term, but the instrument with four courses is generally referred to in the sources as a *guitarra*. Bermudo also refers to the five-course instrument as a guitar. References to seven-course vihuelas are found throughout the century, the earliest being to its use by Luis de Guzmán, and later sources mention the ability of the composer Francisco Guerrero as a vihuelist.[37]

Vihuela *scordatura* occurs only in the books of Pisador and Fuenllana, which both call for the sixth course to be lowered a tone in a number of instances. It is evident from Bermudo, however, that tuning might not have been so immutably standardized. He discusses variant tunings and gives in addition to standard tuning two others: one in which the third course is raised by a semitone as on the modern guitar, which Bermudo describes as having seen in Italian sources, and another that is based on a major triad that ascends G–B–d–g–b–d[1], if G is assumed as the lowest course. Bermudo enumerates four different tunings for the seven-course vihuela, four for the five-course guitar or vihuela, and three for the four-course guitar. He claims that the adventurous vihuelist 'does not content himself with the tuning of the vihuela *común*, but tunes according to his wishes and ciphers according to the tuning, and . . . [that] only he will know how to play on such a vihuela'.[38] In the absence of other evidence, it is difficult to assess whether these tunings are simply theoretical speculation, or were part of a real practice.

[36] Comparative measurements for both instruments are given in Egberto Bermúdez, 'The Vihuela: The Paris and Quito Instruments', in *La guitarra española* (Madrid, 1991), pp. 25–47.

[37] Francisco Pacheco, *Libro de descripción de verdaderos Retratos de Illustres y Memorables varones, c.1599;* facsimile edn (Seville, 1983), p. 204.

[38] *Declaración*, fol. 93v: 'no se contente con el temple de la vihuela común: sino temple a su voluntad, y cifre conforme al temple, y tañendo aquello cifrado, solo el sabrá tañer por semejante vihuela'.

STRINGING

The courses of the vihuela appear to have been tuned in unisons, although we cannot be sure. The literature discusses strings by course, always expressed in the singular – the *prima, segunda,* etc. – rather than by individual string. The unique exception is found in the introduction of Pisador's book where he specifies that the player 'take one of the open fourth strings and tune it in unison with its pair' as the starting point for tuning the vihuela.[39] The only other Spanish evidence favouring unison pairs rather than octaves is the testimony of Covarrubias, who claims unison courses to be one of the features that distinguish the vihuela from the guitar.[40] As has recently been argued, these references are scant evidence upon which to base a general conclusion.[41] Similarly, the question of whether one or two strings were used on the first course also suffers from a similar lack of information. The testimony of Covarrubias and the painting in Barcelona Cathedral of a five-course vihuela that clearly shows a single first course are the only explicit pieces of information. Strings were not always perfect in roundness and diameter. Milán explains a simple manner of testing strings to ensure their true intonation by plucking an outstretched string before putting it on the vihuela, and observing whether its vibration produces an even arc 'as if two strings and not more'.[42] Little is known about string-making in Spain or the importation of foreign strings, and no evidence has been produced to show whether the bass strings of the vihuela were plain gut, or whether the techniques of roping or chemical modification of gut (so-called 'loaded' gut) that have been revived in recent decades are relevant to Spanish practice.

PITCH AND TUNING

Milán's advice on stringing suggests that the true pitch of the vihuela, its *verdadera entonación,* was determined empirically according to the size of the instrument. His advice to novices is to choose a first string according to the size of the instrument; quite simply, this means the larger the vihuela, the thicker the string. This string is raised to just below its breaking point, 'as high as it can bear', and the other courses are tuned from it.[43] Venegas also recommends that the first string be used as the

---

[39]   *Libro de música,* introduction, fol. iii r.

[40]   Covarrubias, *Tesoro,* p. 670 states that the guitar has 'cuerdas requintadas, que no son unísonas, como las de la vihuela, sino templadas en quintas [*sic*]; fuera de la prima que está en ambos instrumentos, es una cuerda sola' ['higher strings which are not unisons like those of the vihuela, but tuned in fifths except for the first of both instruments which is a single string'].

[41]   See Bill Hearn, 'Playing Devil's Advocate: The Shaky Case for Unison-Course Vihuela Stringing', *LSAQ* 29 (1994), pp. 3–10.

[42]   *El Maestro,* fols. Aiii v–Ai v.

[43]   *El Maestro,* fol. A iii v: 'subireys la prima tan alto quanto lo pueda suffrir; y después templareys las otras cuerdas al punto de la prima'.

reference point for tuning since it is easily broken. Milán comments that if the vihuela is tuned too high it goes down, and if it is too low it goes up.

The tuning instructions of Milán and Pisador proceed by unisons and octaves. Milán gives two tuning methods for the instrument: unisons descending from the first string on the fifth and fourth frets of each lower string as required. Pisador varies from this only in that he starts from the fourth course. Milán's second method is based on the octaves II/3–IV/0, III/3–V/0, and IV/2–VI/0. Pisador specifies these same octaves for confirming the tuning done by unisons. Venegas adds to a similar description his observation that some players teach tuning by marking a line across the strings at the nut of a tuned vihuela for students to use as a visual reference point, retuning the strings by aligning the marks with the nut.

FRETS AND TEMPERAMENT

Knowledge of vihuela fretting, temperament, and intonation is principally derived from the precise accounts given by Bermudo. He observes that most vihuelists placed the frets by ear, and moreover that few did it well,[44] so it is possible that he had never seen his scientific method of fretting used in Spain. It can only be hoped that his mathematical formulas accord with the sound world he knew. He gives advice at three levels: a simple fretting system for beginners, more complex systems for advanced players, and a sophisticated system to satisfy the needs of the most inquiring player. While his ultimate system results in an approximately equal temperament, Bermudo's simpler systems are all based on Pythagorean principles of pure fifths, and unequal major and minor semitones.[45]

Bermudo's simplest system specifies only the placement of frets corresponding to the diatonic notes, and he leaves the player to place by ear the frets that correspond to accidentals. For the standard vihuela in G he gives rules for placing frets 2, 4, 5, 7, and 10: fret 2 is placed at ⅑ of the distance from the nut to the bridge, fret 4 at ⅑ the distance between the second fret and the bridge, frets 5 and 7 respectively at ¼ and ⅓ of the full string length, and fret 10 at ¼ of the distance between fret 5 and the bridge.[46] The chromatic frets are initially placed at half the distance between the whole tone frets, and moved towards the nut if a smaller *fa* semitone is desired, or towards the bridge if it is to be a larger *mi*. Bermudo's more advanced systems give the mathematical calculations for all the frets on the seven vihuelas for which he provides intabulation templates. The essentially diatonic frets 2, 5, 7, 9, and 10

---

[44] *Declaración,* fols. 102r ff.

[45] Annoni, 'Tuning, Temperament, and Pedagogy', pp. 132, 135, and 163ff. tabulates equivalents in cents for these systems.

[46] These frets, expressed as decimal fractions (rounded to 4 places) of the distance from nut to bridge, are the following: 0.1111, 0.2099, 0.2500, 0.3333, and 0.4375.

remain constant for all these vihuelas, while the other frets are manipulated slightly to give both diatonic and chromatic notes their correct intervallic distance within Pythagorean temperament. The templates depicted in Bermudo's treatise provide an approximation that allows the reader to see which frets represent both major and minor semitones.

But owing to the intervals between courses, these tunings do not always give the correct semitone at each fret of each string. In G tuning, for example, the first fret should give a small *fa* semitone for E♭ and B♭ on courses II and III, and a *mi* semitone for F♯ on course IV. Theoretical and practical differences are irreconcilable. Bermudo acknowledges the problem and describes practices that can remedy these deficiencies by (1) finding an alternate fingering on another string for the incorrect note, (2) altering the pitch of the string with the left hand, (3) slanting the fret, (4) moving the fret, (5) using double frets of different thicknesses to give both the correct *mi* and *fa* in the manner of the split keys of keyboard instruments, or (6) retuning and playing only one of the strings of a unison course. He is not sympathetic towards some of these practices, but they obviously represent some of the solutions that players used.

References to altering fret positions are found in the books of both Milán and Valderrábano, specifically with regard to the fourth fret. The apparent contradiction between them – Milán recommends moving the fourth fret towards the pegs while Valderrábano requests that it be shifted towards the rose – is reconciled in terms of the modes in question. Within a Pythagorean framework, both instructions result in altering the semitone division to create an effect closer to equal temperament, similar to Bermudo's most elaborate system of fret placement. In Milán's case, the change to the fourth fret specified for his fantasia in modes 3 and 4 serves, in A tuning, to correct the octave b–b^1 (IV/4–I/2) and to decrease the sharpness of the semitones g♯^{1} and d♯^{1} (II/4 and III/4) to something close to equally tempered notes.[47] In Valderrábano's case, his *Fantasía sobre un pleni* in mode 1 assumes E tuning with the final on IV/0.[48] Modification of the placement of the fourth fret sharpens the normally minor semitone between a and b♭ on course III, again approximating equal temperament. Thus, Mark Lindley's argument that Milán played in meantone temperament is without credibility; it completely ignores Bermudo and develops on the assumption that Pythagorean tuning was far too 'Medieval' for the refined 'Renaissance ear'.[49]

While the primary beauty of Pythagorean temperament lies in the purity of fifths, in strategic terms it favours the structure of vihuela music. The cadences that form its essential grammar and punctuation are strengthened – to the modern ear, at least –

[47]   Fantasia 14, fol. D vi r, and *Con pavor recordó el moro*, fol. Qiv v.
[48]   *Silva de sirenas,* fol. 74r.
[49]   Mark Lindley, 'Luis Milán and Meantone Temperament', *JLSA* 11 (1978), p. 46.

by the sharpness and upward insistence of cadential leading notes, and the more strongly plaintive Phrygian cadences that emphasize the flatter *fa* semitone. It seems no surprise that Spanish taste for Pythagorean temperament may have endured longer than in other parts of Europe due to its inherent strong contrasts and affective intensity.

PLAYING POSTURE

All of the writers on the vihuela are silent about how the instrument is to be held. Our observations can be based solely on iconographical evidence and personal experimentation. Illustrations show the instrument most frequently held with the lower bout resting on the right upper thigh. The neck of the vihuela is shown at angles of between 35° and 60° above horizontal. Additional support of the instrument appears to come from the right forearm pressing the instrument against the player's chest. The illustrations from the frontispieces of the Narváez and Milán books (Plates 8 and 9) are representative examples of the positions shown in iconographical sources. They also show the two extremes of right-hand position: Milán's Orpheus apparently plays with thumb-under technique while Narváez's Arion is unquestionably playing thumb-out.[50] Other related illustrations of players of the vihuela, the viola da mano, and of early guitars show only little variation. Some illustrations from both the fifteenth and the sixteenth centuries show players of vihuelas *de peñola* and *de mano* performing in a standing position with the instruments held between the forearm and player's belly without the use of a cord or strap. This position allows the instrument to be played with the forearm virtually parallel to the strings, although it is difficult to play with the same ease as when seated. A similar right-arm position is depicted in Giovanni Raimondi's engraved portrait (ca. 1510) of Giovanni Philotheo Achillini playing the viola da mano, which shows him with the waist of the instrument on his right leg, and with the neck of the instrument almost horizontal to the ground.[51] This illustration offers a variant that appears to be the exception to the norms of both Spanish and Italian practice, and the positions shown by Milán and Narváez's vihuelists indicate a manner of sitting and holding the instrument that appears to have remained constant until at least the end of the seventeenth century.

LEFT-HAND TECHNIQUE

Two issues concerning the left hand receive comment from writers on the vihuela. Venegas de Henestrosa is the only writer to provide advice on fingering patterns. He

---

[50] For a basic definition of thumb-under and thumb-out techniques, see Paul O'Dette, 'Plucked Instruments', in *A Performer's Guide to Renaissance Music*, ed. Jeffrey T. Kite-Powell (New York, 1994), p. 142.

[51] Depicted in Alexander Bellow, *The Illustrated History of the Guitar* (New York, 1970), p. 72.

Plate 8   Orpheus playing the vihuela, from Milán, *El maestro* (Valencia, 1536)

Plate 9   Arion playing the vihuela, from Narváez, *Los seys libros del Delphín* (Valladolid, 1538)

indicates first that it is preferable to use open strings where possible instead of notes stopped at the fifth fret, and he also comments that ascending and descending passages are to be fingered with the 'second and fifth, or the fourth fingers', that is, 1, 4, and 3 in modern terms. No further clarification is offered. The simplest interpretation of this reference is that comfortable fingering patterns are recommended which allow the hand to remain in a natural position without having to be extended more than necessary.

The second matter concerns sustaining polyphonic voices by leaving the left-hand fingers on the fingerboard. Fuenllana exemplifies typical situations by precise description. He refers to chords as in Ex. 7.1, where it is necessary to keep the finger holding V/2 and VI/2 (the bass voice) in place for the duration of each tablature bar. In selecting fingerings, he gives the instance shown as Ex. 7.2, specified by him in E tuning, where it is necessary to sustain the lower voices while the upper part descends from g^1 to f^1. He advocates the fingering shown in Ex. 7.3a in preference to Ex. 7.3b, which unnecessarily curtails the sound of the lower voices. Mudarra uses the sign of the circumflex above tablature ciphers to indicate that 'the finger should not be lifted for the duration of the bar, if it is found at the beginning of it', a statement intended to mean holding the finger in place for the duration of a semibreve.[52] Numerous instances of this occur in Mudarra's tablature at places that alert the player to suspensions, and concur with Bermudo's caution to be attentive to maintaining left-hand fingers in place to allow suspensions to sound properly.[53] As an advanced technique, Fuenllana and Bermudo both allude to stopping only one string of a course, and letting the other sound at its open pitch as a way of fingering difficult chords. Fuenllana indicates that he resorts to this technique only in intabulations of works in five or six voices in order that the integrity of the counterpoint be preserved.[54] Numerous examples are found among his intabulations of five-voice motets.

RIGHT-HAND TECHNIQUE

Iconographical sources, though often unreliable, show vihuelists playing with the right hand held in both thumb-out and thumb-under positions, as they are commonly termed. In six proficiently executed Spanish paintings and four woodcuts that show hand positions clearly, at least five if not seven of the players are using the thumb-out position, and three of them appear to be depicted playing thumb-under. The variety of practice is confirmed by Venegas de Henestrosa, who includes both positions among his 'four manners of redoubling'. His use of the terms *figueta*

[52] *El Maestro*, fol. Aiii v: 'no an de alçar el dedo de la cuerda durante aquel compás, si estuviere al principio de el'.
[53] *Declaración*, fol. 28r.
[54] *Orphénica Lyra*, introductory fols. iv v–v r.

Ex. 7.1

Ex. 7.2

Ex. 7.3

castellana for the thumb-out alternation of thumb and index finger and *figueta extranjera* for thumb-under alternation is indicative of what he believed to be the origins of each style, but no preference is shown towards either the 'Castilian' or 'foreign' way, and each is presented as a legitimate manner of playing.[55] It is also clear from Fuenllana's comments which follow below that some players used their nails to play the vihuela while others did not.

Most of the specific discussion of plucking technique is devoted to the execution of rapid passages. The noteworthy exception occurs in Fuenllana's instructions for playing cleanly, where he makes special comment about the use of the thumb where a string is to remain silent between the strings to be plucked with the thumb and fingers. In such instances, Fuenllana advocates using an *apoyando* thumb stroke to guard against it accidentally striking the intermediate string. He makes it clear that this can only be done when the music is moving in minims and semibreves, and not in diminutions.[56]

Milán, Mudarra, Fuenllana, and Venegas provide commentary regarding the kind of strokes that were used for the performance of *redobles* – rapidly 'redoubled' or paired notes used both in cadential ornamentation and scale passages. All authors distinguish between the single-fingered *dedillo* stroke, and various ways of playing

[55] Anglés, *La música en la corte de Carlos V*, vol. I, p. 159.
[56] *Orphénica lyra*, introductory fols. vi r–viv r.

figueta or with two fingers, *dos dedos*. *Dedillo* was the term used by vihuelists that described the use of the index finger in the manner of a plectrum. As a technique, it appears to be a vestige of the early period of vihuela practice; by the 1550s it was regarded by Fuenllana as no longer the ideal way of playing. From Fuenllana's description of the stroke it may be deduced that the flesh of the finger was used for the accented note of each pair:

> One of the excellences that this instrument has is [the quality of] the attack with which the finger strikes the string. And given that in this manner of *redoble* [= dedillo], the finger when it enters strikes with [this] attack, when it leaves it is impossible to avoid striking with the nail, and this is an imperfection, for neither is it a [properly] formed note, nor does it strike wholly or truly. And it is here that those who redouble with the nail will find ease in what they do, but not perfection.[57]

Milán designed the fourth *cuaderno* of the first book of *El Maestro* to show the difference between playing *dedillo* and *dos dedos*. By indicating at the outset of the *cuaderno* that the playing of *redobles* is 'commonly called playing *dedillo*', he implies this to have been in common currency in the 1530s. He specifies it as the principal technique for the first three fantasias (nos. 10–12), which he explains at the beginning of Fantasia 12 'will better be played with *dedillo* as they are composed for acquiring dexterity'.[58] The remaining two fantasias (nos. 13 and 14) are for playing with *dos dedos*. In comparing these pieces, it is evident that *redoble* passages to be played *dedillo* are concentrated on the upper three courses of the instrument while two-finger alternation is concentrated on the lower three.

Mudarra advocates playing with *dos dedos* but admits that there are occasions when the *dedillo* stroke is useful, and specifies how to use it:

> Regarding the *redoble* I wish to state my view. And it is that I regard the [stroke with] two fingers as good: and he who wishes to play well should take my advice and use it because it is the most secure, and [the one] which gives the best style to the passages. Of *dedillo* I shall not speak ill. He who practices both manner of *redoble* will not encounter difficulties for both are necessary at times. *Dedillo* [is] for passages that are played from the first towards the sixth [course] which is from top to bottom, and *dos dedos* for ascending [passages] and for cadencing. *Dedillo* is for passages that go from the first string towards the sixth which is from high to low, and the two-fingered technique for moving from low to high, and for cadencing'.[59]

---

57 *Orphénica lyra*, introductory fols. v v–vi r: 'vna de las excelencias que este instrumento tiene, es el golpe con que el dedo hiere la cuerda. Y puesto que en esta manera de redoble, el dedo quando entra hiere la cuerda con golpe, quando sale no se puede negar el herir con la vña, y esta es imperfectión, assí por no ser el punto formado, como por no auer golpe entero ni verdadero. Y de aquí es que los que redoblan con la vña hallarán facilidad en lo que hizieren, pero no perfectión.'

58 *El Maestro*, fol. Diii v: 'mejor se tañeran con dedillo pues son hechas para hazer soltura de dedo'.

59 *Tres libros de música*, introductory fol. iii r: 'Acerca del redoble quiero dezir mi parecer. Y es que tengo por bueno el de dos dedos: y que quien quisiere tañer bien de mi consejo dévelos usar porque es redoble más cierto: y que da mejor ayre a los passos. Del dedillo no digo mal quien pudiere tener entrambas maneras de redoblar no se hallará

In line with Fuenllana's implication that the accentuation in *dedillo* playing was done with the flesh stroke, Mudarra's preference is for using the *dedillo* stroke for descending passages where the movement of the finger towards the lower strings on accented notes allows for easy and natural crossing from one string to the next. In the first three of his fantasias, Mudarra uses the abbreviations *dos de* and *dedi* to indicate the passages that are to be played with the respective strokes in accordance with his stated principle. *Dedillo* technique has been maintained to the present day as an integral part of playing the Portuguese guitar.

Regarding two-finger alternation, Venegas and Fuenllana are the most specific. Venegas considers index–middle alternation to be appropriate in pieces where the thumb needs to play a cantus firmus, or its presumed secular equivalent 'making a discant with index and middle *de contado*'.[60] The same texture can also be played with *dedillo* above the cantus firmus, but not with thumb-index alternation.[61] Fuenllana, the master of them all it would seem, deserves the last word. In distinguishing between two-finger *redoble* types, he expresses his preference for middle–index alternation. He praises thumb–index playing, and comments that it is particularly appropriate for the thicker lower three courses, as one can achieve a fullness of tone, and adds that it can be used on all the courses 'as we know is done by strangers to our nation'. Of middle–index alternation he tells us that it should be played in regular alternation using the middle finger on strong beats, and that it can be used in both descending and ascending passages. He adds:

I dare to venture, that in this manner alone resides all the perfection that any manner of *redoble* might contain, both in velocity and cleanliness, and in permitting that which is played with it be most perfect for, as has been said, there is great virtue in plucking the string with a good attack, without needing to use the nail or any other kind of invention, for in the finger alone, as in [any] living material, lies the true spirit, which is brought out by striking the string.[62]

---

mal conellas porque entrambas son menester a tiempos. El dedillo para passos que se hazen de la prima hazia la sexta que son de arriba para abaxo y el de dos dedos para los que se hazen pa arriba y para el clausular. El dedillo para pasos que se hacen de la prima hacia la sexta que son de arriba para abajo y el de dos dedos para los que se hacen de abajo para arriba y para clausular.'

60 Anglés, *La música en la corte de Carlos V*, vol. I, p. 160.

61 Venegas, from Anglés, *La música en la corte de Carlos V*, vol. I, p. 160: 'discantar con dos dedos de contado, o redoblar de dedillo sobre el canto llano: las quales dos vozes, no se podrán llenar con redobles de figueta'. The only reference in musical sources to this term is the title of Mudarra's *Fantasía de pasos de contado* in *Tres libros de música*, fol. 4r, built as running notes above an unidentified or original bass.

62 *Orphénica Lyra,* introductory fol. vi r: 'oso dezir, que en ella sola consiste toda la perfection que en qualquiera modo de redoble puede auer, assi en velocidad, como en limpieza, como en ser muy perfecto lo que con el se tañe, pues como dicho es, tiene gran excellencia el herir la cuerda con golpe, sin que se entremeta vña ni otra manera de inuención, pues en solo el dedo, como en cosa biua consiste el verdadero spíritu, que hiriendo la cuerda se le suele dar'. The 'other manner of invention' may be a reference to thimbles or finger picks of the type that have been documented with reference to Francesco da Milano's playing. See Paul O'Dette, 'Some Observations about the Tone of Early Lutenists', *Proceedings of the International Lute Symposium Utrecht 1986*, ed. Louis P. Grijp and Willem Mook (Utrecht, 1988), p. 87.

For the performer, the development of a historically derived performance practice requires the assimilation of information that I instinctively separate into the categories of mechanics and aesthetics. Regarding the latter, vihuela music itself reveals much of its own story. Our stylistic understanding of the repertory is the first thing that guides us in the application of instrumental technique. A deeper understanding of vihuela music in its larger musical and social contexts sharpens this knowledge: it is easier to make good music on the vihuela if one has a grasp of the sixteenth-century Spanish vocal styles and of music theory of the period. The individuals who played the instrument, their social experience, their musical preferences and traditions, and the working of their minds also form an indispensable part of the backdrop. From other, more fragmentary accounts, we can form a clearer image of the social context in which the vihuela was performed that can help us understand such issues as the role of improvisation, the value that players placed on the authority of the musical texts they used, and the level of stylistic uniformity that social conventions demanded of performers.

For the vihuela, there is no single 'correct' way to play. The central sources reveal a variety of standards and taste in matters such as embellishment (particularly in intabulations), tuning, tempo, and virtually every other dimension of performance. There is no reason to doubt the reliability of these sources, and the very fact that they do not agree simply assists us to define the boundaries of performance practice and instrumental technique. We can only conclude that there was no uniformly consistent manner in which the vihuela was played. Some players used thumb-under while others preferred thumb-out; some evidently played with nails, while others used flesh; there were progressives who expanded existing practice, and conservatives who maintained older traditions. Taken as a whole, the strength of these traditions led to an instrumental technique which was inherited by subsequent generations of guitarists, and which served the new instrument with little alteration for some 300 years.

8

PERFORMING SEVENTEENTH-CENTURY ITALIAN GUITAR MUSIC: THE QUESTION OF AN APPROPRIATE STRINGING

GARY R. BOYE

'In stringing there is variety . . .' states Gaspar Sanz in a well-known passage from his guitar tablature of 1674.[1] He continues with one of the most illuminating discussions of five-course or 'Baroque' guitar stringing from the period, stating that some guitarists use only thin strings on the fourth and fifth courses, with no true *bourdons*, others pair two *bourdons* with thin strings at the octave, and still others use only *bourdons*. While Sanz states his preference for the first method and gives alternative solutions, the large majority of guitar tablatures from the seventeenth century give no indication whatsoever of the manner in which the lower two courses are strung. The question of stringing has been further confused by our indiscriminate use of the term 'Baroque guitar', which fails to distinguish between the variety of individual styles, national and regional traditions, and performance practices that existed for this instrument in Europe for over a century. In reality, each tablature represents a unique stage in the development of particular guitar styles and techniques, and in order to obtain specific answers to questions about performance practice, each one must be studied within its proper musical, historical, and cultural context.

Since much work has been dedicated already to the question of stringing the five-course guitar in the French and Spanish repertories,[2] the primary focus of this article is on seventeenth-century Italian printed sources. This repertory, in fact, predates many French and Spanish sources and accounts for a large percentage of existing Baroque guitar music. These tablatures can be divided into two basic notational types. The first involves music that is made up entirely (or almost entirely) of strummed chords, known in the original sources as the *battuto* (Sp. *rasgueado*) style. The notation for this music consists of a chord alphabet, or *alfabeto*, in which various

---

[1] 'En el encordar ay variedad . . .', Gaspar Sanz, *Instrucción de música sobre la guitarra española* (Zaragoza, 1674 and 1679).

[2] See, for example, Neil D. Pennington, *The Spanish Baroque Guitar* (Ann Arbor, MI, 1979), pp. 46ff.; Sylvia Murphy, 'The Tuning of the Five-course Guitar', *GSJ* 22 (1970), pp. 49–63; and Richard Pinnell, *Francesco Corbetta and the Baroque Guitar* (Ann Arbor, MI, 1980), pp. 28–9, 44–5.

letters and symbols represent a chord to be fretted on the guitar, along with signs indicating the direction of the strums.[3] Tablatures in this style employ only a single horizontal line on which the chord alphabets are placed. The less complex of the *battuto* tablatures are specifically intended for beginners and often contain a good deal of pedagogical information. Sources of the second notational type incorporate the same *alfabeto* in combination with Italian lute tablature, and can therefore indicate both strummed chords *and* individually plucked notes, a style called *battuto/pizzicato* in the earliest sources.

Girolamo Montesardo's *Nuova inventione d'intavolatura* (Florence, 1606) contains one of the most complete discussions of guitar tuning and stringing of the seventeenth century, clearly describing the use of octaves on both the fifth and fourth courses, unison pairs on the third and second, and a single string (*cantino*) for the first.[4] This method of doubling lower courses with a thin octave string while keeping the upper courses tuned at the unison had already been used in sixteenth-century Italian lute music. A similar unambiguous reference to octave basses can be found in Sanseverino's tablature.[5]

At the opposite extreme, Fabritio Costanzo seems to omit *bourdons* in the tuning instructions of his first tablature, *Fior novello* (Bologna, 1627), which are given in Ex. 8.1 in the original tablature and transcribed into modern notation according to the intervals specified. Costanzo explains that the fifth course is tuned to some convenient pitch and then used as a basis for tuning the other four courses, as follows: first the open fifth course is tuned to a 'consonanza' at the second fret of the fourth course; next the fifth and third, then the fourth and second courses are tuned to a 'corrispondenza'; finally, the third and first courses are tuned to an 'ottava'. Since the term for octave is used only on the last pair, one assumes that a 'corrispondenza' can be equated with a unison and that therefore the lower two courses are heard up an octave from Montesardo's guitar. Two additional sources seem to indicate the absence of *bourdons* through a comparison of harp and guitar tuning.[6]

While these sources are reasonably clear in their explanations, the large majority of *battuto* tablatures make no distinction between unisons and octaves in their tuning instructions, perhaps to allow the performer to decide on either stringing method. Other factors influencing the choice of strings would have been the size of the guitar

---

[3] About half of the printed sources in this style also include some rhythmic/metric information.

[4] Montesardo, *Nuova inventione* (Florence, 1606), fol. 5v. See pp. 193–4 of the present volume for a complete list of primary sources cited in this article.

[5] Benedetto Sanseverino, *Intavolatura facile . . . opera terza* (Milan 1620; rpt 1622).

[6] The earlier source is Giovanni Battista Abbatessa, *Intessitura di varii fiori* (Rome and Lucca, 1652), p. 4. Virtually the same instructions can be found in Antonino di Micheli, *La nuova chitarra* (Palermo, 1698), fol. 1r. Both composers match notes on the guitar to successive strings on the harp in a way that implies the use of upper octaves on the lower two courses.

Ex. 8.1   Fabritio Costanzo (1627), p. 5

– many sizes were available in the period, with guitars often being grouped into consorts tuned at various intervals to each other – and the quality and availability of gut for strings. To summarize so far, the earliest Italian tablatures call for octaves on the lowest two courses, while three later sources seem to require upper notes at the unison. Interestingly, each of these three sources can be connected with the south of Italy: Abbatessa's book was printed in Rome, Micheli's book in Palermo, and Costanzo calls himself a 'Napolitano' on his title page.

It is misleading to think of the *battuto* style merely as a precursor to the *battuto/pizzicato*; both were in use throughout much of the century and should be viewed more as contemporary extremes than evolutionary steps. The large repertory of strummed guitar music, mostly for amateur beginners, only hints at what must have been a vital and, in the hands of a professional musician, intricate style, which could exploit variations of chord voicing and rhythmic ornamentation, as well as harmonic progressions. Nor should all of these sources be grouped into one category. In particular, the books from the 1630s by Corbetta, Trombetti, and Sfondrino contain music of much greater interest and complexity than the crude, skeletal works of such guitarists as Abbatessa.

Still, the majority of *battuto* tablatures appealed mainly to beginners. The *battuto/pizzicato* style, on the other hand, is often explicitly designated for more advanced performers, and it requires the full range of right- and left-hand techniques used by lutenists.[7] *Battuto/pizzicato* notation presents the basic information for left-hand finger placement as in any tablature, but with the addition of *alfabeto* chord symbols. For modern performers familiar with Italian lute tablature, the *alfabeto* system can be memorized with relative ease, especially for those already familiar with common guitar chords. But while the notation indicates a fixed position on the instrument and thus a relative pitch, no explicit indication of the octave disposition of the five courses is included in the tablature itself.

Indeed, most composers using *pizzicato* give no information at all about tuning the instrument, but there are two major exceptions: Giovanni Paolo Foscarini and

---

[7]   Francesco Corbetta, *Varii capricii per la ghitara spagnuola* (?Milan, 1643), Angiolo Michele Bartolotti, *Secondo libro di chitarra* (Rome, 1655) and Giovanni Bottazzari, *Sonate nuove per la chitarra spagnola* (Venice, 1663) all contain references to the difficult nature of this music, stating that their works were not intended for *principianti*.

Ferdinando Valdambrini. Foscarini is generally regarded as the originator of *battuto/pizzicato* guitar music, but in reality he cultivated at least three distinct musical styles. The first was the older, *battuto* style, as found in his *Libro secondo*; the second style involved the *pizzicato* manner of playing individual strings with the fingertips, as in lute music, without using strummed chords; the third style combined both strummed chords and individually plucked notes into the true *battuto/pizzicato* manner that is unique to the guitar. All of Foscarini's tablatures begin with the unambiguous tuning instructions stating that the first series of notes should be tuned to the unison ('medema voce') and the second series in octaves ('due corde in ottava'), as seen in Ex. 8.2. The explanation leaves no doubt that Foscarini intended the use of *bourdons* on the lower two courses, almost certainly paired with their customary higher octaves.[8] This places him in the tradition of Montesardo and Sanseverino.

While Foscarini's first five guitar books are currently available in facsimile, the two books by the Roman Valdambrini are almost totally unknown.[9] In the tuning instructions and prefaces to his books, Valdambrini's makes quite clear where unisons and octaves should appear (Ex. 8.3). Once again we have evidence of a tuning without *bourdons* by a guitarist connected with the south. This regional consistency supports the continuation of Sanz's statement that was quoted at the beginning of this article: 'In stringing there is variety, because in Rome the Masters string the guitar only with thin strings, without using any *bourdons*, either in the fourth or the fifth.'[10] Ex. 8.4 shows Valdambrini's tuning compared with that of Foscarini's. No other explicit references are made to this re-entrant tuning in the Italian *battuto/pizzicato* repertory, but Foscarini's tuning instructions (and a large percentage of his preface) reappear in Giovanni Battista Granata's *Capricci armonici* (Bologna, 1646), as well as in works by Calvi and Pesori. Altogether, of the more than thirty printed tablatures in this style, less than a third contain any instructions at all on tuning the instrument. In order to establish some guidelines for dealing with the other two-thirds, the styles of Foscarini and Valdambrini will be compared and contrasted with regard to their use and tuning of the fifth and fourth courses.

At first glance, the tablatures of these two guitarists appear quite similar. Sections of strummed chords alternate with passages of scales, ornamental flourishes, and what appears to be simple polyphony. Two representative examples from a very similar *ciaccona*, in the same key, will demonstrate the varying approaches of the two composers (see Ex. 8.5a and 8.5b). The pieces have been transcribed according to the tuning methods outlined above – Foscarini with *bourdons* and Valdambrini without. Valdambrini integrates the fifth course into the melody, twice doubling the

---

8   The use of two *bourdons* on each of the lower courses seems to be limited to Spain; see Pennington, *The Spanish Baroque Guitar*, pp. 49ff.

9   Ferdinando Valdambrini, *Libro primo d'intavolatura di chitarra* (Rome, 1646) and *Libro secondo* (Rome, 1647).

10   See Pennington, *The Spanish Baroque Guitar*, p. 49.

Ex. 8.2   Foscarini (1629): Tuning in unisons and octaves

Ex. 8.3   Valdambrini (1646): Tuning in unisons and octaves

Ex. 8.4   Comparison of Valdambrini's and Foscarini's tunings

Ex. 8.5(a)   Valdambrini (1646), p. 32, *Ciaccona*, bars 3–6

(b)   Foscarini (1640), p. 107, *Ciacona*, bars 1–5

second course at the unison (marked by the asterisk). It can also be seen that using a lower octave on the fifth course would disrupt the stepwise motion in bar 5. The open third course, the lowest pitched note on the instrument, has assumed the role of a rudimentary bass. In contrast, Foscarini clearly uses the fifth course as a true bass voice, outlining the harmony and creating a sense of dissonance and syncopation. Another short passage demonstrates Valdambrini's characteristically thin, almost monophonic texture, compared to Foscarini's use of two clearly independent voices (see Exx. 8.6a and 8.6b). Valdambrini's passage would be awkward at best if the notes on the fifth and fourth courses were played at the lower octave. On the other hand, the same tuning without *bourdons* would muddle Foscarini's counterpoint and disrupt the stepwise motion of the bass in bars 22–3 and bar 24. The use of unisons may seem superfluous in Valdambrini's examples, but it is actually an integral part of the style, as can be seen in Ex. 8.7, where a unison is played on three different courses. Without a true bass, the guitar can become either a melodic *or* a chordal instrument. Between chordal passages, Valdambrini uses long scales – both across the strings as in campanella passages, and by conventional ascending- and descending-fret movement – in addition to bursts of repeated notes and short melodic sequences. This is the delicate, often thinly textured style used by later Spanish guitarists such as Sanz. *Bourdons* would not only disrupt the melody in passages such as these, they would prove noisy on extended slur passages on the lower courses.[11]

Like many northern Italian guitarists, Foscarini played the lute and was familiar with the music of French lutenists of the early seventeenth century. His music owes as much to the lute as to the guitar, a fact that is acknowledged by the composer himself in his preface: 'Of the pieces called "Pizziccate" I will not say much, having included them more for the embellishment of the work than for other respects; because I know them very well to be more appropriate to the lute than the guitar . . .'[12] Since this often-quoted passage continues with a discussion of the true *battuto/pizzicato* style, it should be pointed out that the composer's comment applies only to those pieces in his tablature that use the *pizzicato* style (i.e. pieces totally lacking strummed chords and *alfabeto*, such as those on p. 15). Far from disparaging the guitar, as some scholars have interpreted the intent of this passage, Foscarini emphasizes the combination of strummed chords and plucked notes as the true style of the instrument.[13]

---

11 As Sanz himself states; see Pennington, *The Spanish Baroque Guitar*, p. 53.

12 'Delle Sonate, dette Pizziccate, non ne parlo più che tanto, havendole poste più per abbellimento dell'opera, che per altro rispetto; poiche sò benissimo esser più proprie del Leuto, che della Chitarra . . .' G. P. Foscarini, *Il Primo, secondo, e terzo libro della chitarra spagnola* (*ca.* 1630), fol. 4v. Translated by the author.

13 These instructions must also be read in the context of their origins in Foscarini's third book, which comprises pp. 1–78 of *Li 5 libri*. The division of the final collection is not made entirely clear in the tablature itself, but a close comparison of other editions indicates that the fourth book comprises pp. 79–102 and the true fifth book pp. 103–35. For a more complete discussion of Foscarini, see the author's dissertation, 'Giovanni Battista Granata and the Development of Printed Music for the Guitar in Seventeenth-Century Italy', Ph.D. diss., Duke University, 1995.

Ex. 8.6(a) Valdambrini (1646), *Ciaccona*, bars 7–10

(b)   Foscarini (1640), p. 107, *Ciacona*, bars 21–5

Ex. 8.7   Valdambrini (1647), p. 19, *Passacaglia Quinto*

His fifth book represents the earliest occurrence of the mature *battuto/pizzicato* style, which was to prove so influential to later Italian guitarists.

Over twenty-five tablatures for guitar were printed in seventeenth-century Italy after Foscarini's collection. Since half of these books can be connected with the city of Bologna, and more specifically with the printer Giacomo Monti, it becomes possible to identify a true 'Bolognese School' of guitarists. Monti's interest in guitar tablatures is evident throughout his career, despite the complexities of printing *battuto/pizzicato* tablature. His publications in this style, half of which were devoted to the works of Giovanni Battista Granata, were the only guitar tablatures to be printed from movable type, as opposed to engraved, during this period.

With regard to stringing, only Pellegrini's *Armoniosi concerti* (Bologna, 1650) and Granata's tablatures of 1646 and 1680 are of pedagogical value, but these books deal mostly with notational questions such as ornaments, slurs, and arpeggios. Granata's use of Foscarini's tuning chart, mentioned above, is the only reference to tuning in the entire Bolognese repertory. To obscure matters further, Monti's tablatures

Ex. 8.8 (a)   Granata (1674), p. 45, *Alemanda* without *Bourdons*
  (b)   with *Bourdons*

Ex. 8.9 (a)   Granata (1674), p. 45, *Alemanda* without *Bourdons*
  (b)   with *Bourdons*

include a dramatic shift after 1650 towards printing music in the French style with French genres and compositional techniques supplanting those of the Spanish. From this time on, the performer was left to decide which stringing fits the music best, with little help from outside sources.

Referring to the different styles seen in Foscarini and Valdambrini, we can now look at a few examples from the Bolognese repertory and confront the problems in stringing that arise. Ex. 8.8 presents a typical situation encountered by performers of this music: the use of cross-string scales on the lower courses. Ex. 8.8 is transcribed using Valdambrini's tuning, first without, and then with, *bourdons*. For clarity, the upper octaves on the fourth and fifth strings have been omitted. Clearly, the first method produces a much smoother melodic line, and one is tempted to conclude that Granata calls for a re-entrant tuning. However, at the end of this work and in other sections as well, awkward octave displacements occur which can be resolved only with the use of *bourdons*, as seen in Exx. 8.9a and 8.9b. In the first transcription, the melodic line leaps up a major seventh and the voice leading of the cadence is corrupted. The second transcription reveals the underlying two-voiced texture, with a much better resolution at the cadence, but also contains an awkward leap of a seventh. Remembering that the fifth course would be sounding the upper octave as well, especially in a downwards slur, this leap would be heard as a much less jarring drop of a half step. Instances such as this occur throughout the repertory, with the lower courses being used as cross-string melody notes in one measure and as stepwise bass notes in the next.

Fortunately, there is a relatively simple method by which the guitarist can play either the *bourdons* with their upper octave or the upper octave alone, without the lower note. James Tyler was one of the first modern scholars to explore the possibilities of this technique.[14] For its execution, it is absolutely essential that the upper octaves of the lowest two courses be strung *above* (i.e. on top of) the lower octaves, so that the right-hand thumb strikes them first. Furthermore, the upper strings can be adjusted so that they are raised slightly above the adjacent string. With this arrangement, an upward stroke of the thumb (equivalent to the modern guitarist's free stroke) will sound only the upper octave of either the fourth or fifth course. If the lower octave is necessary, the normal downward stroke will sound both strings together.

Two objections to this technique might be raised in terms of its historical appropriateness: (1) it is too complex or impractical for amateur guitarists of the seventeenth century, and (2) there is no direct evidence of its use in any contemporary sources. The first objection ignores the fact that most of these tablatures were explicitly intended for more advanced performers, as noted above, and were often looked upon as being difficult by contemporaries.[15] Furthermore, several authentic techniques used by sixteenth-century lutenists and vihuelists were even more complex, including the playing of divided courses in which only one of a pair of strings was fretted with the left-hand finger. It might also be noted that one of the common flaws of beginning lutenists is striking only one of a pair of strings, i.e. they strike a bass note with the thumb but not its corresponding octave. If these two strings are reversed and the thinner string is raised slightly, this technical flaw can be turned to the guitarist's advantage.

The second objection, the lack of evidence, creates more serious problems for the modern performer and scholar. There is, of course, documentary confirmation that the upper octave string was often placed above its bass,[16] which made it at least more possible to accentuate the upper note; but the almost total absence of detailed

---

[14] See James Tyler, *A Brief Tutor for the Baroque Guitar* (Helsinki, 1984), p. 20.

[15] Not without his commercial interests at heart, Granata states in his Op. 6 that he could teach anyone to play his pieces on the guitar, even though some considered them playable only by *maestri*. He even goes so far as to invite interested guitarists to Bologna to study with him.

[16] See Pennington, *The Spanish Baroque Guitar*, p. 53.

pedagogical information in the guitar repertory indicates either that guitarists were already expected to know this technique, or that they would have to learn it directly from a teacher. There were certainly no technical limitations imposed on these guitarists that forced them to write cross-string scales, and one should never underestimate the abilities of past professional musicians or their more advanced students.

Returning to Ex. 8.8 and 8.9, a performer with a properly adjusted guitar could play the thin strings only on the cross-string scales in the 'a' examples and the descending scale and cadence with both *bourdons* and their octaves in the 'b' examples, combining the advantages of both stringing arrangements. While it is certainly possible to play this music with a variety of *bourdon*/octave combinations, composers such as Granata make no effort to avoid scalewise movement from the third course to the lower courses, as does Valdambrini. Furthermore, the contrapuntal nature of Bolognese guitar music, due no doubt to a strong influence of French lute music, indicates that a wider bass range would be required to realize the texture fully.

While the multiple use of octave courses can help the performer by bringing out individual lines, it must be noted that in chordal strumming both strings of the pair will naturally be sounded, sometimes resulting in odd inversions if *bourdons* are being used. Angiolo Michele Bartolotti's books from 1640 and 1655 provide a solution to this problem.[17] Several chords are given in his *alfabeto* with slashes through their letter symbols, called *lettere tagliate*, indicating that the fifth course should not be played. This results in chords sounding in root rather than in $\frac{6}{4}$ position, as shown in Ex. 8.10. The fifth course could quite easily be dampened by the right-hand thumb, or the stroke could be started at the fourth string and moved downwards. Careful notation such as this indicates that the best guitar composers were often concerned with the harmonic voicing of notes in chords, contrary to the views of some modern scholars. Inversions can also be avoided, especially at cadences, by the use of extended arpeggios such as those described by Bartolotti in the same preface.

One final issue will conclude our discussion of the lower two courses of the guitar: Corbetta's use of a *bourdon* on the fourth, but not on the fifth course.[18] Appearing in Corbetta's *La guitarre royalle* of 1671, a full twenty-eight years after his last tablature of Italian origin, this tuning has been connected with Granata and the Bolognese school, and is even considered as the 'standard' tuning for the guitar in the late seventeenth century. Yet there is no evidence for this stringing prior to Corbetta's print; some modern scholars even state that it was invented by the composer specifically for this tablature, which is notated in French tablature without

---

[17]   Bartolotti, *Libro primo* (Florence, 1640), fol. 3r and *Secondo libro* (Rome, 1655), fol. 3r.

[18]   For a complete discussion see Pinnell, *Francesco Corbetta*, pp. 152–5 and Murphy, 'The Tuning of the Five-Course Guitar'.

Ex. 8.10   Bartolotti's *lettere tagliate*

Ex. 8.11   Corbetta (1643), p. 22, *Passachaglia sop[ra] B* (the xs mark
the upper octave that would sound if no *bourdons* are used)

the *alfabeto*. By using the fifth course as a melody note integrated into the texture of the higher strings, the use of the fourth course as both a bass string as well
as a melody note an octave higher, and the avoidance of scalar motion from the
third to the fifth course, the composer could carefully avoid the need for the fifth-
course *bourdon*. This use of only one octave course can be seen as a practical compromise between the two extremes of stringing discussed above, yet the bulk of
the Italian repertory had already been written by the time Corbetta wrote his
preface. It is quite possible that along with the change in notation and musical style
that resulted after his move to Paris, a parallel change in the stringing of his guitar
took place. Rather than adopting the re-entrant tuning common in France at that
time, Corbetta dropped only the lowest *bourdon* from his instrument. Passages
from his earlier works, such as that in Ex. 8.11, make little sense using his later
'French tuning'.

The bulk of the Bolognese repertory generally gives the lower two courses of the
instrument a dual role: as a bass note and, when played on only the uppermost
string, as part of the melody. While the music can certainly be performed without
the fifth-course *bourdon*, there is no systematic avoidance of its use and the performer
gains much by having the lower range of the instrument available. The upper
octaves on the lower courses, on the other hand, must be thought of as essential
throughout the repertory. Other factors, such as the size of the instrument and string
quality, are certainly important, but our information about these topics comes
mostly from French, not Italian, sources. Furthermore, Bolognese guitarists, like

Ex. 8.12   Granata (*ca.* 1650), p. 7, *Passacalli*

Ex. 8.13   Granata (1680), p. 21, *Allemanda*

most musicians of the period, experimented with their instruments, as seen, for example, in Granata's use of a guitar with extended bass strings in his Op. 4, and his extending of the neck and number of frets in Op. 6. It seems doubtful that someone so concerned with the range of his instrument would omit a perfect fourth from the lower range of the guitar by using Corbetta's stringing, especially if the cross-string effects could be obtained by plucking only the upper octaves.

Issues of organology and range bring us to one final topic involving the five-course guitar and its stringing: the not infrequent use of the third course in *campanellas* an octave lower than the prevailing melodic line (see Ex. 8.12). Evidence exists for an octave third course, as first proposed by Tyler, but the two sources he quotes involve rather simplistic *battuto* music, and both use the re-entrant tuning on the lower two courses.[19] The only sources that contain such passages are Corbetta (1643 and 1648), all of Granata's books after Op. 1, Bottazzari (1663), Asioli (1676) (only once), and Roncalli (1692). Granata seems particularly fond of this device. A high octave g^1 string is not impossible to string – it is, after all, equivalent to the g^1 first course of a lute – but the size of the instrument would have to be suited to the

---

[19]   The two sources are Bologna, Ms. AA360 and Modena, Campori Ms. 612; see Tyler, *A Brief Tutor*, p. 7. In the Campori manuscript, notes are written on a staff without a clef sign. If a tenor clef is used, the following tuning results: a–d^1–g/g^1–b–e^1. The Bologna manuscript includes the same series of notes in bass clef, but the fifth, fourth, and second courses are doubled at the unison. Oddly, the third course contains four notes: two at g^1 and two an octave lower. In the middle of these four notes is written 'canto in mezzo'. While this could imply that the higher of the two strings, the 'canto', would be placed in the middle of the other eight strings and thus above the lower octave, there remains no explanation for the other octave pair on the third course. Since the music in both sources is almost entirely in single-line *alfabeto*, little more can be said about the use of this tuning.

extra tension and the string made of sufficient thickness to sound well.[20] Placed above the lower string, the g[1] string can be used in the same manner as the upper octaves on the lower two courses.[21] The sound of such a string in passages similar to Ex. 8.12 is satisfying, but the use of the lower octave cannot be ruled out and will sound equally well at quicker tempos. Once again, we appear to have found musical evidence for a technique not discussed by the composers themselves, and one that was not forced upon the composer by some shortcoming of the instrument. Alternatively, the passages could be played just as easily using the eighth fret of the second string, as in Ex. 8.13, which juxtaposes normal scales with the *campanella* effect.

All of the guitar music connected with Bologna is in the fuller, more contrapuntal style originating with Foscarini. No Italian successors of Valdambrini seem to exist in the printed repertory; even Bartolotti, who calls himself a Bolognese in both of his tablatures, retains the northern style in his Roman book of 1655. If one thinks of Italy in the seventeenth century as a geographical entity and not a true nation state, it is easy to see how different performing traditions could exist in close proximity. The tremendous influence of the French lute tradition in northern cities such as Bologna and Modena contrasts sharply with the more Spanish-influenced Rome and Naples. Even within the corpus of tablatures printed by Monti there exists a large range of musical styles, as in Calvi (1646), which juxtaposes the strict *battuto* style in the first half of the book with archaic *pizzicato* pieces in the second.

In conclusion, the works of Foscarini and Valdambrini are important for the explicit description of two contrasting methods of tuning: the former with octaves on the fourth and fifth courses, and the latter with unisons at the upper octave. Later guitarists from northern Italy continue in the style of Foscarini, using the lowest courses both as bass strings and as upper octave melody notes. The successors to Valdambrini have yet to be explored, but Gaspar Sanz and some later French and Spanish guitarists also use the re-entrant tuning. Since tablature is not pitch-specific, both tuning methods were notated in exactly the same manner; modern performers and editors, however, must make a more binding decision. Lacking information on tuning in the original sources, such as those of Granata and his Bolognese contemporaries, performers should choose a tuning and performance method that enables them to use both upper and lower octaves on the lowest two courses of the instrument.

---

[20] Twentieth-century folk guitarists in Calabria use a high octave g[1] string attached to a peg driven through the fingerboard from the back of the neck. See Roberta Tucci and Antonello Ricci, 'The Chitarra Battente in Calabria', *GSJ* 38 (1985), p. 78. While this shortened string may be of use as a high drone in strummed music, there are serious problems involving its use in more complex music. Still, it serves as an example of the ingenuity of luthiers and guitarists.

[21] Note the similarity between a hypothetical stringing with upper octaves on the lower three courses and the re-entrant tuning of the theorbo, an instrument that was played by several Bolognese guitarists.

The reconstruction of an important and vital performance tradition cannot be based solely on individual works or references studied in isolation, or on what may well be unrelated sources from diverse eras and countries. The complicated issue of stringing for the five-course guitar, as well as other unresolved issues in its performance practice, must therefore be resolved through a judicious combination of three related areas of study: (1) textual references by composers or theorists; (2) the music in the tablatures themselves; and (3) practical experimentation with the original instrument.

PRIMARY SOURCES CITED IN THIS CHAPTER

Abbatessa, Giovanni Battista. *Intessitura di varii fiori* (Rome and Lucca, 1652)

Asioli, Francesco. *Primi scherzi di chitarra* (Bologna, 1674)

    Concerti armonici per la chitarra spagnuola . . . opera terza (Bologna, 1676)

Bartolotti, Angiolo Michele. *Libro primo di chitarra spagnola* (Florence, 1640)

    Secondo libro di chitarra (Rome, *ca.* 1655)

Bottazzari, Giovanni. *Sonate nuove per la chitarra spagnola* (Venice, 1663)

Calvi, Carlo. *Intavolatura di chitarra e chitarriglia* (Bologna, 1646)

Corbetta, Francesco. *De gli scherzi armonici* (Bologna, 1639)

    Varii capricci per la ghitarra spagnuola (Milan, 1643)

Costanzo, Fabrizio. *Fior novello Libro I* (Bologna, 1627)

Foscarini, Giovanni Paolo. *Intavolatura di chitarra spagnola . . . libro secondo* (Macerata, 1629)

    Il primo, secondo, e terzo libro della chitarra spagnola (n.p., *ca.* 1630)

    I quatro libri della chitarra spagnola (n.p., *ca.* 1635)

    Li 5 libri della chitarra alla spagnuola (Rome, 1640)

Granata, Giovanni Battista. *Capricci armonici sopra la chitarriglia spagnuola* (Bologna, 1646)

    Nuove suonate di chitarriglia spagnuola picciate, e battute . . . opera seconda (Bologna, *ca.* 1650)

    Nuova scielta di capricci armonici e suonate musicali in vari tuoni opera terza (Bologna, 1651)

    Soavi concenti di sonate musicali per chitara spagnuola opera quarta (Bologna, 1659)

    Novi capricci armonici musicali . . . opera quinta (Bologna, 1674)

    Nuovi sovavi concenti . . . opera sesta (Bologna, 1680)

    Armoniosi toni di varie suonate musicali per la chitarra spagnuola (Bologna, 1684)

Micheli, Antonino di. *La nuova chitarra di regole* (Palermo, 1698)

Montesardo, Girolamo. *Nuova inventione d'intavolatura* (Florence, 1606)

Pellegrini, Domenico. *Armoniosi concerti sopra la chitarra spagnuola* (Bologna, 1650)

Pesori, Stefano. *Galeria musicale* (Verona, 1648)

    Lo scrigno armonico . . . opera seconda (Mantua, *ca.* 1648)

    Toccate di chitarriglia . . . parte terza (Verona, *ca.* 1660)

    I concerti armonici di chitarriglia (Verona, *ca.* 1660)

    Ricreationi armoniche overo toccate di chitarriglia (n.p., *ca.* 1675)

Roncalli, Ludovico. *Capricci armonici sopra la chitarra spagnola* (Bergamo, 1692)

Sanseverino, Benedetto. *Intavolatura facile . . . opera terza* (Milan, 1620)

    Il primo libro d'intavolatura per la chitarra alla spagnuola . . . opera terza (Milan, 1622)

Sfondrino, Giovanni Battista. *Trattenimento virtuoso . . . sonate per la chitarra* (Milan, 1637)

Trombetti, Agostino. *Intavolatura di sonate . . . libro primo* (Bologna, 1639)

    Intavolatura di sonate . . . libro due (Bologna, 1639)

    Libro secondo d'intavolatura di chitarra (Rome, 1647).

9

ESSENTIAL ISSUES IN PERFORMANCE PRACTICES OF THE CLASSICAL GUITAR, 1770–1850

RICHARD SAVINO

The intent of this chapter is to serve as a succinct, practical guide to performing classical guitar literature on a 'period' instrument. A significant amount of research into this topic has already been accomplished, most notably by Paul Cox, who gives a comprehensive survey of classical guitar tutors in his 1978 doctoral dissertation.[1] While valuable, however, Cox's work is essentially a summary of what these tutors profess and not a guide to performance practice; furthermore, there is little discussion of interpretive issues, such as ornamentation. To his credit, Cox remains objective and rarely comments from a personal or 'experiential' perspective. In contrast, the present chapter is highly subjective and frequently based on personal experimentation with the many diverse instruments of the guitar family that were used between 1770 and 1850. While I shall certainly refer to Cox's work, as well as to other research by Heck, Turnbull, Evans, and Wade, I shall also examine primary source material, including new information that has come to light since these studies were published.

When addressing the issue of classical guitar performance practice the guitarist encounters problems that do not exist for other instrumentalists. What is commonly referred to as the apex of the classical guitar period is, in fact, the early Romantic period, *ca.* 1800–40. In reality, the Classical period of *ca.* 1740–90, as it is described by most music historians, is a time of transition for the guitar, during which at least four kinds of guitars were in common use, each requiring somewhat different tuning, stringing, and playing techniques. Therefore, when performing a work from the *Classical* period one must first determine the instrument for which the repertory was originally composed. Two other questions must then be asked: (1) is it too great a compromise to perform these works on another, but different, instrument of the period, and (2) how does one go about performing these works from an informed perspective on a modern guitar?

---

[1] Paul Cox, 'Classic Guitar Technique and its Evolution as Reflected in the Method Books ca. 1770–1850', Ph.D. diss., Indiana University, 1978.

INSTRUMENTS AND STRINGING

The four kinds of guitars that existed in the late eighteenth century are the five-course, six-course, five-string, and six-string varieties.[2] Other guitar variants such as the English, lyre, and extended-range guitars are of peripheral import to this chapter and do not warrant discussion here. The five-course guitar, commonly referred to as a Baroque guitar, was developed during the late sixteenth century and was the primary guitar in use throughout the seventeenth and early eighteenth centuries. By the late 1700s this instrument had lost much of its popular appeal, as the lack of published music for the instrument during this period suggests. This is not to imply that the guitar was completely abandoned; on the contrary, it is probably safe to assume that the instrument was still the favoured companion of the travelling singer and lay musician, as it was – and still remains – an easy instrument with which to accompany simple songs. One of the last examples of a five-course guitar is an instrument that bears the label 'Joseph de Frias, Sevilla, 177[?]', which is housed at the Museo de la Festa at the Patronato Nacional del Misterio de Elche, Alicante. There is also another instrument by the same maker, dated 1793, which is in the collection of the Biblioteca Real, Palacio Real, Madrid.

With the exception of a tutor by Andre de Sotos (1764) and the above-described instruments by Joseph de Frias, evidence of the instrument at this time is scant and printed music limited. Yet, contrary to Paul Cox's explanation that there was a large gap in the guitar repertory and that a new period for the guitar was ushered in by the works of 1799,[3] recent discoveries reveal a continuous production of guitar music during this late eighteenth-century 'transitional period', most of which is only now slowly re-emerging.

Some of the earliest examples of a newly developed six-course guitar were made by Francisco Sanguino of Sevilla in the late 1750s. One of these instruments, dated 1759, is housed at the Gemeentemuseum, The Hague, and another is housed at the Museu de la Música in Barcelona. While these guitars may have been isolated examples of a newly emerging instrument, by the early 1770s the six-course guitar had become firmly established in both Spain and Latin America. In particular, newly discovered manuscripts by Juan Antonio Vargas y Guzmán clearly show the evolution from the five- to the six-course guitar. One of these manuscripts bears the date 1773 and identifies the author as being a resident of Cádiz. Two others are dated 1776 and identify Vargas y Guzmán as a resident of Veracruz, Mexico.[4] In his preface Guzmán discusses the tutors by previous masters of the guitar, all of whom

---

[2] This article adopts the common terminology in which 'courses' are defined as double strings and 'strings' as single.

[3] Cox, 'Classic Guitar Technique', p. 23.

[4] A copy of one of these manuscripts is presently housed at the Newberry Library in Chicago. For more information see Robert Stevenson, 'A Neglected Mexican Guitar Manual of 1776', *Inter-American Music Review* 1 (1979), pp. 205–10.

composed for the five-course instrument. Besides Guzmán's another important eighteenth-century manual for six-course guitar was published in 1799 by Fernando Ferandiere.[5] While this corresponds with the date Cox gives as a turning point in guitar music, it must be noted that at the conclusion of Ferandiere's manual is an extensive list of his compositional output in which he clearly specifies which of his works are older and which were composed during the previous ten years.[6] Other eighteenth-century Spanish composers who wrote for this instrument include Isidro La Porta, Antonio Abreau, and Jimenez. The six-course guitar remained in use throughout Spain and Latin America until approximately 1810, when the six-string guitar became the standard. Furthermore, disputing Cox's claim that the earliest surviving six-string guitar made in Spain is that of José Recio (Cadiz, 1831), a recent exhibition at the Metropolitan Museum of Art in New York displayed three six-string guitars that predate the Recio instrument.[7] More important though, are the comments from Frederico Moretti's tutor published in Madrid in 1799: 'The French and Italians use single strings for their guitars, and in this way achieve a faster tuning and a longer life for their strings before going bad. It is difficult to find two equal strings giving exactly the same pitch. I follow this system, and I advise beginners to do the same thing, having known its great utility.'[8]

In France, the guitar of five courses was being restrung with single strings. In his *Traité des Agrèmens de la Musique executés sur la Guitarre* (1777), Giacomo Merchi provides an interesting and enlightening commentary: 'I am taking advantage of this foreword to say a word about the way to string the guitar with single strings. It is very easy now to find a great number of true strings. The single strings are very easy to tune and pluck cleanly. They make a pure sound, strong and mellow, and approach that of a harp, especially if one uses thicker strings.'[9] An illustration from Charles Doisy's *Principes Généraux de la Guitare* (Paris, 1801) shows that single strings were clearly in vogue (see Plate 10). The instrument described and illustrated in this tutor has none of the features that are characteristic of the later, true *classical* guitar, such as a raised fingerboard and a more exaggerated body shape; it is simply a five-course baroque guitar that has been restrung with single strings, as one can see by the number of pegs relative to strings. Doisy explains that 'As far as I am concerned, I adopted so much the more willingly the single strings on which the resulting sound is purer, the difficulty of pairing strings is eliminated, and which takes less time to tune.'[10] Most French guitar music of the true Classical period was composed

---

[5] Fernando Ferandiere, *Arte de Tocar la Guitarra Espanola por Musica* (Madrid, 1799; facsimile edn London, 1977).

[6] *ibid.*, pp. 31–2.

[7] *The Spanish Guitar* (New York, 1991), pp. 131–2 (catalogue of an exhibition at the Metropolitan Museum of Art in New York).

[8] Quoted in Cox, 'Classic Guitar Technique', p. 12.

[9] *ibid.*

[10] Charles Doisy, *Principes généraux de la guitare* (Paris, 1801) pp. 9–10.

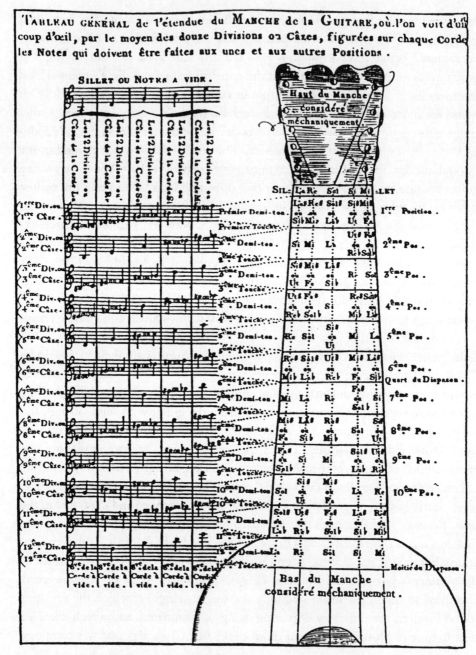

Plate 10   Charles Doisy, *Principes Généraux de la Guitare* (Paris, 1801)

for this type of instrument; in one collection of pieces for five-string guitar by Pierre Porro, there is even an arrangement of the overture to *Iphigénie en Aulide* by Gluck.[11] Another French composer who wrote for this instrument was Antoine L'Hoyer, who eventually made the switch to the six-string guitar. L'Hoyer's works for five-string guitar have recently taken on greater significance since it was discovered that he was the actual composer of the *Five Preludes*, Op. 83 which were often credited to Mauro Giuliani.[12] Giuliani may have appropriated music from the five-string guitar repertory on other occasions. Many of the arpeggios found in his Op. 1 *120 Right-Hand Studies* appear to have been directly 'lifted' from a collection published in 1792 by Federico Moretti.[13] By 1780, six-string guitars were regularly being built in southern France and the popularity of the five-string guitar was fading fast.

Even though the guitar is usually considered a 'Spanish' instrument, it is in Italy where the transition of the five-course Baroque guitar to the six-string Classical guitar seems to have been the most direct. To my knowledge the sole Italian evidence of a five-string guitar comes from the same Moretti manuscript mentioned above. In this manuscript, Moretti gives a tuning chart that clearly shows a five-single-string instrument (see Plate 11), which is the most direct precursor of the 'classical' guitar of the late eighteenth and early nineteenth century. When the Italians Mauro Giuliani and Ferdinando Carulli emigrated north to Vienna and Paris, respectively, they created in these cities a mania for the instrument that would last for over fifty years. In fact, evidence of significant interest in the Valencian guitar in Germany or eastern Europe prior to the arrival of Mauro Giuliani is scant at best. The exception appears to be Christian Gottlieb Scheidler, who was one of the few lutenists of the late eighteenth century to have also composed for the guitar.[14] As was the case with other stylistic developments, England lagged furthest behind, owing in no small part to its geographic isolation from the rest of Europe. The classical guitar does not appear there until approximately 1810, and its popularity peaked only after the arrival of Fernando Sor in 1815. Almost all references to the guitar prior to 1810 should be considered as referring to the *English* guitar, a type of cittern. To summarize our main points thus far:

- The five-course Baroque guitar lasted into the early Classical period, where it played a limited role in the music of that time.
- The five-string guitar enjoyed a brief period of popularity *ca.* 1777–1808, almost exclusively in France.
- The six-course guitar was widely used in Spain and Latin America, and flourished during the years *ca.* 1759–1805.

[11]   Pierre Porro, *Ouvertures arrangées en Sonates pour Guitare et Violon*, facsimile edn (Monaco, 1981).
[12]   See Matanya Ophée, 'The Guitarist's Album', *Soundboard* 17 (1990), pp. 80–7.
[13]   See Frederico Moretti, *Principi per la Chitarra* (Naples, *ca.* 1792; rpt Florence, 1983), Tavola XVII.
[14]   Christian Gottlieb Scheidler, *Two Sonatas for Guitar* (Mainz, *ca.* 1800; facsimile edn Monaco, 1981).

- The six-string *classical* guitar emerges at different times from different cultures, yet if Europe is considered as a whole, we can recognize that the six-string guitar is established *ca.* 1780 in a form that is an extension of the earlier five-course Baroque guitar – that is, with a fingerboard that is flush with the top of the instrument and bridge without a saddle. It should be noted that many five-course Baroque guitars were expanded to six strings during the late eighteenth century.

This transformation of the guitar from the five-course Baroque instrument of the seventeenth and early eighteenth centuries to the six-string instrument of the early nineteenth century represents a remarkable metamorphosis that parallels the larger changes taking place in Western art music. Further developments took place from around 1780 to 1850, during which the instrument evolved to encompass a number of interesting features: seven, eight, or ten single strings; bridges with a saddle upon which the strings rested; the introduction of tuning machines; the replacement of movable gut frets with fixed frets; a variety of raised fingerboards; the internal reworking of the instrument; and the eventual standardization of construction materials. Accompanying this transformation was a dramatic shift from tablature, through the intermediary violin notational system with its specific lack of voice-leading, to the present system of staff notation.[15] Although tablature is still used today, especially in popular guitar songbooks, methods, transcriptions, and, of course, by lutenists, it was falling out of favour during the mid eighteenth century.

PERFORMANCE PRACTICE

The subject of performance practice on the guitar is a most complex issue. With every variable that one encounters in tuning, instrument construction, nationalistic tendencies, and style, there is a corresponding technical and aesthetic judgement to be made. These decisions, if they are to be of any import, cannot be made in a vacuum. Thoughtful consideration and deliberation can lead to interpretations that acknowledge, but do not blindly follow, historical practices. What follows are suggestions based on personal experience and a close examination of relevant treatises and tutors. They are not prescriptions to imitate but rather alternatives to liberate and demystify the important points of this literature.

Technique and seating position

Tutors and iconographic evidence show that there was little standardization in how the guitar was held during the late eighteenth and early nineteenth centuries. For instance, many paintings portray the guitarist in a leisurely position when playing

---

[15] See Thomas Heck, 'The Birth of the Classic Guitar and its Cultivation in Vienna, Reflected in the Career and Compositions of Mauro Giuliani (d. 1829)', Ph.D. diss., Yale University, 1970, pp. 153–68.

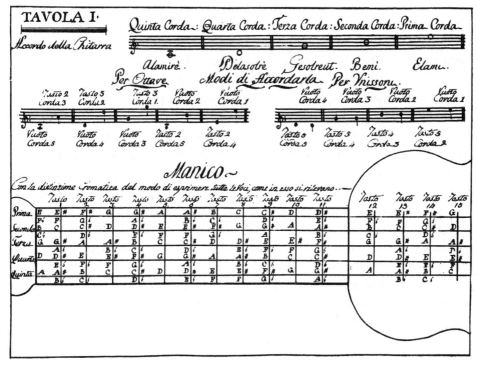

Plate 11   Frederico Moretti, *Principi per la Chitarra* (Naples, *ca.* 1792), Tavola I

what appear to be simple chordal accompaniments to a song. But when it comes to performing art music of a more complex nature, proper support of the instrument is essential. How this support is provided has been a subject of discussion from the seventeenth century to the present day.

One of the main issues in holding the guitar is determining the angle at which each hand will meet the instrument. Specifically, how will the right hand meet the strings, and by extension, at what angle will the instrument be held? Complicating this decision is the question of whether or not the player chooses to use right-hand fingernails. Nail players of early plucked instruments often attack the strings at an oblique angle, thereby avoiding a sharp metallic sound and the hooking of the string that can result when plucked at a perpendicular angle; it may benefit the player, in this case, to hold the instrument at a more horizontal angle. Players who use only the flesh will usually try to achieve a brighter sound and therefore can afford to pluck the string more 'straight on', holding the guitar at an angle of approximately 45° from the floor. Naturally, this is a rule of thumb only, and some performers can use either angle and still achieve their desired result.

The conventional sitting position of modern guitarists involves the use of some sort of footstool to elevate the left leg upon which the guitar rests. For some, this manner of sitting results in persistent back, shoulder, or neck pain (and it can be theorized that upper-body physical discomfort and tension were also experienced by the players of earlier times, all the more so given the variation in size and shape of their instruments). The main drawback to the raised-left-foot/footstool position when playing the small late eighteenth- and early nineteenth-century guitars is that the instrument will still sit quite low and, in certain instances, cause the player to use an excessively curved left-hand wrist and a hunched back. A solution is for guitarists to place a small piece of sponge or foam padding between the guitar and their leg, similar to what many Baroque violinists use to help support the violin between their chin and collarbone.

Many tutors from the seventeenth to the nineteenth century include instructions or engravings showing that a popular sitting position was one in which the base of the guitar rests on the lap of the right leg, while the neck of the instrument is supported by a strap that is then draped over the player's shoulder and either sat on or attached to the bottom of the guitar. There are a number of guitarists (and lutenists) presently performing on period instruments who use this seating position to good effect. I have yet to share their enthusiasm since I find that the instrument is not adequately stabilized and tends to shift. In addition this position places the end of the guitar neck at a point that is too far removed from the body and causes me to bend and over-extend my left wrist, resulting in an occasional inflammation of the wrist tendons. A second alternative is a standing position. While never advocated outright in tutors, the inclusion of strap buttons on most late eighteenth- and early nineteenth-century instruments suggests that this could be a possibility with historical precedent. One advantage of this position is that since the guitar is raised an additional two feet at least, the instrument can project more sound, an improvement that I can attest to from experience. If supported by the weight and pressure of the right arm, the instrument can be adequately stabilized, though still not as securely as when seated and supported by the left leg.[16]

The position generally used by lutenists, in which the player crosses the left leg over the right and rests the instrument on both legs, is a possible alternative for some players. While this position can be very useful when playing on smaller instruments, it can inhibit circulation in the left leg and cause the back to be hunched over, producing a certain degree of discomfort and upper body tension. In attempts to

---

[16] The title page of Johann Nepomuk Hummel's *Sérénade en potpourri*, Op. 63 (Vienna, *ca.* 1814–15) for piano, violin (or flute), guitar, clarinet, and bassoon (or 'cello) contains a miniature engraving showing an ensemble with these instruments and the guitarist standing. This work is a 'potpourri' based on themes by Mozart and was composed for a series of concerts that were given in the Schönbrunn Botanical Gardens in Vienna during the summers of 1814–16. The guitarist at these concerts was none other than the famed Mauro Giuliani, who also composed much of the guitar part; this is indicated in the guitar part itself. Although this engraving presents a romanticized picture of how these performers might have appeared, might it not also suggest that Giuliani performed from a standing position?

resolve the issue, some peculiar contortions were advocated by some of the most responsible pedagogues, including Fernando Sor, who suggests resting the instrument against a table while playing,[17] and Dionisio Aguado, who recommends sitting on the far left corner of a chair and resting the base of the guitar on the chair's right side.[18] Finally, there is the apparatus designed by Aguado that was called the tripodium. This device secured the guitar on a large tripod that was placed in a position that enabled the player to perform while standing and without the guitar actually touching the player's body (see Plate 12). According to Aguado, this 'sitting' method resulted in increased volume and projection. Sor thought so highly of the tripodium that he published his *Elegiac Fantasy,* Op. 59, with the comment that it could only be performed effectively if using this device. Regardless of the sitting position one finally chooses, primary consideration should always be given to comfort and playing ease. It should be remembered that many of the famed pedagogues of the early nineteenth century advocated more than one kind of seating, much in contrast to most modern teachers who prefer a single, standardized position.

The right hand and fingernails

Rarely has there been an issue that has so divided the guitar and lute world than the question of using right-hand fingernails in the performance of 'early music'. It is important to point out that there is evidence for playing both with and without nails from the seventeenth to the nineteenth century, provided by lutenists and guitarists such as Alessandro Piccinini, Sylvius Leopold Weiss, Domenico Pellegrini, Fernando Ferandiere, and Dionisio Aguado. Ferandiere, an advocate of nail use, writes that 'our guitar is played with at least three fingers of the right hand, without any more nail than is necessary to strike the string'.[19] Aguado's more thorough comments on this subject recognize that technical differences exist between the two manners of execution:

The right hand can pluck the strings with the tips of the fingers only, or with the fingertips and then with the part of the nail which protrudes beyond the fingertip. These two forms of plucking require different uses of the fingers of the right hand. Without the nails, the fingers must be bent so as to grip the strings; with the nails, the fingers are less bent so that the string will *slide* along the nail.[20]

---

[17] Fernando Sor, *Method for the Spanish Guitar*, trans. A. Merrick (London, 1850; facsimile rpt New York, 1980), p. 10.

[18] Dionisio Aguado, *Méthode Complète Pour la Guitare* (Paris, 1826), plate 1.

[19] Ferandiere, *Arte de Tocar la Guitarra*, p. 6.

[20] Dionisio Aguado, *Nuevo Mètodo para Guitarra* (Madrid, 1843), trans. Brian Jeffery (London, 1981), p. 10 (hereinafter, *New Method*).

Plate 12   Dionisio Aguado, *Nuevo Método* (Madrid, 1843), Plate 1, 'tripodium'

Aguado goes on to recount his modification to this technique after having heard the playing of Fernando Sor: 'I had always used the nails of all the fingers I used to pluck, including the thumb, but after listening to my friend Sor I decided not to use the nail on the thumb, and I am very pleased to have done this . . .'[21] In subsequent paragraphs, he gives reasons for why he prefers to play with nails, how they should be shaped, and against their being too long. His comments about nails are remarkably similar to those made by the lutenist Alessandro Piccinini in 1623, and his concluding statements on the subject are interesting and refreshingly non-dogmatic: 'If the nails are used, runs can be performed very rapidly and clearly. There is an important exception, however. Persons with very long fingers should not play with the nails, because this gives each finger more leverage on the strings and thus diminishes the force used.'[22] Aguado clearly accepts that playing without nails is also a legitimate technique.

Writing as an advocate of flesh technique, Fernando Sor remarks that 'Never in my life have I heard a guitarist whose playing was supportable, if he played with the nails. The nails produce but very few graduations in the quality of the sound: the piano passages can never be singing, nor the fortes sufficiently full.'[23] About Aguado, Sor then states: 'It is necessary that the performance of Mr Aguado should have so many qualities as it possesses, to excuse his employment of the nails; and he himself would have condemned the use of them if he had not attained such a degree of agility, nor found himself beyond the time of life in which we are able to contend against the bend of the fingers acquired by a long habitude.'[24] Although later in this section Sor claims that Aguado had confessed to him that 'if he were to begin again he would play without using the nails',[25] there is no evidence in any of his writings to support this, other than the removal of his thumbnail. Interestingly, the reasons for Aguado's use of nails are precisely why Sor occasionally recommends Aguado's method: 'His master played with the nails, and shone at a period when rapid passages alone were required of the guitar, when the only object in view was to dazzle and astonish.'[26] A few pages later he confesses: 'As to the right hand, I have never aimed to play scales staccato, or detached, nor with great rapidity . . .', concluding that 'should the reader wish to learn to detach notes with rapidity in a difficult passage, I cannot do better than refer him to the method of Mr. Aguado, who, excelling in this kind of execution, is prepared to establish the best rules respecting it'.[27] Later, he makes one last reference to this subject: 'When it is [a] question of a staccato passage

---

[21] *ibid.*

[22] *ibid.*, p. 11.

[23] Sor, *Method*, p. 17.

[24] *ibid.*

[25] *ibid.*

[26] *ibid.*

[27] *ibid.*, pp. 21–2.

without accompaniment, I have heard several guitarists (and chiefly Mr. Aguado) who make them with surprising neatness and velocity, by employing alternately the first and second or third fingers.'[28]

Which technique, then, is the most appropriate? I propose that one keep an open mind regarding both. To be sure, a certain degree of commitment to either nails or flesh is essential in order to develop one's own technique to its fullest potential; yet, as Sor and Aguado themselves recognize, both techniques are appropriate and allow for unique interpretive results. Sor put it most succinctly when he commented on Aguado's performance of one of his works: 'he succeeded in playing all the notes very distinctly; and if the nails did not allow him to give the same expression as I did, he gave one peculiar to himself, which injured nothing'.[29]

More crucial than the issue of nails is the manner in which sound is produced on early plucked instruments. From personal experience, I can state unequivocally that a nail player (as I am) can produce a sound that is close to, if not entirely indistinguishable from, that of a flesh player. Nails can produce a harsher, brighter sound, but this depends on how the nails are used as well as the type of instrument. Among the specific advantages of using nails are an increased volume and a more well-defined articulation. Given today's performing venues, and because I enjoy playing in a variety of ensemble settings, I choose to play with nails. Historically, this appears to fall into line with the practices of certain guitarists. Fernando Sor, for example, who played without nails, was not known for his chamber and concerto performances, and all of his published music that remains is either for solo or two guitars. At the opposite end there is Aguado, whose method specifically recommends the use of right-hand fingernails and describes a variety of techniques for their employment as a means of creating timbral diversity. Aguado's close friend François de Fossa, who edited Aguado's method and translated it from the original Spanish to French, composed some extraordinary chamber music for guitar and multiple strings, and there are accounts of his having performed these works in concert. This, coupled with his obvious familiarity with Aguado's method, suggests that he too played with nails.[30] Then there is Fernando Ferandiere, who advocates the use of nails in his method for six-course guitar and composed many works for guitar and multiple instruments, including some six concertos for guitar and full orchestra.[31] There is never any mention of the issue of nails in the methods or writings of either Giuliani and Carulli, although it would have been logical for these guitarists, both of whom were active in chamber music circles, to use right-hand nails rather than flesh. Giuliani regularly performed with some of the greatest virtuosos of early

[28]   *ibid.*, pp. 32–3.
[29]   *ibid.*, p. 17.
[30]   It should be noted that six of Luigi Boccherini's guitar quintets have come down to us only in de Fossa's hand.
[31]   Ferandiere, *Arte de Tocar la Guitarra*, pp. 31–2.

nineteenth-century Vienna, including the pianists Johann Nepomuk Hummel and Ignaz Moscheles, and the violinist Joseph Mayseder. Some of these performances even took place out of doors (see n. 16, above), and it seems that Giuliani would have used whatever means necessary to ensure that his instrument was clearly heard at these concerts. These circumstances coupled with the numerous chamber works and full concertos that flowed from his pen, suggest that he, too, used right-hand fingernails. But it is the nature of Giuliani's writing that provides the most persuasive evidence of his use of nails. Unlike Sor, who specifies that many of his scale passages are to be slurred, Giuliani's compositions (like Aguado's) contain many rapid, unslurred passages, which are most effectively executed with nails.

Right-hand technique and sound quality

Once the issue of performing with or without nails is resolved, the player must then confront the issues of timbre, hand position, and fingering. Timbre is an important subject since both Sor and Aguado, although employing very different techniques, describe various effects that are possible on the guitar, including imitations of the harp and wind, brass, and percussion instruments. The most important issues to consider regarding sound production include determining where the point of articulation begins, the angle of the stroke, and its follow-through or release. The angle at which the guitar is held will usually impact on the angle of the finger stroke when plucking. Contemporary guitarists playing on modern instruments, which are for the most part larger and strung with thicker strings of a higher tension, will usually hold their right-hand wrist at an angle that is arched an inch or two above the soundboard, and then pluck at an angle that is more perpendicular to the string. While this technique is easily applied to the later instruments of the period *ca.* 1815–40, and is clearly advocated in Aguado's tutor of 1843, it is less appropriate for instruments of the earlier period. For the most part, pre-1815 guitars are set up with the strings fairly close to the soundboard with a very small saddle on the bridge, and those prior to 1800 usually have no bridge saddle whatsoever. This results in very little room between the strings and the soundboard for a stroke follow-through, which is essential for a resonant sound production.

Similar problems exist when performing on instruments that are strung with double courses. A perpendicular, or 'straight-on', stroke that is coupled with a highly arched wrist and fingernails that are on the 'long' side will usually produce a tinny or metallic sound. Furthermore, in order to avoid hitting and scratching the top of the guitar, the perpendicular modern stroke is often executed on a plane that is more parallel to the plane of the strings and is usually too forceful for more lightly strung period instruments. This tends to be more of a problem with instruments strung with double courses. The modern guitar stroke will often cause the strings of these instruments to be displaced to an excessive degree and cause them to rattle against each other. This is less of a problem with single-strung guitars, though the strings on these instruments are still very close to the top of the instrument. Consequently, players using modern technique with long nails will still have a problem of their fingers hitting the top of the instrument when the strings are plucked.

There is, however, a solution to this dilemma that does not require any radical overhaul of modern guitar technique. First, one must recognize that modern guitar technique, even with its diverse 'schools', is the logical extension of mid-nineteenth-century guitar technique. With the emergence of the Tárrega 'school' and its modification and further transformation by the twentieth-century guitarists Emilio Pujol, Miguel Llobet, Andrés Segovia, and their apprentices, right-hand guitar technique became dominated by the *apoyando*, or 'rest', stroke. When executed on later instruments with high-tension strings and ample clearance between the strings and soundboard, this stroke produces a very loud, full-toned pitch. On many late eighteenth- and early nineteenth-century instruments, however, this stroke is too strong and can result in rattling, buzzing, and a generally unpleasant sound. On these instruments it is important that the angle of the stroke be more oblique and towards the top of the instrument. This can easily be accomplished with a 'free' stroke that presses into and 'springs' off the string. A similar position is described in 1799 by Federico Moretti: 'The right hand should be held horizontally with the strings, because in this situation the fingers can play more easily and the fingernails do not get in the way.'[32] The result is a full-toned pitch that is similar to a rest stroke on a modern guitar but has the unique timbral characteristics of an early, or 'period' instrument. I have found that this is most easily accomplished by holding the right hand in a position that resembles a semi-circle, thus enabling the player to grasp the string securely, press it towards the top, and then release with a spring-like motion. To facilitate this hand position I suggest that the player experiment with one of the earliest classical guitar right-hand positions: the placing of the little finger on the soundboard of the instrument and holding the hand in what is most commonly described by lutenists as a 'thumb-over' position, in which the thumb is held above and at a right angle to the fingers. This position shapes the fingers into the above-described semi-circle by placing the hand closer to the instrument's top.[33]

The placing of the right-hand little finger on the soundboard of the instrument is a position that has existed throughout the history of plucked string instruments, from lutenists of the early sixteenth century to present-day electric guitarists and country

---

[32] Quoted in Cox, 'Classic Guitar Technique', p. 45.

[33] This is very similar to what was already described in Alessandro Piccinini's *Intavolatura di Liuto, et di Chitarrone* (Bologna, 1623; facsimile rpt Florence, 1983), pp. 2–3.

'pluckers.' As is well known, this technique was abandoned by mid-nineteenth-century classical guitarists and is no longer a part of modern classical guitar technique. This change in hand position occurred gradually, and paralleled the changes in musical styles and instrument making. It is easier to use this technique on the earliest classical guitars, whose fingerboards are flush with the instrument's top and whose bridges lack a saddle. On these instruments the strings are very close to the soundboard and the right-hand little finger serves as a support that prevents the fingers from constantly hitting the top. This hand position is advocated by most pre-1820 guitar tutors. P. J. Baillon (1781) states that the 'right hand must be fixed on the little finger between the bridge and the rosette so as to be able to pluck near the latter'.[34] To this we can add Carulli's comments that 'The hand must rest lightly on the little finger, which must lie almost next to the E string, and precisely in between the bridge and rosette', and that 'This hand has no fixed position, because when one wants to soften the sounds and imitate the harp, one must play closer to the rosette, and closer to the bridge to play *forte*.'[35] This last statement demonstrates Carulli's increased awareness of the guitar's timbral diversity. Sor is a partial advocate for this hand position, stating that 'sometimes I employ the little finger, pressing it perpendicularly on the sounding-board below the first string, but taking care to raise it as soon as it ceases to be necessary'.[36]

The drawbacks of this position are that an *apoyando* forefinger stroke becomes very difficult to execute and it limits the use of the right-hand ring finger. Most tutors acknowledge this by rarely advocating the former, and carefully discussing the use of the latter. In his brief method for six-course guitar, Fernando Ferandiere writes that 'our guitar is played with at least three fingers of the right hand'[37] – I interpret this as referring to the thumb, index, and middle fingers – and according to Carulli, 'One must pluck the sixth, fifth and fourth strings with the thumb of the right hand, and the three other strings with the fore-finger and the middle finger, alternating with each note. The ring finger is used only when playing chords and arpeggios.'[38] Carulli goes on to give a series of exercises for playing scales on the bass strings with the thumb alone.[39] In a more analytical discourse from his method, Sor writes: 'I therefore establish as a rule of my fingering, for the right hand, to employ commonly only the three fingers touched by the line A B, and to use the fourth only for playing a chord in four parts of which the part nearest to the base leaves an intermediate string.'[40] An illustration (see Plate 13) accompanies this comment.

34 P. J. Baillon, *Nouvelle Méthode de Guitarre* (Paris, 1781), p. 4.
35 Ferdinando Carulli, *Méthode Complète pour Guitare*, Op. 241 (Paris, 1825), p. 6.
36 Sor, *Method*, p. 33.
37 Ferandiere, *Arte de Tocar la Guitarra*, p. 6.
38 Carulli, *Méthode*, p. 7.
39 *ibid.*, pp. 8–10.
40 Sor, *Method*, p. 11.

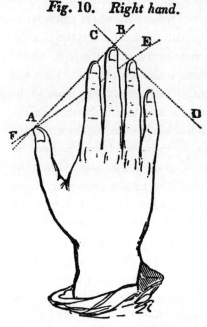

Plate 13   Fernando Sor, *Method for the Spanish Guitar* (*ca.* 1850), p. 11

While some might question the wisdom of adopting such a technique, there are benefits to be obtained from its employment. For instance, it gives greater flexibility to the thumb in the execution of certain passage work, as some passages from works by Sor clearly demonstrate (Exx. 9.1a–b).

Aguado describes the same technique in detail: 'Instead of using four digits of the right hand to pluck chords played on four consecutive strings, the thumb is applied firmly to the lowest string and is then forced *rapidly* across the next after the first has sounded. The same can be done in cases where two consecutive strings must be plucked at one time.'[41] Personal experience has shown that it helps if one performs these kinds of passages with a short or no thumbnail, as advocated by both Sor and Aguado. In addition, many tutors recommend using the thumb in the treble and melodic contexts, and in another homage to lute technique, both Sor and Doisy clearly state that articulated scales are to be played by alternating the thumb and index fingers.[42] It is precisely for these reasons that I advocate experimenting with and, to some extent, adopting this hand position of placing the little finger on the top of the instrument, for it forces the player to come to grips with the benefits offered by early classical guitar fingerings and strokes.

[41]   Aguado, *New Method*, p. 58.
[42]   Sor, *Method*, p. 33; Doisy, *Principes*, p. 63.

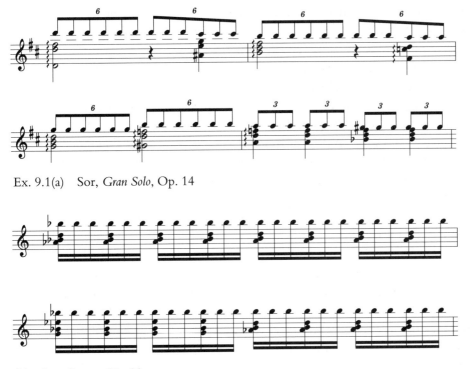

Ex. 9.1(a)   Sor, *Gran Solo*, Op. 14

(b)   Sor, *Sonata*, Op. 22

Two guitarists who clearly broke with the above traditions are Giuliani and Aguado. Although Giuliani never states a position, his Op. 1 right-hand studies show a thorough and active use of the ring finger to an extent that would be all but impossible if the right-hand little finger were placed on top of the guitar. Aguado makes a clear, forceful, and repeated argument against this right-hand placement of the little finger as early as 1825: 'By no means should the little finger or any other be rested on the table, because the hand must be free and completely loose.'[43] Later, in 1843, he tempers his tone somewhat:

Some rest the little finger of the right hand on the soundboard so as to give sureness to the hand when plucking. This may have been useful for some people while the guitar was not in a fixed position, but now that it is played on the tripod I do not consider this support necessary because the fingers of the right hand depend on the support given by the forearm and wrist. Two more disadvantages are avoided in this way – the weight this finger lays on the soundboard which is a real impediment to its vibration, and the danger of staining it with the contact of the finger. Another advantage is that the hand is more nimble and able to perform all the movements desired.[44]

---

[43]   Dionisio Aguado, *Escuela de Guitarra* (Madrid, 1825), p. 3.

[44]   Aguado, *New Method*, p. 11.

Yet Aguado still recommends the use of the middle over the ring finger: 'In order to obtain from the strings all the tone they can give, I generally prefer to use the middle finger of the right hand rather than the ring finger since it is stronger',[45] and almost all the exercises that follow, including those that are arpeggiated, confirm this preference. Curiously, the engravings in this method appear to show Aguado resting his little finger on the bridge of his instrument. It was not until the appendix to his method was posthumously published in 1849 that the engraving clearly shows the little finger *not* resting on the instrument.[46] This appendix also contains Aguado's suggestion for using the right-hand little finger: 'The direction and firmness of these fingers [right-hand index and middle] are also useful when the ring finger and even the *little finger* are used, because they successively give support to those which follow.'[47] In a footnote, he adds that he has 'thoroughly considered the great force needed to enable the ring and little fingers to pluck strongly keeping the hand in the position explained; however, after experimenting with my pupils, I have observed that this difficulty can be overcome'.[48] To my knowledge Aguado is also the first author to advocate an *apoyando* stroke for the forefingers of the right hand. Describing a passage consisting of consecutive thirds, he writes: 'The forefinger can also pluck the first and second strings when they have to be sounded together, for example in intervals of a third. If the nails are used, the first string must be plucked sharply so that the finger passes over the second string, sounding it and then coming to rest on the third.'[49] While certainly unconventional, it is still an *apoyando* stroke, and it must be remembered that when this method was published in 1843, Aguado was playing on a guitar that was much closer in design to our modern guitar than that which was used in the first decades of the nineteenth century.

The left hand

Left-hand guitar technique for performance of 'classical' works is for the most part similar to left-hand Baroque or modern guitar technique. The exceptions to this are (1) the use of the left-hand thumb, and (2) the frequency with which modern performers finger passages in high positions that are more easily played in the lower positions. Whereas today it is commonplace to use the left-hand thumb for fingering notes on the sixth string when playing guitars with narrow necks, such as acoustic steel-string and electric, it is no longer a part of classical guitar technique, because of the size and thickness of the modern classical guitar neck. On early nineteenth-

[45]   *ibid.*, p. 11.
[46]   *ibid.*, Plate 1.
[47]   *ibid.*, p. 170.
[48]   *ibid.*
[49]   *ibid.*, p. 58.

century guitars with narrow necks this was not as much of a problem, and many authors, including Giuliani, Mertz, and Carulli, call for reaching around the neck with the thumb and using it in this manner. This was not a universally accepted technique, however, and Carulli specifically refers to this in his method:

In certain manuals the authors absolutely forbid their students to use the left-hand thumb, opposite the other fingers on the sixth and sometimes on the fifth strings. Music is all the more pleasant in that it is rich in harmony, and four fingers do not suffice to play at the same time a melody and a figured bass in different keys. To achieve this one must use the thumb; therefore, I invite all those who wish to play the guitar with greater ease to do so.[50]

Interestingly, Carulli suggests that there are players who use the left-hand thumb to finger notes on not only the sixth but the *fifth* string, *and* he also speaks about figured bass as if it were standard training for classical/early Romantic guitarists. Sor clearly opposes this technique,

because I could not press a string with the thumb without contracting my shoulder, without bringing my hand behind the neck (and consequently annulling in a great measure the play of the fingers shortened by one half), and putting the wrist into a position far from easy, in order that the tendons which should actuate the joints may have the room and direction suited to the liberty of their action.[51]

In Aguado's case the fact that he neither advocates nor condemns this technique might lead one to assume that he held no opinion on the subject. But a close examination of his left-hand recommendations clearly places him in Sor's camp. Speaking subjectively, I agree with Sor, but it is also true that many modern guitarists have employed this technique with great effect.

Regarding the second exception, the fingering of passages, it has become clear after examining many late eighteenth- and early nineteenth-century manuscripts and editions, that most authors expect the performer to execute difficult passages using the most efficient and least difficult means. At the conclusion of his method Sor gives a list of general maxims that reinforce this principle, which form the result of all that he has previously stated in his method. Maxims 3, 4, and 5 state the following:

To be sparing of the operations called barring and shifting.

To consider fingering as an art, having for its object to make me find the notes I want, within reach of the fingers that are to produce them, without the continual necessity of making deviations for the purpose of seeking them.

Never to make any ostentation of difficulty in my playing, for by doing so, I should render difficult what is the least so.[52]

---

[50] Carulli, *Méthode*, p. 6.
[51] Sor, *Method*, p. 13.
[52] *ibid.*, p. 48.

One final point about left-hand technique should be mentioned. Whereas Aguado preferred playing scales in a detached manner, Sor is an advocate for playing such passages in a much more legato fashion, similar to Baroque lute technique. He states that he plays 'only the note which commences every group composing the passage',[53] and then directs the reader to look at an example clearly showing a scale passage that is made up of slurs. Interestingly, Sor makes no attempt to begin these on a strong beat, but always begins these slurs on the next most convenient note. His greater concern is for an overall legato sound.

Ornamentation

The subject of ornamentation is far too complex to cover in a chapter of this length. Therefore I will address those issues which I feel are most relevant to the previous discussion. What follows, then, is a general guide to realizing certain specific ornaments found in the classical guitar literature.

The trill

This is one of the most common and most misinterpreted ornaments found in the repertory. With the exception of late eighteenth-century French tutors such as Baillon and Doisy, which are obviously indebted to earlier French Baroque practices, almost every source I have examined advocates the use of main-note trills starting on the consonant harmonic tone.[54] This holds true for Giuliani, Aguado, and Carulli. Both Carulli and Giuliani suggest two means of executing this ornament: (1) slurring or 'hammering' on a single string, and (2) using a 'cross-string' technique, that is to say, plucking two separate strings in rapid succession.[55] Carulli often goes a step further by writing out measured main-note trills, as in his *Grand Sonata,* Op. 83 (Ex. 9.2).

Although he uses the same sign for each, Carulli differentiates between the *trille* and the *cadence,* the former being a trill that is executed as an ornament in passage work, and the latter a kind of trill that is employed at cadences. Carulli defines the *trille* as 'an ornament and one executes it by slurring the note on which it is placed with the note above, but very quickly, and as many times as one can manage for the duration of the note'.[56] He then gives an example (Ex. 9.3). From this I have concluded that Carulli is an advocate of 'double-dotting' in such passages. Note, in the

---

[53] *ibid.,* p. 21.

[54] One additional exception to this is Niccolò Paganini, who gives a written-out, cross-string, upper auxiliary trill to the guitar in bars 99 and 247 of the first movement of his *Terzetto in D* for viola, cello, and guitar (Zimmerman edition (Frankfurt, 1980)). This is the only occasion of which I am aware where Paganini writes out a trill; and that it is specifically of the upper auxiliary kind might simply be an example of his violin vocabulary being adapted to the guitar.

[55] This is the technique that was often used by Baroque guitarists such as Giovanni Battista Granata and Francisco Corbetta.

[56] Carulli, *Méthode,* p. 51.

Ex. 9.2   Carulli, *Grand Sonata*, Op. 83, bars 170–3

Ex. 9.3   Carulli, *Méthode Complete pour Guitare*, Op. 241, p. 51

realization, how he adds value to the note being trilled and compensates by taking value from the next note.

Concerning the *cadence,* or cadential trill, Carulli gives three different realizations (Ex. 9.4). Aguado advocates only the 'slurred' trill and describes it as 'a beating of two notes at intervals of a tone or semitone, played by a single voice or two at a time and repeated many times at great speed, plucking *only* the first note with the right hand, and then slurring the rest, but all must be heard equally'.[57] He then gives two separate signs for its use: *tr* and ⌣. The accompanying example to this instruction clearly shows that he is referring to a main-note trill.

Doisy describes three types of *cadences* (see Ex. 9.5):

the *cadence parfaite* [perfect], the *jetée* [thrown] and the *feinte* [faked]. Two ornaments played quickly together, the *son porté* [hammer-on slurs] and the *chute* [pull-off slur] make up the cadence, which is only ever made up of two notes separated by a half-step or, at the very most, a step.

The *cadence parfaite* is indicated by a *trait tremblé* (~) turned up at one end, indicating the manner in which to end the cadence.

The *cadence jetée* is indicated by a small cross (+), meaning without preparation:

The *cadence feinte* is indicated by a *trait tremblé simplement* (~), as if to mean something imperfect.[58]

---

[57]   Aguado, *New Method*, p. 44.
[58]   Doisy, *Principes*, pp. 62–3.

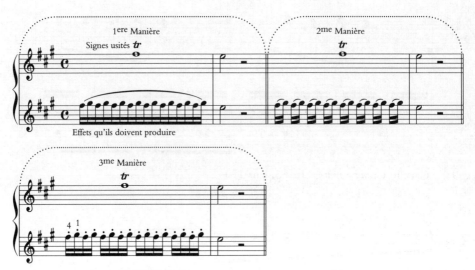

Ex. 9.4   Carulli, *Méthode Complete pour Guitare*, Op. 241, p. 51

He then goes on to give some practical advice regarding the execution of these ornaments:

One must avoid, as much as possible, having one of the notes in the cadence on an open string, the sound being less pleasant than elsewhere. When one wishes to have an open string, the cadence must be on a whole step. On a half step it would sound dull, because the finger, being too close to the nut, would rob the string of its elasticity. As for the rest of all the ornaments, the most essential and difficult element is neatness; this is why one must attach particular care to playing cleanly in order to make beautiful sounds.[59]

Grace-notes and agréments

There appears to be less agreement among the central treatises on the manner of executing ornaments. Some tutors, Giuliani's in particular, are vague when explaining how to execute the appoggiatura or mordent, for example. Giuliani gives examples, but no detailed instructions as to on what part of the beat the ornament begins. By contrast, Carulli is quite specific. Of grace-notes and ornaments he writes: 'The *Petites notes* and *agréments* serve to embellish the music. They have no time value, but take up half the value of the note which follows them, and one must slur both ornament and the note together.'[60] He then gives an example (Ex. 9.6), in which it is clear that such ornaments are to be played long and *on* the beat.

Doisy gives specific instructions on how to execute ascending and descending grace notes, which he calls, respectively, the *son porté* and the *chute,* but like Giuliani

59   *ibid.*, p. 63.
60   Carulli, *Méthode*, p. 50.

Ex. 9.5   Doisy, *Principes généraux de la guitare*, pp. 62–3.

gives no indication of their time value or beat placement.[61] He follows this with specific instructions on how to execute a vibrato *(son tremblé)*:

The *son tremblé* is played with the left hand, which must stay very relaxed. The fingers must press hard against the strings, the hand must move back and forth very quickly, the fingers must stay within the box and must not rise above the strings. This action, together with the touch of the right hand fingers on the notes which must be played, produces a kind of pleasant vibration. The *son tremblé* sounds brighter towards the bottom [upper positions] of the neck, because at this spot, there remains on the nut side a long stretch of string which can vibrate . . . To execute this example press the third finger of the tenth box of the B string. Touch this string with a finger of the right hand which gives us the A. Flutter the hand without raising the finger which has played the A, and you have the *son tremblé*.[62]

In many of Doisy's other comments and descriptions about ornamentation he shows an indebtedness to the seventeenth-century guitarist Robert de Visée. It was not until the arrival of Sor, Aguado, Carulli, and Carcassi, representing the

[61]   Doisy, *Principes*, p. 61.
[62]   *ibid.*, pp. 61–2.

Ex. 9.6   Carulli, *Méthode Complete pour Guitare*, p. 50.

competing Spanish and Italian guitar schools, that a clear break from the French
Baroque guitar tradition in Paris was finally achieved.

Continuo practice

Although this topic is too extensive to address in a chapter of this nature and size, it
is important to point out that many pedagogues provide a basic grounding in
harmony as it applies to the guitar. Some eighteenth-century writers, such as Vargas
y Guzmán, go a step further by creating a true continuo treatise for six-course guitar.
But even more interesting are the previously mentioned comments by Carulli,
where he refers specifically to playing from a figured bass and performing Diabelli's
arrangements of Giuliani's concertos for guitar and fortepiano. In these arrangements
the guitar is provided with a written-out, continuo-like realization that is be played
during the tutti sections. In Giuliani's original the guitar does not play during these
parts, but the arrangement might suggest that Giuliani performed along with the

orchestra during the tutti sections, like the soloist in Mozart piano concertos, whose part contains a continuo bass line during the ritornellos. A similar situation exists in the *Symphonia a Grande Orchestre,* No. 21, by Luigi Boccherini. In his autograph, Boccherini writes out a part that alternates between solos and a single-voice accompaniment, which is in reality a bass part written in treble clef. On closer examination of the original source, one can see a lightly pencilled-in realization of the chords that should accompany such a bass part. Since this work was dedicated to his wealthy guitar patron, the Marquis de Benevente, it was most probably the Marquis himself who played from the part, and not being a professional musician, his continuo playing was possibly less than adequate, thereby necessitating the pencilled realization. This suggests that guitarists should know the principles of continuo practice on their instrument and take the liberty to apply it in those circumstances where it seems appropriate.

As we mentioned at the beginning of this chapter, there are many variables one encounters when approaching the early classical guitar. The co-existence of a variety of stringing, techniques, and nationalist styles demonstrates a greater diversity of 'performance practices' than what is usually encountered in today's concert hall, be it on period or modern instruments. Furthermore, in a world dominated by 'definitive' recordings and instant communications a degree of homogeneity has infiltrated our art. How, then, does one develop an individual voice with respect to past practices? Clearly it would be too much to ask that for each of these variables one should play a different instrument with a different technique; one would spend more time studying these different practices than employing them. More importantly, it is an awareness of these issues, combined with a rejection of dogma, that can allow the performer to embrace the spirit, musical sensibilities, and *Gestalt* of this art no matter what instrument or technique is employed.

GENERAL INDEX

Abbatessa, Giovanni Battista 181n, 182, 193
Abreau, Antonio 197
Achillini, Giovanni Philotheo 173
Adriaensen, Emanuel 22, 85–8, 97, 99–100, 102–4
Agazzari, Agostino 103
Agricola, Martin 20
Aguado, Dionisio 203–7, 210–15, 217
Albariel, Lope de and Juce de 160
Aldobrandini, Pietro 124
Alfonso della viola 92n
Alighieri, Dante 90
Allacci, Leone 133n
Allegri, Lorenzo 109
Amphiarco, Vespasiano 8n
Amphion 69
Andriolo, Giovanni Geronimo de 31n
Anerio, Felice 87, 89, 103–5
Anerio, Giovanni Francesco 76n, 78, 87, 89, 96
Anglés, Higinio 161n, 176n, 178n
Annoni, Maria Theresa 161, 164n, 171n
Antonelli, Cornelio 77, 79–80, 88, 97, 98n
Aolst, Nicolo van 42
Apollo 63, 76
Aquila, Marco dall' 23
Aragon 159
Arcadelt, Jacques 125
Archilei, Antonio 90
arciviolata lira 90
Arion 76, 173–4
Aristoxenus 28n, 69
Artusi, Giovanni 28, 41

Ascham, Roger 64n
Asioli, Francesco 191, 193
Attaingnant, Pierre 5, 20, 22
Aucert, Alí 160n
Augsburg 82

Bach, Johann Sebastian 68
Baglioni, Giuseppe 109
Baillon, P. J. 209, 214
Bal y Gay, Jesús 166n
Ballard, Pierre 144–6, 156
Banti, Anna 88n, 93n
Barberiis, Melchiorre de 18, 23–6, 29n
Barbetta, Giulio Cesare 76n, 78, 92n
Bargagli, Girolamo 90
Bari 45n
Bartolotti, Angiolo Michele 182n, 189–90, 192, 193
basse danse 1, 163
Bassano, Giovanni 93–5
Basset, Jehan 142–4, 146, 148–9, 151, 156
basso continuo, see continuo practice
Basso, Alberto 44n
Bath, Michael 56n
Becchi, Antonio 92n
Beier, Paul 16n, 36n, 46n
Bellasio, Paolo 78, 87, 97
Bellow, Alexander 173
Berio, Luciano 44n
Bermúdez, Egberto 169n
Bermudo, Juan 22, 161–6, 168–9, 171–2, 175
Bertacchini, Pietro 20

Besard, Jean-Baptiste 19, 37, 81, 83, 86, 93, 95, 145n
Bianconi, Lorenzo 135n
Biblioteca Real (Madrid) 196
Biondi, Tempesta 18, 29
Blanchot, Maurice 67
Boccherini, Luigi 206n
Bollini, Alessandra 45n
Bologna 18, 41, 120, 186, 188–9, 192
Borrono, Pietro Paolo 23, 25, 30
Bossinensis, Franciscus 43, 74n, 91–2, 97n
Bottazzari, Giovanni 182n, 191, 193
Bottegari, Cosimo 87, 99
Bottrigari, Ercole 31n, 32–3
Bouchard, Jean-Jacques 122
Bourdelot, Jacques 108
Bouvier 157n
Boye, Gary R. 180–94
Brambilla, Ambrogio 18, 43
Brancaccio, Giulio Cesare 92n, 93
Bream, Julian 128
Brescia 18, 29
broadside sheets 42–5
Brown, Howard Mayer 11n, 16n, 20, 22, 23n, 37n, 43n, 45n, 73n, 74n, 75n, 76n, 79n, 92n, 96n, 161n
Brown, Kate 111n
Brueghel, Jan 55–6
Buch, David 153n, 154n, 157n
Buetens, Stanley 37n
Burton, Robert 54n, 58n
Burwell Lute Tutor 148–51, 153, 156

Cabezón, Antonio de 22
Cabezón, Hernando de 161n
Caccini, Giulio 89, 105
Cádiz 196
Caffagni, Mirko 37n, 45n, 130n
Cairns, Huntington 66n
Calabria 191n
Calasso, Roberto 63
Calvi, Carlo 183, 192–3
Campion, Thomas 47, 48, 50, 54, 68–9, 71
Canguilhem, Philippe 35n, 109n
canzonetta 77–8, 82–3, 89, 93, 96, 99, 109, 124
Capirola, Vincenzo 1, 2, 18, 24, 26–7

Cara, Marco 3
Caravaggio 120
Carcassi, Matteo 217
Cardamone, Donna 75n, 84n, 92n
Carey, Sir George 68
Caroso, Fabritio 124–5
Carrara, Michele 18–19, 24, 43, 45n
Carter, Tim 90n, 106n
Carulli, Ferdinando 199, 206, 209, 213–18
Casares, Emilio 159n
Casey, W. S. 17n
Castaldi, Bellerofonte 29, 72–3, 107, 120, 133n
Castellani, Marcello 34n
Castiglione, Baldassare 27, 162
Castiglione, Giovanni Benedetto 57n
Castillo, Rodrigo 160n
Cavalieri, Emilio del 90
Cavaliere del Liuto (see also Laurencini) 18, 36, 124
Celano, Orso da 19
Cerone, Pietro 19, 33, 34n
Cerreto, Scipione 19, 33–4, 39, 41, 44
Chancy, François, Sieur de 143–4
Chatton, M. 37n
Chiesa, Ruggero 118n
Chilesotti, Oscar 77, 81
Christiansen, Keith 120
ciaccona 129–30, 184
Clavijo, Bernardo 162
Coelho, Victor 19, 20, 45n, 46n, 57n, 74n, 75n, 83n, 92n, 94n, 108–41, 157n
Como 27
continuo practice, 19, 41–2, 72–107, 122, 213, 218–19
Conversi, Girolamo 87
Corbetta, Francesco 182, 189–91, 193, 214n
Córdoba, Juan Sánchez de 159n
Corona-Alcalde, Antonio 159n, 164n
Corradi, Flamminio 72–3, 107
Correa, R. 37n
Costa, Gasparo 87
Costanzo, Fabritio 181–2, 193
Covarrubias, Sebastián de 160, 170
Cox, Paul 195–7, 208n
Crema, Joan Maria da 23–5
Cristoforetti, Orlando 26n, 35n, 37n, 40, 41n, 42n, 120n, 124n

Dalhousie, Lord 145n
Dalla Casa, Filippo 20, 41–2
dalla Casa, Girolamo 85
Dalza, Joanambrosio 1, 26
Daniels, Samuel 48
Danner, Peter 1, 2
Darbellay, Etienne 135n
Dart, Thurston 17, 148n, 149n
Davis, Walter 50–1, 68n, 69n, 70n, 71n
Daza, Esteban 22, 83n, 161–3, 165–6
DeFord, Ruth I. 83n, 93n
Denss, Adrian 85–7
Dentice, Fabritio 79n
Diabelli, Anton 218
Disertori, Benvenuto 43n, 74n
Doisy, Charles 197–8, 210, 214–16
Donaire, Rodrigo 160n
Dorico, Valerio 18
Doughtie, Edward 51, 60n, 68n, 69n
Dowland, John 19, 37, 47–8, 51–3, 60n, 64–5,
        68, 126
Dowland, Robert 36–7, 53, 64, 69
Dubut, Pierre 144, 157n
Dufaut, François 144
Dugot, Joël 37n
Durante, Sergio 37n, 135n
Dürer, Albrecht 54

Einstein, Alfred 92n
Elizabeth, Princess, see Stuart, Elizabeth
Elizabeth I (Queen of England) 60
ensemble music (lute, guitar, and vihuela) 2, 40,
        86, 96–7, 109, 120, 166, 206, 214n
Entheus 69
Espinel, Vicente 162
Este, Isabella d' 96n
Eurydice 63–4, 66–7
Evans, Tom 195

Fabriano 3
Fabris, Dinko 16–46, 75n, 79n, 118n, 125n,
        127n, 129n
Facoli, Marco 76n
Falconieri, Andrea 109, 129
Fallamero, Gabriel 77, 79, 81, 83–5, 88, 97
Fallows, David 2, 21

fantasia (see also ricercar) 111, 124, 128, 165–7,
        172, 177–8
Fenlon, Iain 42n
Ferand, Ernst T. 93n
Ferandiere, Fernando 197, 203, 206, 209
Ferrabosco, Alfonso 69, 87
Ferrara 92, 126
Ferrari, Alfonso 76n, 78
Ferretti, Giovanni 87
Ficino, Marsilio 64–5
Filangieri, Gaetano 31n
Finé, Oronce 22
Fiorino, Gasparo 77, 80, 85, 87–8, 96–8
Fischlin, Daniel 47–71
Florence 18–19, 46n, 88, 90
Forin, Elda Martellozzo 45n
fortepiano 218
Foscarini, Giovanni Paolo 182–7, 192–3
Fossa, François de 206
Francesco da Milano, 18, 23, 27, 64–5, 109,
        111–18, 122, 124–5, 178n
Freis, Wolfgang 161
Frescobaldi, Girolamo 135
Frias, Joseph de 196
frottola 3, 74, 91, 97
Fuenllana, Miguel de 22, 74n, 83n, 161–3,
        165–6, 169, 175–8

Galilei, Vincenzo 18, 34–6, 39–40, 45, 75–7,
        79, 83, 87, 90, 93–5, 97, 109, 122
Gallo, Franco A. 33n
Gallot, Jacques 142, 151, 156
Ganassi, Silvestro 18, 27, 30, 31
Gardano (publishing firm) 79n
Garsi da Parma, Santino 109, 124–6
Garsi, Donino 125
Gasp[aro] 10
Gasser, Luis 162n
Gastoldi, Giovanni 78, 87
Gaultier, Pierre 121n, 149n
Gautier, Denis 142, 148, 151–6
Gautier, Ennemond ('le Vieux') 144, 148, 149,
        152–5
Gayangos, Pascual de 162n
Gemeentemuseum (The Hague) 196
Genoa 19, 45n

Gerle, Hans 22
Gesualdo, Carlo 68
Ghizeghem, Hayne van 14
Giancarli, Heteroclito 76n, 78
Giazotto, Remo 45n
Giorgione 58
Giotto 139
Giovanelli, Ruggiero 79n, 87–9, 99–100
Giuliani, Mauro 199, 202n, 207, 211, 213–14,
        216, 218
Giunta (catalogue) 44n
Giustiniani, Vincenzo 88, 92–3, 95, 122
Glixon, Jonathan 45n
Gluck, Christoph Willibald 199
Golding, Arthur 62–3
Göllner, Theodor 6, 11n, 12
Gombert, Nicolas 165
Gombosi, Otto 2n, 4n, 26n
Gorzanis, Giacomo de 77, 79, 87, 88n, 96–8
Grammatica, Antiveduto 120
Granata, Giovanni Battista 183, 186–93,
        214n
Griffiths, John 125n, 158–79
Grijp, Louis P. 178n
Gruppo di Studio del Conservatorio di Milano
        18n
Guardiani, Francesco 128n
Guernica, Juan Pérez de 159n
Guerrero, Francisco 169
guitar
        Baroque 28, 75n, 122, 149, 160, 180–94,
                196–7, 199–200, 212, 218
        classical 127, 195–214
        folk (incl. acoustic) 5, 10, 26, 191n, 200, 212
        jazz 5, 10
        Portuguese 178
        Renaissance 75n, 169–70, 173
        rock (incl. electric) 5, 10, 27, 200, 208, 212
        vihuela (sizes) 162, 169
Guzmán, Luis de 162, 169

Haar, James 73n, 92n
Hainhofer, Philip 37n, 42, 82
Hambreus, Bengt 74n
Hamilton, Edith 66n
Handel, George Frideric 118
harp 2, 27, 75n, 161, 181, 207, 209

harpsichord 19, 42, 76, 152
Harrán, Don 21n
Hearn, Bill 170n
Heartz, Daniel 16n, 17
Heck, Thomas 195, 200
Heckel, Wolff 22
Hefling, Stephen E. 151n
Hellewig, Friedemann 14n
Henning, Rudolf 2n
Henning-Supper, Uta 82
Hollander, John 57n, 62–3
Horsley, Imogene 76n
Horvat, Marco 37n
Hove, Joachim van den 85–8
Howell, Almonte C. 161n
Hubbell, Leslie Chapman 76n, 83n
Hultberg, Warren E. 161n
Hummel, Johann Nepomuk 202n, 207

iconography 55–9, 120, 127
Imparato, Giovanni Alfonso 31n
improvised tradition 91–2
intabulations 13–14, 31–32, 34–6, 40, 42, 44,
        76, 82–7, 94–5, 97, 107, 120, 128,
        164–6, 175, 179
Ivanoff, Vladimir 1–15, 20n, 29n
Ives, Charles 68

Jackson, Holbrook 54n
Jacobs, Charles 161
Jacquot, Jean 4n, 16n, 74n
Japart, Johannes 14
Jeffery, Brian 203n
Jimenez 197
Jiménez, García 159n
Jobin, Bernhart 22
John IV (King of Portugal) 79n
Jones, Lewis 4n, 74n
Jones, Robert 51
Jonson, Ben 69
Judenkünig, Hans 20, 22

Kapsberger [Kapsperger] Giovanni Girolamo 19,
        28, 39, 72–3, 107–9, 120, 122–6, 129,
        131, 133–5
Kargel, Sixtus 45n
Kastner, Macario Santiago 161n

Kircher, Athanasius 120
Kirsch, Dieter 125n
Kite-Powell, Jeffrey T. 173n
Knighton, Tess 2n, 160n
Körte, Oswald 1n

L'Hoyer, Antoine 199
La Porta, Isidro 197
Landa, Iñigo García 159n
Lanfranco, Giovanni 18, 29, 33, 41
Lasso, Orlando di 82, 87
Laurencini (Lorenzini; see also Cavaliere del
          liuto) 19, 36, 37, 126
Le Roy, Adrian 22, 144
Ledbetter, David 143n
Lee, Sir Henry 60
left-hand technique 14, 25–26, 30, 34, 38–40,
          145–6, 173–5, 212–14
Leo X (Pope) 23
Leonardo da Vinci 139
Leppard, Raymond 111n
Lesure, François 4n
Levine, Laura 50n
Lieto, Bartolomeo 18, 31–2, 34
Lindley, Mark 28n, 172
Linus 69
lira 92n
lira da braccio 3, 76
Livy 124
Llobet, Miguel 208
Luisi, Francesco 74n, 97n
Lundberg, Robert 122n
lute (lute family: specific categories)
     archlute 19, 28, 36, 38, 40, 42, 108, 119,
          122, 124–6, 128–9, 139
     chitarrone, see theorbo
     cittern 41, 44, 75, 93n, 199
     eight-course 40–1, 44, 121–22, 124, 126
     eleven-course 108, 126, 145n
     five-course 14
     kithara 63, 75
     leuto alla Francese 40
     leuto grosso (see also theorbo) 90
     leuto teorbato (see also archlute) 40
     lyre 63
     pandora 39

plectrum 1–15
seven-course 109, 120–2, 124–6
six-course 36 (benefits of), 122, 125
ten-course 121n, 125, 145n
theorbo (chitarrone) 19, 28, 38–41, 45n, 59,
          72–3, 90, 106–7, 109, 119,
          122–30, 135–9, 192n
tiorbino 120
'ūd 14
Luzzaschi, Luzzasco 76n, 90–1
Lyon 19

MacClintock, Carol 76n, 79, 88n, 91n, 96, 97n,
          109n, 122n
Mace, Thomas 151n
Madrid 197
Maes, Philippe 123
Malvezzi, Christofano 90–1
Mania (goddess of madness) 69–70
Mantua 106
manuscript sources
     Buxheim Organ Book 2, 13
     Königsteiner Liederbuch 3n, 20
     Bassano del Grappa,
          Biblioteca civica
               Ms. without shelf mark (Chilesotti) 81, 83
     Berkeley, University of California Music
               Library
               Ms. 757 (Berkeley 757) 120, 124
               Ms. 759 (Berkeley 759) 123–4
               Ms. 774   22n
     Bologna, Archivio di Stato
          Fondo Malvezzi-Campeggi, Ms. IV-
               86/746 (Bologna) 123
     Bologna, Biblioteca Universitaria
          Ms 596.HH.2⁴ (Bologna) 3n, 18, 21
     Bologna, Civico Museo Bibliografico
               Musicale
               Ms. AA360   191n
               Ms. B 44 [Bottrigari] 33n
               Mss. EE.155.I, II [Dalla Casa] 20, 41n
               Ms. B 145   43n
     Brussels, Bibliothèque du Conservatoire
               Royale de Musique
               Ms. Littera F. No. 704 (Brussels 704) 73,
                    90n, 107

Ms. Littera S. No. 16.662 *(Brussels 16.662)* 123

Ms. Littera S. No. 16.663 *(Brussels 16.663)* 125

Brussels, Bibliothèque Royale de Belgique
    Ms. II, 275 D *(Cavalcanti)* 81, 83–4, 92–4, 97n, 103

Castell'Arquato, Chiesa Collegiata
    Ms. w/out shelf mark 76n, 83n

Chicago, Newberry Library
    Acq. No. 107501 *(Capirola)* 1, 2, 3, 8, 11, 18, 25–7

Como, Biblioteca comunale
    Ms. 1.1.20 *(Como)* 124, 126

Edinburgh, National Library of Scotland
    Panmure mss., acq. 2763 no. 5 *(Dal. 5)* 145–8, 156

Florence, Biblioteca Nazionale
    Ms. Ant. di Galileo 1   90n
    Ms. Fondo Magl. XIX 45 *(Florence 45)* 120–1, 129
    Ms. Magl. XIX 66   90n
    Ms. Magl. XIX 106   19
    Ms. Magl. XIX 109 *(Florence 109)* 81, 83–4, 88n, 92n, 98n
    Ms. Magl. XIX 168 *(Florence 168)* 81, 83n, 103n
    Ms. Banco Rari 62 *(Florence 62)* 81
    Landau-Finaly Mus. Ms. 2 *(Landau-Finaly)* 79, 84, 93–4, 97n

Frankfurt-am-Main, Private library of Matthias Schneider
    Ms. w/out shelf mark *(Frankfurt)* 120

Fribourg, Bibliothèque cantonale et universitaire
    Ms. Cap. Rés. 527   4

Genoa, Biblioteca Universitaria
    Ms F VII 1 *(Genoa)* 19, 81

The Hague, Gemeentemuseum
    Ms. 28 B 39 *(Siena)* 111–18

Haslemere, Dolmetsch Library
    Ms. II.C.23 *(Haslemere)* 82, 84, 93

Kraków, Biblioteca Jagiellonska
    Mus. Ms. 40032 *(Kraków 40032)* 125
    Mus. Ms. 40153 *(Kraków 40153)* 109, 125, 127

Mus. Ms. 40591 *(Kraków 40591)* 120, 130

London, British Library
    Add. 31389   4

Lucca, Biblioteca statale
    Mus. Ms. 774 *(Lucca)* 79, 82–4, 93–4

Modena, Archivio di Stato
    Ms. Archivio Ducale Segreto per materie, musica, e musicisti, Busta IV [Fascicle B] *(Modena B)* 109, 120, 123, 126, 135–8

Modena, Biblioteca Estense
    Mus. 239 *(Modena 239)* 20, 130
    Ms C 311 *(Bottegari)* 79, 84, 87, 88n, 89–90, 92, 96–7, 98n, 99
    Ms. x.k.6.31 *(Modena)* 79
    Ms. F. 1367   79n

Montreal, Bibliothèque du Conservatoire de Musique
    Ms. without shelf mark *(Montreal)* 82, 84, 93–4, 124

Munich, Bayerische Staatsbibliothek
    Cod. lat. 7755   6n

Nuremberg, Bibliothek des Germanischen National-Museums
    Ms. 33748/M.271 [2] *(Nuremberg 2)* 109, 120, 139
    Ms. 33748/M.271 [3] *(Nuremberg 3)* 109, 120, 139
    Ms. 33.748/M.271 [4]   19

Paris, Bibliothèque du Centre National de la Recherche Scientifique
    ['Reymes'] *(CNRS)* 145, 148, 156

Paris, Bibliothèque Nationale
    Mus. Rés. Vmd. Ms. 27 *(Thibault)* 3, 4, 8, 9, 27n, 74n, 97n
    Mus. Rés. Vmd. Ms. 29 *(Paris 29)* 124–5, 130
    Mus. Rés. Vmd. Ms. 30 *(Paris 30)* 109, 126, 135–8
    Mus. Rés. Vmd. Ms. 31 *(Paris 31)* 130
    Mus. Rés. Vmf. Ms. 50   19
    Mus. Rés. Vmf. Ms. 51 *(Pa. Viée)* 156
    Ms. Vm7 6211 *(Vm7 6211)* 156
    Ms. Fonds Conservatoire National Rés. 941 *(Paris 941)* 125, 130

manuscript sources (*cont.*)
  Perugia, Archivio di Stato
    Archivio Fiumi-Sermattei della Genga,
        Ms. VII–H–2   127, 129–32
  Pesaro, Biblioteca Oliveriana
    Ms. 1144 *(Pesaro)* 1–15, 18, 20–1, 29
  Pesaro, Bibioteca musicale statale del
        Conservatorio di Musica 'G.
        Rossini'
    Ms. b.10 *(Pesaro b.10)* 130
    Ms. b.14 *(Pesaro b.14)* 125
  Prague, Univ. knihovna
    Ms. IV G 18   145n
  Rome, Biblioteca Apostolica Vaticana
    Ms. Barb. Lat. 4145 *(Rome 4145)* 19, 123,
        129
    Ms. Barb. Lat. 4395 [Valentini] 19, 40n
    Ms. Barb. Lat. 4433 [Valentini] 20, 40,
        120n
    Ms. Mus. 570 (*olim* Casimiri 36) *(Rome
        570)* 125
  San Gimignano, Biblioteca comunale Fondo
        San Martino, Ms. 31 *(San
        Gimignano)* 82, 88n, 98, 103n
  Stockholm, Kungl. Biblioteket, Kart och
        bildsektionen Musikalier
    Skap 6c, Hylla 23   44n
  Turin, Biblioteca Nazionale
    Ms. Mus. IV/ 43/2   19
  Uppsala, Universitetsbiblioteket
    Vocalmusik i handskrift 87   74n
  Venice, Biblioteca Marciana
    Ms. Italiano classe IV, no. 1793 *(Venice)*
        127, 129
    Ms. Lat. 336, coll. 1581   21n
  Verona, Accademia Filarmonica
    Ms. 223   28, 74n, 97
  Vienna, Österreichische Nationalbibliothek
    Ms. codex 18821 *(Vienna)* 82–3, 92n
  Wolfenbüttel, Herzog-August-Bibliothek
    Codex Guelph.18.7–8 Aug. 2°, pt. III
        (Wolfenbüttel) 37n, 42, 82,
        84
    [Brown 1530₂] 21
    [Brown 1546₅ / Sorau copy] 18
    [Brown 1546₁₃ / London copy] 18
Marcolini, Francesco 112, 117, 118n

Marenzio, Luca 79n, 86–89, 95
Maria, Giovan 45
Maria Maddalena of Austria, 139
Marincola, Federico 26n
Marino, Giambattista 128
Marmi, Giacinto 121
Marquis de Benevente 219
Mason, Kevin 72–107, 120n, 126n
masque 59n
Mauro, Alberto Di 42n
Maynard, John 51
Maynard, Winifred 48n
Mayseder, Joseph 207
Medici, Cosimo II 139
Meierott, Lenz 125n
Mel, Rinaldo del 89
Melii, Pietro Paolo 19, 28, 39, 126
Mellers, Wilfrid 63n
Mendoza, don Pedro de 160n
Merchi, Giacomo 197
Merlo, Alessandro 93
Merrick, A. 203n
Mersenne, Marin 122, 142–5
Mertz, Johann Kaspar 213
Mesangeau, René 143–8, 156–7
Metropolitan Museum (New York) 197
Micheli, Antonio di 181n, 182, 193
Milan 17n, 44, 110
Milán, Luis 22, 83n, 91n, 161–2, 165–8, 170–4,
        176–7
Minamino, Hiroyuki 2n, 17n
Mirandola, Pico della 64
Mischiati, Oscar 43n, 44n, 79n
Modena 192
Molinaro, Simone 122, 126
monody 89–90, 95
Montarcis, M. de 153
Monterosso, Raffaello 111n
Montesardo, Girolamo 181, 183, 193
Monteverdi, Claudio 67n, 111n
Monti, Giacomo 186, 192
Mook, Willem 178n
Moors 159–60
Morales, Cristóbal de 165
Morelli, Arnaldo 78
Moretti, Frederico 197, 199, 201, 208
Morrow, Michael 2

Moscheles, Ignaz 207
Mounson, Sir Thomas 51
Mouton, Charles 142, 143n, 151, 156
Mozart, Wolfgang Amadeus 118, 202n, 218
Mudarra, Alonso 21, 83n, 91n, 161–2, 165–7,
    169, 175–8
Murano, Putaturo, A. 45n
Murphy, Sylvia 180n, 189n
Museo de la Festa (Alicante) 196
Museu de la Música (Barcelona) 196
Myers, Joan 161

Nagler, George 43n
Nanino, Giovanni Maria 87, 89
Naples 18, 21, 30n, 33, 38, 46n, 110, 112, 160n,
    182, 192
Narváez, Luis de 21, 83n, 91n, 161–3, 167, 169,
    174
Nashe, Thomas 50n
Ness, Arthur J. 111n, 112n, 118
Newman, Joel 76n
Newsidler, Hans 15n, 22
Nutter, David 45n, 73n, 89n

O'Dette, Paul 118, 126, 173n, 178n
Ohlsen, Oscar 16n
Ophée, Matanya 199n
organ (organists) 2, 11–12, 14, 20, 23, 40, 42
Orgel, Stephen 56n
Orologio, Alessandro 78
Orpheus 48, 62–71, 76, 173–4
Osthoff, Helmuth 45n
Ovid 62, 76

Pacheco, Francisco 169n
Päffgen, Peter 2
Paganini, Niccolò 214n
Pagano, M. 18
Pagano, Mutio 43
Page, Christopher 2, 21
Paladin, Jean-Paul 22
Palermo 31, 182
Palestrina, Giovanni Pierluigi da 87, 89, 97
Palisca, Claude 76n
Pallarés Jiménez, Miguel Angel 159n, 160n
Paris 190, 199

Parise, Francesco di 88
Parks, Tim 63n
Parma 45n
passacaglia 130
Pati, Mossé 160n
Pauman, Conrad 20
Pausanias 63
Pavan, Franco 21n, 45n
pavane 163
Peacham, Henry 52–4, 69
Pellegrini, Domenico 186, 193, 203
Pennington, Neil D. 180n, 183n, 185n
Peres, D. 45n
Peri, Jacopo 90
Perret, D. 37n
Perrine 151–5
Pesori, Stefano 183, 193
Petrarch 65, 124
Petrucci, Ottaviano 8n, 9, 17–18, 21, 23, 44, 45
Phaedrus 66–7
Phalèse, Pierre 22
Piccinini, Alessandro 19, 37–41, 45n, 108–9,
    112n, 123–8, 131, 133, 203, 205, 208n
Piccinini, Filippo 123
Piccinini, Girolamo 124n
Pigna (catalogue) 45
Pilkington, Francis 68–9
Pinel, Germain 149
Pinnell, Richard 180, 189
Pirrotta, Nino 73n
Pisador, Diego 22, 74n, 83n, 161–7, 169–71
Plato 65–7
Plutarch 124
Pluto 63
Pohlmann, Ernst 79n
Polk, Keith 2n, 3n
Pomponazzi, Piero 62n
Porro, Pierre 199
Porter, William V. 105n
Poulton, Diana 16, 17n
Praetorius, Michael 120
Prizer, William F. 45n, 92n, 96n
Pujol, Emilio 167n, 208
Purcell, Henry 64–5
Puttenham, George 49n, 52–53
Pythagoras 69

Quagliati, Paolo 89

rabel 159
Raimondi, Giovanni 173
Raimondi, Pietro 126
Raphael 27
Rave, Wallace 142–57
Recalde, Ramón 159n
Recio, José 197
Reese, Gustave 76n
Renaldi, Giulio 94
Rey, Juan José 159, 162n
Ricci, Antonella 191n
ricercar (recercare; *see also* fantasia) 3, 7, 11–14,
        112–18
right-hand technique 5, 9–10, 25, 27, 30, 34,
        38–40, 127–8, 143, 145–6, 149, 151,
        153, 163, 173, 175–8, 188–9, 200–1,
        203–12
Ripa, Cesare 55, 56n, 57
Rippe, Albert de 22
Robarts Lute Book 154–6
Rogers, John (*see also* Burwell Lute Tutor) 151
Rognoni, Francesco 95n
Rollin, Monique 144n
Rome 18, 36–7, 40, 42–4, 85n, 88–90, 92, 120,
        122–3, 128, 182, 192
Roncalli, Ludovico 191, 193
Rooley, Anthony 48, 64–8, 111n
Rore, Cipriano de 87, 97
Rosseter, Philip 51
Rossi, Franco 76n
Rossi, Salamone 72, 107
Ruberti, Ettore 43
Ryan, Lawrence V. 64n
Ryding, Erik 48n

Sadie, Stanley 73n, 119n
Sanguino, Francisco 196
Sanseverino, Benedetto 181, 183, 194
Santa Maria, Tomás de 22, 161
Santucci, Pitio (Pizio) 80, 88, 98
Sanz, Gaspar 180, 183, 185, 192
Sappler, Paul 3n
sarabande 149, 151
Sartori, Claudio 74n

Savino, Richard 195–219
Scaletta, Orazio 89
Scheidler, Christian Gottlieb 199
Scheit, Karl 16n
Schmidt, Henry L. 2n
score formats 76, 79–80, 82–3, 89, 91
Scotto, Girolamo 23
Segovia, Andrés 208
Sellas, Matteo 121
Sermisy, Claudin de 163
Seville 196
Sfondrino, Giovanni Battista 182, 194
Sforza, Queen Bona 45n
Shrine to Music Museum (South Dakota) 14
Silbiger, Alexander 129n
Smith, Hopkinson 2n, 126, 139
Smock, Ann 67n
Snow, Robert 76n
Sommer, Heinrich 17n
Sor, Fernando 199, 203, 205–7, 209–11,
        213–14, 217
Soriano, Francesco 89
Sotos, Andre de 196
Souris, André 144n
Spaar, Kenneth 44n
Spencer, Robert 47, 55n, 148n, 154n
Spinacino, Francesco 1–2, 8n, 9n, 23,
Steane, J. B. 50n
Stearns, Roland 16n
Stevenson, Robert 196n
Stockholm 18
Strambi, Antonio 18, 43
Striggio, Alessandro 67n, 87, 106
Stuart, Elizabeth (Princess Elizabeth, later Queen
        of Bohemia, daughter of James I) 69
Sultzbach, Johannes 112–17, 118n
Sutton, Julia 37n

tactus (*tactus puri*) 6–8, 11, 168
Tárrega, Francisco 208
Taruskin, Richard 110n
Tasso, Torquato 124
Taylor, Andrew 60n
temperament, *see* tuning
ter Borch, Gerard 59
Terzi, Giovanni 81, 84, 93–4, 97

Tessier, André 154n
Thibault, Geneviève 4n, 74n
Thynne, Ioane 51
Timotheus 76
Tinctoris, Johannes 159–60
Tischler, Hans 3n
Titian 58, 139
toccata 128–9, 131, 133–5
Toft, Robert 48–9, 51–2, 54, 55n
Tomlinson, Gary 62n
Trombetti, Agostino 182, 194
Tromboncino, Bartolomeo 3
Tromboncino, Ippolito 79n, 87, 89
Tucci, Roberta 191n
tuning (incl. pitch) 6, 14, 32–3, 41–4, 72–3, 76,
       95–7, 119–22, 130, 144n, 149n, 164,
       168–73, 181, 183
Turnbull, Harvey 195
Tyler, James 159n, 188, 191

Vaccaro, Jean-Michel 2n, 17n, 74n, 124n, 144n
Valdambrini, Ferdinando 183–7, 189, 192
Valderrábano, Enrique de 22, 74n, 158, 161–8,
       172
Valencia 160
Valentini, Pier Francesco 19, 20, 39–41, 120,
       130
Valera, Ottavio 95n
Vander Straeten, Edmond 108n, 123n–4n
Vargas y Guzmán, Juan Antonio 196–7, 218
Vecchi, Giuseppe 33n, 78
Vecchi, Orazio 77–8, 82, 84, 87, 93–4, 103, 106
Vega, Garcilaso de la 162
Vendrix, Philippe 108n
Venegas de Henestrosa, 22, 161, 163, 170, 173,
       175–8
Venere, Vendelio 28n, 120
Venice 3–4, 14, 16, 18–19, 23–4, 36, 79, 88
Veracruz 196
Verdelot, Philippe 97
Vermeulen, Philippe 123–4
Verovio, Simone 76n, 77n, 78n, 79, 84, 87, 89,
       98, 103, 107
Vicentino, Nicolò 31n
Vidal, Pierre 25

Viée, Johanes 155
Vienna 199, 202n
Vigio (singer) 92
vihuela 33, 45n, 74n, 76, 83n, 158–79, 188
vihuela de arco 159–60
villancico 166
villanella (incl. villanesca) 78, 81, 83, 88–9,
       92–3, 96, 98–9, 166
Vincenti, Giacomo 77–8, 79n, 89n, 103n, 105
viola da gamba 31n, 90
viola da mano 41n, 159, 173
violin 150, 200, 202
Virchi, Paolo 75n, 93n
Virdung, Sebastian 20, 22
Virgil 63
Virgiliano, Aurelio 34n
Visée, Robert de 217
Vitoria, Juan de 159n
Vogel, Emil 76n

Waissel, Matthäus 22
Walker, Alice 49n
Walker, D. P. 90n
Ward, John 6n, 96n, 159, 161, 162n, 164n
Warden, John 65
Wardrop, James 8n
Weiss, Sylvius Leopold 203
Wells, Robin Headlam 48n, 62
Wert, Giaches de 87
Wessely-Kropik, Helene 120n
West, M. L. 63n
Willaert, Adrian 74n, 97
Willcock, Gladys Doidge 49n
William, Earl of Derby 68
Witten II, Lawrence C. 14
Woodfield, Ian 159–60
Wyssenbach, Rudolf 22

Young, Crawford 2n

Zacconi, Ludovico 16
Zapata, Luis 162
Zaragoza 160
Zarlino, Gioseffo 14, 41
Ziryāb ('ūd player) 14

INDEX OF FIRST LINES AND TITLES

120 Right-Hand Studies, Op. 1 (Giuliani) 199

A Ladri (e Ladre) 6, 10–11
Adoloratta, La 125
Al suon non posa il core (Anerio) 103, 105
Allemande (Mesangeau) 146–7
Al[l]emanda (Granata) 187, 191
Anchor che col partire (Rore) 80, 85, 94, 97–8
arecercare 7–8, 10–13
Aria di Fiorenza (Kapsberger) 129
Aria della Folia 40

Barriera (Caroso) 109, 124–5, 130
Battaglia 130

Che faro o che diro? (Caccini) 90n
Ciaccona (Valdambrini / Foscarini) 186
Come again: sweet loue doth now enuite (Dowland) 60
Conde Claros 163
Contento in foco 6
Corrente 3ᵃ (Kapsberger) 127
Corrente prima (Piccinini) 126
Corrente quinta (Piccinini) 126
Corrente terza (Piccinini) 126
Corrente XII (Piccinini) 126
Corrente XIII (Piccinini) 126
Così nel mio cantar (Galilei) 90n
Courante Mr Pinel (Pinel) 149

Dalle più alte sfere (Archilei) 90
De tous biens playne (Ghizeghem) 6, 10, 13–14

Donna mi fuggi ogn'hora 94n
Dunque fra torbid'onde (Peri) 90
Dura legge d'amor' 91

Elegiac Fantasy, Op. 59 (Sor) 203
Et io vo' pianger (Anerio) 95

Fantasía de pasos de contado (Mudarra) 178n
Fantasía sobre un pleni (Valderr‡bano) 172
Fere selvaggie (Caccini) 90n
Fiamenga freda (Adriaensen) 99, 101–2
Five Preludes, Op. 83 (L'Hoyer) 199
Folia (Kapsberger) 129, 136
Fortuna desperata 6

Gagliarda 3ᵃ (Kapsberger) 127
Gagliarda 12ᵃ (Kapsberger) 136
Gagliarda dele cinque mentite 125n
Gagliarda della Marchesa di Sala (Garsi) 125
Gassenhauer (Newsidler) 15n
Godi turba mortal (Cavalieri) 90
Gran Solo, Op. 14 (Sor) 211
Grand Sonata, Op. 83 (Carulli) 214–15
Guárdame las vacas (Romanesca) 163

His golden locks time hath to siluer turnde (Dowland) 60
Hor ch'io son gionto quivi (Vecchi) 94

In darknesse let mee dwell (Dowland) 52–3
In exitu Israel (Galilei) 95n
Io che dal ciel cader (Caccini) 90n

Io che l'onde raffreno (Malvezzi) 90
Io dicea l'altro (Anerio) 95

J'ay pri(n)s amours 6, 11n, 13
Ja pregamore (Japart) 10–11

Mentre il mio miser core (Anerio) 103–4
Mentre io campai (Vecchi) 94
Mentre io campai 84
Méthode Complete pour Guitare, Op. 241 (Carulli) 215–16, 218
Mi parto, ahi sorte ria! (Giovanelli) 99
Monica, La (Une jeune fillette) 124, 130

Occhi dell alma mia 94n
Ocultamente 6

Paduana discordata (Capirola) 26
Passacaglia (Piccinini) 126
Passacaglia Quinto (Valdambrini) 186
Passacalli (Granata) 191
Passachaglia sop[ra] B (Corbetta) 190
Passamezzo (Kapsberger) 129, 136
Passionata, La 125n
Pavana d'Espana 109
Pavana de Alexandre (Mudarra) 167
Pavaniglia 130
Principes généraux de la guitare (Doisy) 217

Qual miracolo Amore (Galilei) 95n
Quando mirai sa bella faccia d'oro (Vecchi) 103, 106

Recercate d. Gasp. 10
Romanesca (Kapsberger) 129
Romanesca (Mudarra) 167
Ruggiero (Kapsberger) 129–30

Se di dolor io potessi (Renaldi) 94
Se mai per maraveglia (Bossinensis) 91
Se scior si vedra il laccio (Santucci) 80, 88, 98
Sérénade en potpourri, Op. 63 (Hummel)   202n
Sfogava con le stelle (Valera) 95n
Sian fiumi e fonti 94n
Sonata, Op. 22 (Sor) 211
Spagnoletta 109, 124, 130
Symphonia a Grande Orchestre, No. 21 (Boccherini) 219

Tamburina, La 125n
Tant que vivray (Sermisy) 163n
Terzetto in D (Paganini) 214n
Toccata 1ª (Kapsberger)130, 133–5
Toccata 5ª (Kapsberger) 129

Vermiglio e vago fiore (Giovanelli) 99–100
Vestiva i colli (Palestrina) 97
Vola vola pensier (Adriaensen) 103–4